DARTMOOR
365

An exploration of every one of
the 365 square miles in the
Dartmoor National Park

by

John Hayward

Curlew Publications

First published
by Curlew Publications
© Copyright John Hayward 1991
All rights reserved
Reprinted 1993, 1997

Other Books by the same author:
    A New Key to Wild Flowers, 1987
    101 Dartmoor Letterboxes, 1988
    An Hour's Stroll on Dartmoor, 1988
    Your Dartmoor Century, 1989

ISBN 0 9514037 2 9

Typeset by Exe Valley Dataset Ltd, Exeter, Devon
Printed by BPC Wheatons Ltd, Exeter, Devon

FOREWORD

The coincidence of there being 365 days in a year and 365 square miles in the Dartmoor National Park was the acorn that grew into the oak tree of exploration that resulted in this book. It must also be admitted that the satisfaction of collecting things, and of knowing that a complete collection was easily attainable, spurred me on and made the visiting of every one of those square miles a labour of pleasure.

Except for only about three squares where I had already wandered and made notes, every one was visited during 1989 or 1990. Whether I was tramping the remote hills on foot or exploring the border lanes in a car I kept to an average of four square miles explored on every excursion. I made numerous sketches on site and took even more photographs. These were black and white ones that I processed myself. Thus I could use the photos to finish off any drawings that rain, mist, wind or time had prevented me from completing in the open.

During my wanderings I met many farmers and householders who often went out of their way to show me things of interest. To these I owe my thanks as well as memories of pleasant encounters. As background reading on topography and history I found the numerous books by Harry Starkey, Eric Hemery, and William Crossing indispensable. For plant lore I dipped happily into the works of Anne Pratt, Geoffrey Grigson, and a collection of notes I had made over many years.

At no time was it difficult to find something of interest to include: more often there were problems of what to omit. The vast expanses of open moorland merely offered a different set of choices from the enclosed farmlands of the border country. Some omissions may be surprising: for example Dartmeet, Widecombe, and Princetown are not featured. You cannot explore the Moor without passing these crowded places frequently, so I deliberately looked for something else in those square miles.

All you need then is a map, compass for use in wild and lonely places, a determination to colour in all 365 squares on page 9, and a longing to find out what such places as Deadman's Bottom, Ephraim's Pinch, Hangman's Pit, Bloody Pool, Look and Weep, The Crock of Gold, The Elephant's Nest, The Dancers, and Cowflop Bottom are really like.

... And if it happens to be a leap year?
Even that has been taken into account ....

INTRODUCTION

THE 365 SQUARES

Dartmoor National Park has an official area of 365 square miles. An inch grid drawn on a 1″ map, whose edge follows as accurately as possible the Park boundary shows that this is true. Small areas of the Park outside the grid exactly balance small areas of "non park" that are inside.

Apart from the Museum of Dartmoor Life in Okehampton—and no exploration of the Moor would be complete without a visit to it—only one site in this collection lies outside the Park boundary: the Finch Foundry is a hundred yards or so beyond the border.

In general a distance of about a hundred yards has been allowed as a "margin of manipulation" when deciding into which square to place any item that fell right on a grid line. Only rarely has this limit been exceeded: once to avoid trespassing in Okehampton military camp, and perhaps three times to include a particularly interesting site that otherwise would have had to be omitted.

MAPS

The Ordnance Survey "Outdoor Leisure" map of Dartmoor (in a yellow cover) is by far the best map for exploring the Moor. It covers 99% of the National Park on a scale of two and a half inches to a mile. Any reference in the text is to this map.

GRID REFERENCES

In almost every case a six figure reference is given to pinpoint the principal item featured in any square. Occasionally, when a wide expanse of landscape is intended, a four figure reference is used. The area concerned would then lie mainly to the north and east of the grid reference.

SPELLINGS

The spelling of place names is normally taken from the map. This forms an obvious standard, even in cases where a "better" spelling exists. Alternative spellings, found on signposts for instance, are usually mentioned.

FIRING RANGES

The perimeter of the three contiguous army ranges is shown on the maps on pages 8 and 9. The red and white boundary poles, the occasional unsightly notice boards (see Square I 6), and the red flags flown when live firing is taking place are all very obvious. In general the ranges are open to walkers during all holiday periods (from mid July to mid September on the largest range), at all weekends (except one weekend a month at Willsworthy) and on many other days as well. Firing schedules may be consulted at information centres, post offices, police stations, many pubs, and in the local press every Friday.

If the red flags marking any range are not flying by 10 a.m. there will be no firing that day.

The military freely admit that their ranges offer the best walking on Dartmoor. But do confirm that they are open before venturing on to them.

RIVER BANKS

The left and right banks of a river are the ones you would have on those sides if you were to stand in the middle of the stream and face the way the water is flowing.

ENTRANCE FEES

With reluctance a few places have been included where entrance fees are charged. This has only been done when it has seemed that these sites are the ones most worth visiting in any particular square mile. Even so you may find that at most of them you can see all that interests you without having to pay, especially if you are on foot.

VERSES

These light hearted pages are included to add variety to both the features to be noticed in the landscape and the reading matter. The essence of enjoying them is to have at least a nodding acquaintance with the original songs and poems on which they are based. Some of them have already appeared in two earlier books.

THE 365 SQUARES

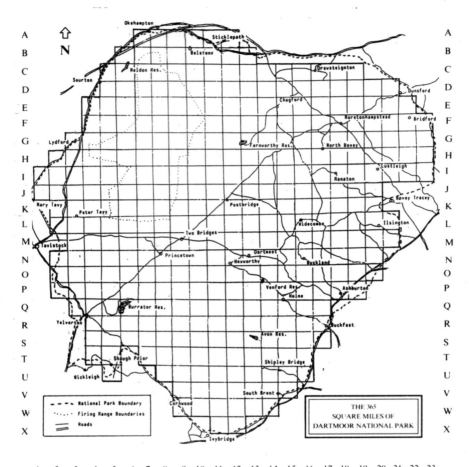

Only the most useful roads are shown on this map. There are many more especially in the border country.

The map referred to in the text is always the widely available Ordnance Survey "Outdoor Leisure" map number 28 of Dartmoor, at a scale of two and a half inches to one mile.

THE 365 SQUARES

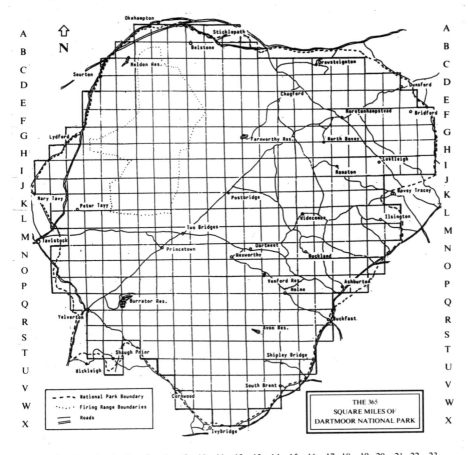

This second map is provided so that those who like collecting things and recording excursions can colour each square after it has been visited and the items described in it have been identified. For this purpose it would be reasonable to allow yourself occasionally a little latitude. For example, if you have climbed Amicombe Hill and have seen a Red Grouse (somewhere else on the Moor), then you would be entitled to colour Square F 7. The many squares containing wild flowers might also fall into this category.

OKEHAMPTON CASTLE

When seen from near the car park the crooked remains of the keep, teetering drunkenly on the summit of the great motte, give this castle a real fairy tale atmosphere.

The original castle was built very soon after the Norman conquest by the first sheriff of Devon, and the walls facing you as you climb the steep slope date back to about 1068. A lot of alterations and extensions were made over the centuries, and most of the remains that now stand were 14th century additions. By the end of the Tudor period many of the buildings had been abandoned, although there was sporadic use of some parts for another 200 years.

While wandering round the grounds you may come across "LADY HOWARD'S WALK". If you dally there after midnight you may see the lady herself, or at least her ghost. Lady Mary Howard spent much of her life (in the time of James I) at Fitzford near Tavistock. She worked her way through four husbands, and legend says that she murdered each one. For her sins she was condemned to ride out every midnight to Okehampton Park and pick a blade of grass. Not until all the grass has gone will she be freed from her punishment. The carriage she rides in is made of the bones of her murdered husbands, the horses drawing it are headless, as also is the coachman. As for Lady Mary she may be the huge black dog that runs in front.

It is about sixteen miles from Fitzford to Okehampton, so perhaps after all it might be best not to linger in the castle grounds much after midnight.

Strictly of course this museum is not within the boundary of the National Park, but it is so much a part of Dartmoor that no exploration of the Moor would be complete without a visit to it—and an unhurried one at that.

A half hour or so spent here will furnish a wealth of information about Dartmoor's geology, archaeology, history, past and present industries, wild life, and the lives and homes of moorland people. The exhibits will enable you to furnish many of the places visited in this book with imaginary but informed pictures of tin miners, clay diggers, peat cutters, toolmakers, quarrymen, farmers, foresters, millers, Bronze Age villagers, and even archaeologists.

The museum is housed in an old mill, set at the end of a cobbled yard which is a delight in itself. Flanking the cobbles are some nineteenth century cottages and a printers' workshop, all carefully restored and now housing a Victorian teashop and a well stocked information office.

For about half a mile between Okehampton and Belstone the National Park boundary follows the railway. Just here, within less than a hundred yards, there are five routes across the East Okement.

Fatherford Viaduct

The drawing shows the view through one of the arches of the railway viaduct towards the bypass road. In between, to the right, are a footbridge, some stepping stones, and a ford. Trains still run on the line every working day, but the service is no longer for the public. The terminus is only about three miles away at Meldon quarry, from where considerable amounts of ballast are carried to Exeter.

The iron way here is supported on five arches, while the road makes do with four legs.

The village seen from the Cleave

The "Cleave" is the cleft or gorge through which the River Taw leaves the high moor to make its way north to the Bristol Channel. There are paths along each side, sometimes by the river, sometimes at a higher level. The views are at all times entrancing, perhaps especially so during the seasons when the trees are not in full leaf.

About half way along on the southern side is a granite outcrop called Ivy Tor. This is a delightful spot to rest: it makes a fine vantage point for looking down into the cleave in either direction.

Power from water

In the village of Sticklepath is a fascinating "working museum".

The three waterwheels, still operating, used to provide power for the making of such tools as scythes, bill hooks, picks, shovels, and axe heads.

SOUTH TAWTON

The parish of South Tawton is one of the largest in Devon. The village of South Zeal is also in the parish; and the boundary extends far enough south to include all of Cosdon Hill, from the summit of which, if you are lucky with the weather, you can see both the English Channel and the Bristol Channel.

The Church House

In the village itself the two outstanding buildings are the large church and the Church House, illustrated above. This has been in use for five or six hundred years for all manner of parochial activities. At festival times it used to become bakery, brewery, ale house, and meeting place. In front of it was the village green, so that in fine weather there was plenty of opportunity for communal merry making.

Since the days of Elizabeth I a tree has grown on the site where the young Oak now stands. This replaces a centuries old Elm which succumbed to Dutch Elm disease in the early 1980s.

This impressive viaduct was built during the 1870s to carry a railway from Okehampton to Tavistock, the former London & S.W. Railway. It is about 180 yards long and stands 150 feet above the river.

The line was closed in the 1960s, but the viaduct is not open to the public. However there are paths beneath it on each side of the river (the West Okement), and a stroll along either of them is well worth taking.

The path leads down from above the car park at the dam, and a footbridge over the river near Meldon Pool (an old limestone quarry) allows exploration of some of the industrial archaeology in the valley.

MELDON QUARRY

From this enormous hole comes one sixth of all the railway ballast used in Britain. The rock is not granite but a sort of mud originally laid down in the sea. It was compressed, elevated, buckled, and then cooked when the nearby granite rose up from the earth's molten interior. This unimaginable heating and compression affected all the rocks bordering the Dartmoor granite, completely changing their characteristics—a change known as metamorphism. In this locality the result was a particularly hard rock, ideally suited, when broken up, to form the bed of a railway track. The quarrymen can tell the quality of their product by the sound made when two pieces are clinked together.

Almost all the output from the quarry is transported along the old Southern Railway line that still runs (for goods only) to Exeter.

A stone crusher at work

This well and also the one called Fice's Well, near Princetown, are both named after Sir John Fitz of Fitzford near Tavistock. In the late 16th century he owned also a large area around Okehampton Park. He was the grandfather of Lady Mary Howard, whose story is told on the page about Okehampton Castle.

The spring, a natural one, was protected by Sir John at about the same time as the other one. (See square M 7). The cross he had erected beside it was almost certainly an old one, even then. It possibly came from a chapel about a quarter of a mile away which had been demolished during the Reformation.

This well too has magical properties, of which the best known is that any girl drinking of its water early on the morning of Easter Day will be married within a year. Unfortunately the well cover—a comparatively recent one needed to prevent pollution and accidents—makes things very difficult for girls at Easter time.

THE NINE MAIDENS

Also known as "The seventeen Brothers"

These stones are all that remain of a Bronze Age burial site.

It is difficult to be certain how many there are, even if you count them yourself. Most authors go for either sixteen or seventeen.

One legend says that they were once maidens who were foolish enough to dance here on a Sunday, and were turned into stone as a punishment. Another says that they were practising witchcraft and fell foul of the local coven.

It is often claimed that the stones still dance, usually at noon, and that if atmospheric conditions are right they really can be seen to move. It is quite certain that some movement has taken place for there is a published photograph to prove that in 1985 one of the stones had moved temporarily to the centre of the circle.

The easiest approach to the Nine Maidens is along the track that runs from Belston village to Cullever Steps.

The moorland marches right up to the cottage gardens in this village. Ponies graze within a stone's throw of the inn, and rooks squabble in the Beeches behind the church. To buy postage stamps you have to go to the Zion Chapel, where the large woolly Belstone Tat will gaze soulfully at you from behind the counter.

Just round the corner is an old granite seat with two comfortable holes in which to rest your legs. Perhaps Moses Arscott was the sort of sailor who used to spend his time there when he returned home from piratical voyages.

A headstone in the churchyard

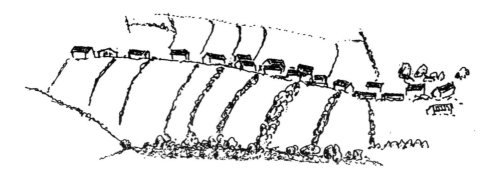

Mediaeval fields at South Zeal

The huge bulk of Cosdon (named Cawsand Hill on some older maps) ensures that it stands up boldly on the horizon from many distant points of the compass.

On the northeast flank the map marks Foxes' Holt, but it is not easy to decide which particular patch of clitter this refers to. Even this stone, which stands nearly 7 feet high, is surprisingly difficult to spot from any distance. It is one of two bond stones set up to mark a special boundary between the Duchy of Cornwall lands and the parish of South Zeal. This is several hundred yards outside the "Forest" proper—the vast area of the Moor which has belonged to the Duke of Cornwall since 1377, when Edward III gave it to his eldest son, The Black Prince.

The view north from here across the village of South Zeal shows very clearly the long narrow fields that run out from the main street. These field boundaries date back to the 14th century, when each family owned one plot.

The road running through the village was once the main Okehampton to Exeter highway. The thatched "King's Arms" has welcomed travellers for some 300 years, and the grander "Oxenham Arms" for perhaps twice as long, though the front of the building is of much later date.

The most unusual feature of this inn is to be found in the small public room behind the bar. It has been suggested that the original house was built round this giant menhir. Its top reaches the ceiling, but nobody has been able to find its base.

Sitting room at the "Oxenham Arms"

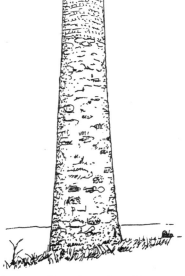

Ramsley mine chimney

This brick capped granite chimney on the hillside above the main road (the old A 30) marks the site of Ramsley mine. This was operating from 1860 to 1880 and again from 1900 to 1909. During these two periods the mine produced in all 9,788 tons of copper.

Some of the spoil heaps are still bare of vegetation owing to the toxicity of the material thrown out.

23

ADDISCOTT CROSS

G.R.667933

This is one of a number of wayside crosses in the vicinity that probably marked an old route to South Tawton church. It is known to have been moved twice during the last century and a half, but only a very short distance.

One of the plants growing at the foot of the cross and also by the drinking trough outside Addiscott House on the other side of the road is Feverfew.

The flowers are daisy-like, and the bright green dissected leaves have quite a pungent smell. Crush one to check. The aroma is not unpleasant, though it may not be to everyone's taste. The plant was probably once cultivated in local gardens because a decoction of the leaves was a recognized cure for fever.

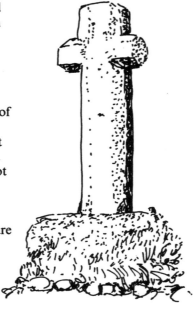

Feverfew

The herbalist Gerard, writing in the days of Charles I, says that a small quantity of dried leaves stirred into honey "purgeth melancholy, and is very good for them that are giddie in the head."

A few years later Nicholas Culpeper described a great many other virtues of this plant, from getting rid of freckles to "remedying such infirmities as careless midwives might cause".

Even well into the twentieth century it was noted in a Cyclopaedia of Botanical Drugs that Feverfew was used in "hysterical conditions".

The one common statement among the writings of all the herbalists was the description of the taste as bitter.

This magnificent 8 foot high cross was removed for safety while the nearby roundabout was being constructed. It now stands again on the verge almost exactly on its old site.

The unusually short arms give the impression that the cross was made by adapting a rectangular slab. This indeed may well be the case, for some ancient lettering can be seen running vertically down the face of the shaft. It is thought that this refers to the name of a local dignitary who possibly lived as far back as the sixth century. If this is so then this adapted cross must be the most ancient inscribed waymark on Dartmoor.

The letters O, H, L, T cut one into each face of the shaft are of much more recent date. They refer to the towns of Okehampton, Hatherleigh, Launceston, and Tavistock. Each letter faces roughly the direction in which the original roads to those places went off.

There is a large car park with toilets and an information board just a few yards from the top of the dam. Footpaths encircle the valley, mainly high above the water, and a circum-navigation of the reservoir makes a pleasant half day walk.

The dam was completed in 1972. It is about 220 yards long and 145 feet high. The reservoir covers about 55 acres and can deliver well over five million gallons of water a day.

The southern end of the reservoir, including the small island, is a wild life reserve, managed by the Devon Wildlife Trust. The West Okement valley is an important bird migration route and many species may be seen here at migration times. The marshy area near the bridge at the far end supports a typical range of bog and aquatic plants.

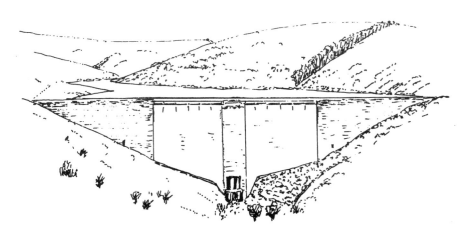

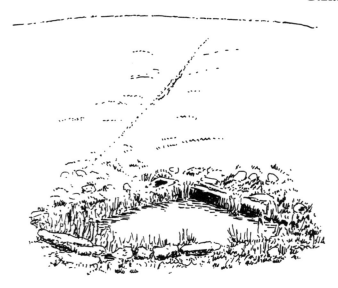

Where the Red-a-ven Brook cascades down among tumbled boulders on a steep slope lies this tiny reservoir. Though it is only about ten yards across it once served to supplement Okehampton's water supply.

There is an iron pipe that takes water from the head of the falls and disappears underground beside the reservoir. At some time two of the joints in this pipe have been refitted with nylon coated clips, but even these now show signs of weathering. Fragments of a stoneware pipe are also to be found. Above the pool, which is slowly being invaded by rushes, stands a solitary Hawthorn.

Tormentil

Just below the pool is the end of a dismantled military railway which runs almost due north for a thousand yards up the gentle slope to Black Down. A target mounted on a trolley used to be hauled up and down. This was operated from the upper end.

The drawing does not show the most picturesque view of the little reservoir and waterfall. The viewpoint was chosen in order to include the faint line of the railway.

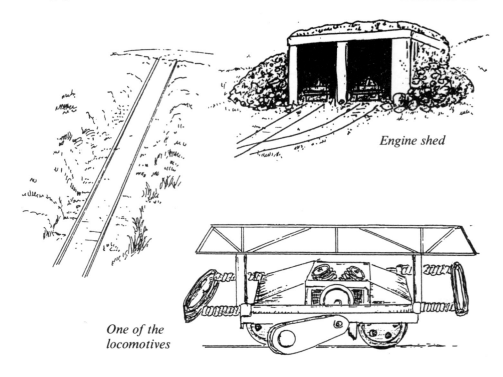

Engine shed

*One of the
locomotives*

This little railway, only about 200 yards long, is surely a "must" for railway enthusiasts. It was once used to haul military targets to and fro behind a protecting bank. At each end of its run the track loops back again, the engine being self guided by spring loaded points. There are two locomotives still in the engine shed, but they are no longer in working condition.

The rifle butts are between here and Row Tor. They are kept in good repair and are still used.

Near the loco shed is this massive iron target, pock-marked by shells of many calibres.

*Stepping stones
and paved ford*

The track that comes down here from the direction of the military camp crosses first the Black-a-ven Brook and then the East Okement river, about thirty yards above their confluence. So there are two fords, two sets of stepping stones, and two bridges. Even more unusual is the paving of the track where it approaches and fords the two streams. The carefully bedded small slabs were laid down at some time during the last century by the army so that horses could draw gun carriages through the water. Without these cobbles the heavy vehicles would soon have gouged deep ruts into the river bed, making their passage unnecessarily difficult.

On the west side of the steps, just a little way back, is a fine bond-stone. The letters OP B stand for Okehampton Parish Boundary. The stone marks the spot where Okehampton and Belstone parishes meet along the line of the old "Forest of Dartmoor" boundary.

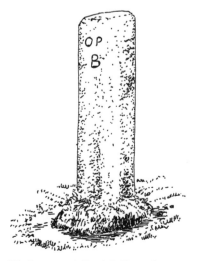

Okehampton Parish Boundstone

The story is told that round about the year 1800 two gentlemen desirous of enclosing a large tract of the Moor for their own profit hired a gang of Irish labourers to build the necessary walls. The local folk viewed the project with dismay for it would severely affect their right to graze their own stock on the open moor. But a gang of tough Irishmen who so scorned the hardships of the terrain as to go to work barefooted would call for planned and concerted action if their schemes were to be thwarted.

The men of Okehampton and Belstone (for both parishes were involved) therefore got together and laid plans. One night, when the Irishmen's wall was nearing completion, they turned out in force, and armed with stout poles threw down enough of the wall to render it useless. The "gentlemen" took the hint and paid off their labourers who quietly disappeared from the story.

The map shows that the wall runs from the Taw up over Belstone Hill and down almost to the East Okement, a distance of over 1,000 yards. The stretch illustrated below is about four yards long and is probably in its original condition. It contains almost a hundred stones. This would indicate something like twenty thousand stones in the whole length.

COSDON ROW

These stones are known as "The Graveyard"

This is probably the best of the triple stone rows on the Moor. It is easily found because the stones descend almost to the peatcutters' track that runs along the eastern flank of Cosdon. Once the rows crossed it and continued down the slope, but most of the lower stones have now disappeared.

At the upper end of each row is a large "blocking stone" set at right angles to all the others. It is curious that these do not stand in line with each other, but are slightly staggered. A little way above them is a kistvaen and the remnants of the circle that once enclosed it.

Stone rows like this arouse all sorts of interesting speculations. Which came first, the kistvaen or the rows? . . . And why are there three of them? There are ten times as many single or double rows as triple ones on Dartmoor, so this must be something of a special site. What sort of person would be buried at the head of a triple row? Did he demand (or even prepare) three rows before he died?

Is there any significance in the varying length of the Dartmoor rows? There are over fifty all told, ranging from about 30 yards to over two miles. Can these all have had the same original purpose?

SHILLEY POOL

On a sunny summer afternoon in holiday time the shallow waters of this almost natural pool are disturbed by the cheerful splashing of children of all ages, while round the banks watchful parents enjoy a warm hour on the grass or the boulders.

The Blackaton Brook has its source only about a mile away in Raybarrow Pool. This is not a pool in the usual sense but a deep and watery mire with a reputation that ensures that no moor-wise walker would try to cross it. About three quarters of the way from its source the brook plunges into a deep, steep, and narrow valley known as Blackaton Hole. Here under the shade of Rowan and Willow the waters tumble over numerous boulders into swirling pools, and then dance on down to emerge at the ford, where they slide over long, gently sloping slabs of granite to fill this pool.

The lower end has been loosely damned so that the depth of water remains constant—up to about two and a half feet. The bottom is stony.

For twenty yards above the pool there is often only an inch of water flowing over the wide, smooth stream bed. Here small stones and aquatic mosses make excellent materials for youthful dam builders to exercise their talents.

VIVAT CAROLUS SECUNDUS

There is a soothing air of calm in this village. You cannot imagine anyone being in a hurry or rushing noisily about. There is just no need to. The inn has gone and the smithy has gone, and the tiny shop and post office sit inconspicuously beside the old forge. The tithe barn has become a dwelling house; so has the Barton farm. The well in the wall opposite is no longer in use.

The thatched lych gate is comparatively modern: it was built as an exact reproduction of the much older one that had been demolished in the nineteenth century. Together with the adjacent Church House it makes an attractive picture.

The slate sundial above the church porch quietly records the passing hours and still wishes long life to King Charles II.

There has been a farm here since Saxon times. When Harold was King of England the manor belonged to his mother, but after the Conquest William appropriated it for himself, together with the six families who lived on the estate. The house, of course, does not date from Norman times, but it is several hundred years old, and has many attractive features.

Along the roadside here grows one of those flowers that are "something like a Dandelion", difficult to identify, and often ignored. It is Nipplewort, one of a number of plants of which a part bears a resemblance to some human organ. Herbalists used to believe that a medicine, made usually from the leaves, would be a certain cure for any inflammation of the appropriate part of the body.

In this case it is the buds that resemble nipples. Then there are also such plants as Lungwort, Toothwort, Spleenwort, Mugwort . . . !

Nipplewort

SPINSTERS' ROCK

A NEOLITHIC BURIAL CHAMBER ERECTED AROUND
3500-2500 B.C. THE CHAMBER PROBABLY
CONTAINED MANY BURIALS AND WOULD ORIGINALLY
HAVE BEEN COVERED BY A LONG EARTHEN MOUND.
THE STONES FELL DOWN IN 1862 AND WERE
RE-ERECTED IN THE SAME YEAR.
TRADITIONALLY THE MONUMENT WAS ERECTED BY
THREE SPINSTERS ONE MORNING BEFORE BREAKFAST.

The spinsters in the story were not necessarily unmarried: they were ladies who earned their living by spinning. They certainly made a good job of setting up these huge boulders!

Rosebay
Willowherb

The first quarry here was a limestone one, but that is now dark and water filled. The sketch shows one of the limekilns perched precariously above the present quarry. This now supplies broken stones for making tarmac and other similar purposes. The rock is a metamorphosed shale. (See Square B 7)

The older waste heaps are alive with wild flowers, yellow Mullein, red Valerian, pink Rosebay, and the great white Bindweed being specially noticeable.

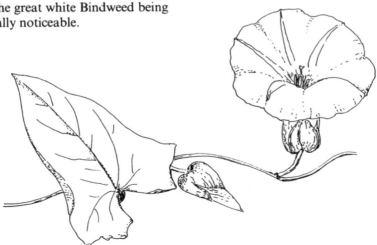

Large Bindweed or American Bellbine

This is a restful village. In the large square time moves only slowly. The church has stood here almost unchanged for 500 years, and the cottage in front of it for over 450. The inn nearby has a thatched roof, and mine hostess has been serving good beer in her front room since before some of her O.A.P. customers were born.

Inside the church hangs this reminder to the bellringers about their conduct.

THE RINGERS ARTICLES

Whoever in this place shall swear
Sixpence he shall pay therefore.
He that rings here in his hat
Threepence he shall pay for that.
Who overturns a bell before
Threepence he shall pay therefore.
Who leaves his rope under feet
Threepence he shall pay for it.
A good ringer and a true heart
Will not refuse to spend a quart.
Who will not these rules agree
Shall not belong to this belfree.

JOHN   HOLE   WARDEN
1816 - 1824

GREYSTONE

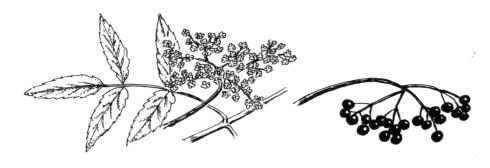

Elder

Greystone Farm hides behind a great barn which stands at the crossroads. In the barn wall is a Victorian letterbox, set there it would seem, for the exclusive use of the farmstead.

Of more recent age, on the other side of the crossroads, is to be found a "living medicine chest" in the form of an Elder tree. It may be that less frequent use is made of it than the letterbox, but by reputation it could provide a greater range of comforts, cures, medicines, lotions, salves, unguents, beverages, amulets, charms, musical instruments, household articles, toys, garden requisites, stories, old wives' tales, and free insurance than any other natural object in the neighbourhood. One modern comprehensive herbal devotes more pages to Elder than to any other plant.

Elderberry wine may not be to everyone's taste, but it was once used to adulterate other red wines because it eased the pains of sciatica and neuralgia. From the flowers a fast maturing champagne is often made; but above all it is the white wine made from fresh flowers that reigns supreme as the most pleasant wild drink of the countryside. Lotions prepared from the flowers have a cooling effect, and have been used to ease both sunburn and sore eyes. Then there are Elderflower pancakes. Dip a spray of flowers in batter and fry lightly. Sprinkle on sugar to taste.

It is a pity that the leaves when crushed impart a disagreeable aroma, but this too has its uses. A sprig of leaves worn in the hat will keep flies away, and an infusion made from them is a reputable garden insecticide.

This account of the useful and proven properties of Elder could go on for several pages, even omitting all the legends and superstitions.

The only possible hazard to keep in mind comes from the burning of Elder logs in your bedroom fireplace. This acts as an invitation to the Devil to come down the chimney . . . and a bedroom is no place for such a visitor.

WOODBROOKE

There are many miles of narrow, deeply sunken lanes running through the steep hills of Dartmoor's "in" country, discreet routes connecting hidden hamlets, worn down below field level by pack horses centuries ago. Many have now been surfaced to suit cars and lorries, but even some of those coloured yellow on the map have a surprise in store for the explorer—a notice at each end saying "Unsuitable for motors". The lane into Woodbrooke is not one of those, but it does provide problems when vehicles meet. Indeed occasionally there are even difficulties if a large car has to pass a pedestrian.

If you are driving you may get the impression that Woodbrooke consists of only two cottages, one pink and one cream: but there is a third one hiding at the back.

Just below the hamlet a ford is marked on the map, but there will only be water flowing across the road in times of flood. The footbridge is supported on a pair of rails.

Here grows Meadowsweet.

Before the days of factory made carpets Meadowsweet was one of the most popular plants for strewing on the floor. It was collected when in blossom, and simply spread out on the floor. The flowers and leaves when crushed each give off a different scent. It is said to have been a favourite of Elizabeth I, though it is no longer in use at Hampton Court.

If you like the almondy smell of the flowers you could stir some in water (one ounce of flowers to a pint), add a little honey, and have a home made tonic recommended to "make the heart merrie". Added to wine or beer it will be even more effective.

Meadowsweet

SOURTON

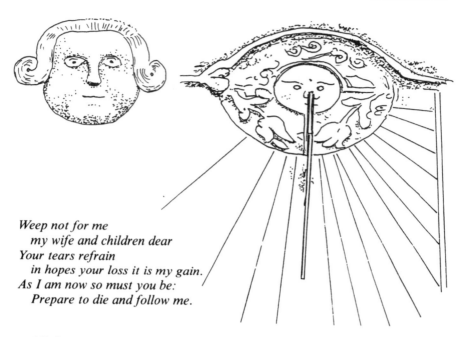

Weep not for me
    my wife and children dear
Your tears refrain
    in hopes your loss it is my gain.
As I am now so must you be:
    Prepare to die and follow me.

All these treasures are to be found within a minute's stroll of each other on or near the tiny village green, which lies beside the road just within the Park boundary.

The "cross" is a Saxon one, very different from the more common Mediaeval ones. It was found, half buried, not far away, and was set up here in 1985.

In the churchyard several of the older headstones bear similar carved faces, and the face of the sundial on the church porch also looks as if the same hand—or perhaps the same spirit of fun—might have been responsible.

The verse above, from a gravestone near the church door, expresses an odd reflection by a husband waiting for his wife to join him.

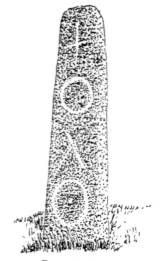

Saxon cross

BRANSCOMBE'S LOAF

The story of how this rock got its name should be sung to the tune of "Good King Wenceslas".

Bishop Branscombe once set out
From the town of Tavy,
Wined and dined on mead and stout,
Meat, two veg and gravy.
Reg his pageboy went with him,
Helped to keep him merry,
Fortified with Eau de Plym
And a cask of sherry.

Soon they climbed the Western slope,
Toiling through the heather,
But they went on buoyed with hope
Braving wind and weather.
Then their way grew steeper still:
Now they found it tiring:
Plodding on with steadfast will
They were both perspiring.

"Sir, I can't last out the day
Now the wind blows stronger,
I am sure we've lost the way,
I can go no longer."
"Cheer up Reggie", said the Bish,
"I espy a stranger,
Just the person we would wish,
'Tis a Dartmoor Ranger."

On they hurried 'cross the moor,
Stumbling through the clitter,
Oozing sweat from every pore,
Wishing they were fitter.
"Mornin' all", the Ranger said,
"Where be you a-walkin'?"
But the Bish was puffed and red,
Hardly fit for talkin'.

" 'Pon my word", the Bishop said,
"Us be tired an' weary,
Trudgin', thirsty and unfed,
O'er this landscape dreary."
"Take this loaf", the stranger cried,
"Put some food within you.
Once you've got it safe inside
You can then continue."

Bish, he took the bread to eat,
Thanked the gen'rous stranger.
Just then Reggie saw the feet
Of the so-called Ranger:
Poking out from 'neath the coat
'Twas not shoes he wore there:
Two feet cloven like a goat
Worthy Reggie saw there.

Sprang he into action quick,
Smashed the loaf asunder,
Hurled invective at Old Nick
In a voice of thunder.
"Well done, Reg", the Bishop cried,
"Thanks for your devotion.
When we reach the other side
You will get promotion."

Satan fled with muttered curse,
"Bother and damnation."
On they plodded, none the worse,
To their destination.
Page and Bishop on they went
Through the dreary weather,
Left the loaf without lament
In the purple heather.

Still it lies on Cornridge brow,
Gives this story credit,
'Branscombe's Loaf' they call it now
Though 'tis made of granite.
Page and Bishop they're not here,
They have gone to Heaven,
But Old Nick is much more near,
He still lives in Devon.

HIGH WILLHAYS
2,038 feet

The cairn on the summit

There is always something satisfying about standing on the highest possible summit in any landscape. You would have to travel about 250 miles to find another English height to exceed this one; though the Welsh mountains are rather nearer.

Nevertheless the climb up here from the military road is an easy one.

The stupendous views are cut off to the north by Yes Tor, the only other Dartmoor height to rise above 2,000 feet. Although its recorded height is seven feet lower than High Willhays it will appear just a little higher from wherever you view it—just another of the Moor's illusions, like the leats that run uphill!

The little cairn on the summit was not included when the official height was calculated!

The highest bench mark in Devon

It is cut into the west face of the summit platform.

Yes Tor
in the background

This pool lies under the evening shadows of High Willhays and Yes Tor, not far from the source of the Red-a-ven Brook.

When it was first given its name, uncounted years ago, it would have been considerably larger. The natural invasion of such pools by rushes, sedges, and bog-mosses advances slowly but surely. However it only needs a little imagination to increase the area of open water and bring in some pixies to play.

The valley bottom is peat filled, and the area round the pool is miry. A close approach will be rewarded with wet feet.

One of the plants to be seen here during much of the year is Hare's-tail Cottongrass. This is a daintier plant than the Common Cottongrass: it has only one boll of cotton on each stem.

Hare's-tail
Cottongrass

Here is an easy tor to reach: it's just a short climb up from the military road.

Quite a number of huge boulders have been hurled about or split apart to make caves, arches, doorways, passages, and rocky fingers pointing to the sky.

Just below the rocks on the eastern side is the track that comes up from Belstone, past the Nine Maidens, and on to Knack Mine Ford.

If you enjoy a really stiff climb then clamber up Steeperton Tor from the northwest.

If you prefer a gentle route then walk up from the south.

Observation Post

The outcrops along the ridge are not high, but from whichever direction the wind is blowing they will provide shelter for a picnic with a magnificent view . . .
. . . . and if it is raining there is always the army lookout cave on the eastern side!

Steeperton Brook runs down to join the Taw

WHITE MOOR CIRCLE

This is a very pleasing circle to visit. Although it stands in a lonely part of the Moor it is easy to find, because the well worn peatcutters' track which runs from South Zeal along the eastern flank of Cosdon, passes close by. The circle stands on firm heathery ground in the dip between Hound Tor (which is locally called Round Tor) and Little Hound Tor (which is not a tor at all).

There are seventeen stones standing, one fallen, and one fairly obviously missing. If the original number was indeed nineteen then the builders chose a figure unlikely to be considered by modern planners. But there were doubtless good reasons. It is not difficult to think of several. One entertaining speculation arises from the fact that the distance between any two more or less opposite stones is the same as that between the wickets on a cricket pitch!

If you stand in the centre of the circle and look out over the broadest stone (roughly southeast) then about 200 yards away will be seen a menhir. This was long ago adopted as a boundary mark between the Duchy of Cornwall land (DC) to the west and the parishes of Throwleigh (TP) and Gidleigh, which both run up to this point from the east.

This superb cluster of farm buildings is set into the hillside only just below the open moor. In their work *The Buildings of Devon* Cherry and Pevsner say that the farmhouse "expresses Devon's local building traditions as perfectly as any one structure can: it is perhaps the most architecturally distinguished of all surviving Dartmoor longhouses."

To the original mediaeval building a new wing was added in the 16th century, windows were replaced, and later extra stabling was built on at right angles. This is the wing behind which the road runs. The doorway to the cross passage is particularly fine. Above it are carved a pattern of Oak leaves and the date 1656. Beside this door is a separate entrance to the shippon, and beside that are steps to the hay loft.

It is a pity that these delights are not visible from outside the farmyard gate. It must be remembered that this is a private home and a working farm; and that the yard is also the home of geese, turkeys, chickens and dogs. The sketch is drawn from a photograph taken by permission of the owner.

There is however a typical Dartmoor longhouse which can be visited by the public. For details see *The Dartmoor Visitor* magazine published annually, and available free at all the Information Centres and many shops as well. That longhouse is featured in Square O 15.

WONSON

About half way between the small village of Throwleigh and the even smaller village of Gidleigh lies the hamlet of Wonson. Since neither village is large enough to support an inn it is to the "Northmore Arms" at Wonson that the villagers must go for refreshment. The inn is named in memory of the family who once owned Wonson Manor on the other side of the lane.

The exceptionally high gateposts at the entrance to the manor farm seem out of place in this rural scene, but when the manor house was a fortified one they probably had a more important role to play.

Almost adjoining the inn is a former longhouse, part of which is still used on such festive occasions as the annual ram roast. In the lower part of the building the great doorway into the barn has a magnificent pair of matching doorposts which rise nine feet above ground level.

A very short way up the hill are more surprises: a Nissen hut which is Throwleigh village hall, a wheelwright's shop that has become a coach depot, a Victorian letterbox, a conker tree planted in 1897, and the wheelwright's stone leaning against a hedge.

So tiny is this hamlet that just about everything has been mentioned. In the sketch are: the Northmore lion.

Alkanet (See also Square L 2)
Shining Crane's-bill (also in Square L 21)
Wall Pennywort (also in Square O 7)

Alkanet   *Shining Crane's-bill*   *Wall Pennywort*

WAY DOWN

An evocative name, this, but there is not much open down left. Two road junctions 200 yards apart are each labelled WAY DOWN CROSS on the signpost. The one visited also sports a slender radio mast.

Among the wild flowers to be found here is YARROW. If you haven't a clue about identifying plants this can be a tricky one, because it looks something like the many wild Parsleys. But it belongs to the Daisy family, or Compositae. A close look at the inflorescence will show that each flower is like a Daisy usually with five short petals.

For thousands of years all over Europe Yarrow has been a well used and respected plant. Its most widespread use was to staunch the flow of blood from a cut. The dark green, feathery leaves were applied directly to the wound; or as in Scotland, an ointment could be made from them for the same purpose.

A tea made from the dried leaves used to be recommended for both colds and rheumatism, while a similar decoction of fresh leaves steeped in hot water could be wiped over a bald head to encourage new hair growth.

If you have toothache then chew a few leaves. If you have a nosebleed then stuff some into the nostrils.

Another of Yarrow's virtues, of quite a different kind, was made use of by girls who were concerned about their sweethearts. If a maid were to pick the first head of Yarrow seen in spring and put it under her pillow she would dream of her love that night.

Alternatively she could rise at dawn, pick a spray of Yarrow while reciting this verse:

"Good morning, good morning, good Yarrow,
 And thrice good morning to thee:
Pray tell me before tomorrow
 Who my true love is to be."

and put it in her left glove or shoe. This would ensure that before the day was over one of the men she would meet would be her future husband.

This belief has entertaining possibilities.

Yarrow

DOGMARSH BRIDGE TO RUSHFORD MILL

D 15

G.R.713893

This delightful walk follows a very short part of the Two Moors Way. (See Square X 11). It starts by the Mill End Hotel, so called because one end of the building was once a mill. The leat still runs out from beneath it.

The path runs at first through woodland with the Teign for company on the left. The pale yellow flowers, mostly in pairs, under the trees in summer are Cow Wheat. These are illustrated in Square D 19. Just after passing the weir that directs water into the mill leat the path emerges into a meadow lined with Alders along the river bank. Across the river is a set of stepping stones, and later a ford. The skeleton of an Oak that fell many years ago lies in the open like a fantastic piece of sculpture. The stretch between the wood and the next mill is particularly rich in bird life.

Footbridge near Mill End Hotel

At Rushford Mill, now a farm, are more stepping stones and another ford. Here too the mill leat runs out from beneath the building, now a barn. By the stile is a discarded millstone and a deep granite trough. In front of the cottage are six more troughs, and by the barn another four, one of which is circular.

Both of these mills were working well into the twentieth century.

Rushford Steps

DROGO NOMEN
ET VIRTUS ARMA DEDIT

THE NAME IS DROGO AND COURAGE HAS GIVEN IT ARMS

England's newest castle was built between 1910 and 1930 of local granite. The exterior stone came from Whiddon Park on the opposite side of the Teign, and the interior from the quarry under Blackingstone Rock (Square G 20).

If castles appeal to you then a visit to this one is bound to provide architectural contrasts and comparisons with any others you may know. Yet even twentieth century castles have their upkeep problems. In recent years much of the roofing has had to be replaced, and in 1990 a massive replumbing operation was about to start.

The site is a magnificent one, high on a bluff above the Teign gorge. Steep footpaths lead up from the river, starting from either Dogmarsh Bridge (D 15) or Fingle Bridge (D 17). Vehicle access is from the lane running west from Drewsteignton. The drive runs through a mile of parkland before reaching the castle itself.

The property is owned by the National Trust, and offers everything one would expect of a visit to a stately home.

This is a picturesque and popular "end of the road" spot for spending a day or even just a couple of hours. Hidden down here in the Teign gorge are a free car park, toilets, a meadow for games and picnics, a licensed restaurant of high reputation open throughout the year, an old bridge, a weir up which salmon leap, paths along the river, paths through the woods, flowers in Spring, trees in Summer, toadstools in Autumn, and sparkling water at all seasons.

The bridge was built in the days when packhorses were the chief means of transporting goods, perhaps in the 1600's. It carried a busy track from Moretonhampstead to Drewsteignton. The niches let in to the parapet are to allow pedestrians to step aside while horses with wide loads are crossing.

The weir is a short distance upstream from the bridge. From there a leat led down to the mill, whose ruins are not far beyond the carpark.

A popular walk from here, of about three miles, runs up through the woods along Hunters' Path, past Castle Drogo, and back along Fisherman's Path which keeps close to the river. Both of these paths go off from the lane not far from the "Anglers' Rest".

Grey Wagtail

This square and the next provide two miles of sheltered walking at any time of the year, following the riverside path along the right bank, between Fingle Bridge (Square D 17) and Clifford Bridge (D 20).

Dipper

This page shows four of the woodland or waterside birds that may be seen. The next page deals with wild flowers.

Green Woodpecker

Great Spotted Woodpecker

TEIGN WOODS walk: 2

This covers the same 2-mile walk as Square D 18.

Wood Anemone and *Wood Sorrel* both have white flowers.
Cow Wheat has pale yellow ones, and *Golden Saxifrage* yellowish green ones.
Cuckooflower, also known as *Lady's Smock*, is pale violet.
Indian Balsam, which may grow up to six feet high, has purplish flowers. This magnificent plant comes from the Himalayas and during the last fifty years has spread along most lowland Devon river valleys.

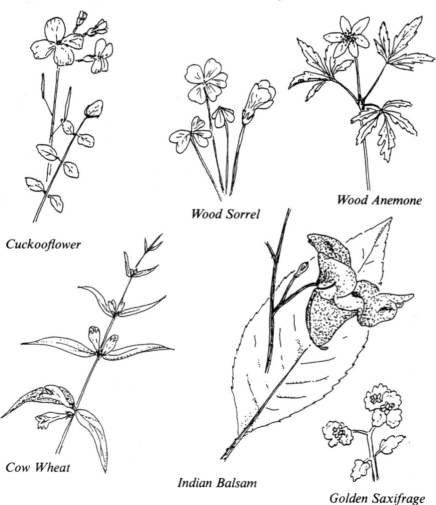

Wood Anemone

Wood Sorrel

Cuckooflower

Cow Wheat

Indian Balsam

Golden Saxifrage

CLIFFORD BRIDGE

This is a surprisingly fine old bridge to find on such a minor road. It was certainly built for horse traffic rather than lorries. The Teign has here left its gorge, and the valley has become much wider.

Near the edge of the wood on the south side a footpath heads up valley. This is a delightful riverside and woodland walk to Fingle Bridge (Square D 17) which is about two and a half miles away.

To find the river path downstream to Steps Bridge (Square E 21) walk up to the cross roads just north of the river and turn right. The path runs off this lane after about a quarter of a mile. It is about two miles to Step Bridge.

This delicate trailing plant can be found growing on the stonework of the bridge. It is Ivy-leaved Toadflax. The flowers are pale lilac with darker veins and little yellow humps. Just before the seeds become ripe the stalk of the capsule bends down towards a crevice so that the seeds may be deposited in a safe place which perhaps contains a little humus, and not scattered at random on the ground where they would be overwhelmed by more vigorous plants.

Single flower enlarged

Ivy-leaved Toadflax

DUNSFORD

Dunsford has the happiness of not lying on a main road. The highway from Exeter to Moretonhampstead once passed along the narrow street below the church but nowadays it runs nearer the river, leaving the village to live its life unjostled by hurrying vehicles. Though outwardly all may seem quiet there is nevertheless unseen activity here. A school, a church, an inn, a shop and post office, a village hall, and several societies all help to keep things moving. The village is not as sleepy as it sometimes appears.

There is quite a bit of cob and thatch among the buildings, and in summer tubs of flowers and hanging baskets add colour to the walls.

In the church one memorial in particular commands attention. It is to past members of the Fulford family. The family, who still live in the parish, are claimed to be the only one in Devon with uninterrupted descent in the male line since the time when Richard Coeur de Lion was crusading in the Holy Land.

LAKE VIADUCT

This handsome viaduct used to carry the former Southern Railway line from Tavistock via Lydford to Okehampton. There are nine arches all told, built throughout of granite. This part of the line was opened in 1874 and not closed until 1968. It was renowned for its scenic views.

A footpath coming up from the main road at Lake runs under the line and out on to the open moor. A few steps aside from the path will provide pleasing views of the viaduct, from both below and above.

On the moorland side of the viaduct an unusually deep, steep, and narrow valley comes down from the northeast. This is Deep Valley. Beneath its thick woods was once a copper mine.

There are some fine stands of Angelica in the wet patches beside the footpath from the road and the viaduct. This is not the Angelica used to flavour cakes and sweets. That species is even bigger.

Wild Angelica

This iron nail found by the track is 5" long

Following this track offers an easy—but stony!—way of reaching the high moor. The best place to start is from "The Fox and Hounds" on the main road.

The railway was built in 1879 to enable the large quantity of peat available in the vicinity of Amicombe Hill to be brought down to Bridestowe station. Horses were used to haul the trucks.

About half way up are "the points" where the line changes direction abruptly. Here the trucks were hauled on to a short siding, the horses unhitched and rehitched at the other end. They then continued along the other arm of the zig-zag.

The enterprise did not last long. It was followed by several others during the next eighty years, and about 1937 the rails were removed and lorries used instead. Perhaps this was when the points were changed into the tight loop that exists there now. The track and the works at its head were finally abandoned about 1955.

The works site is described in Square F 6.

SNIPE IN TIGER'S MARSH

The chances of seeing a tiger in Tiger's Marsh are not at all good. One suggestion about the exotic name for this boggy area where the Lyd has its birth is that it once had some connection with a peat cutter whose nickname was Tiger.

But if there are now no tigers there are certainly snipe.

The most frequent view of a snipe in places like this is to see a bird zigzagging away after it has been disturbed. No other ground nesting bird up here flies off in quite the same way.

The nestlings can run almost as soon as they are dry after hatching, but often they remain still, relying on their camouflage to conceal themselves among patches of Cottongrass or Heather.

Part of a snipe's nuptial display, or sometimes apparently just an expression of joie de vivre, includes "drumming". In carrying out this manoeuvre the bird rises steeply into the air, and suddenly dives with its wings only half open but its tail widespread. The outer tail feathers are held out beyond the others and vibrate during the descent to make a noise described as drumming or sometimes as bleating.

Here is a tor that has great character, presenting a fascinating shape from whichever side you view it. The climb up to it is an easy one, and if you come here from Meldon car park then it is at the end of as picturesque a walk as you can find on the high moor. You would be hard put to discover more colour and variety in a couple of hours' stroll than by exploring Meldon Reservoir, Vellake Corner, The Valley of Rocks, Black-a-tor Beare, Sandy Ford, and the banks of the West Okement on the way.

The tor, where Ravens sometimes nest, caps a comparatively low hill set among the giants of the Northern Moor. On the brow of the great hill to the north is High Willhays; on its shoulder is Fordsland Ledge (with two army huts); and from its hip projects Black Tor. To the west the pimple of Kitty Tor is to be seen on the skyline of Amicombe Ridge. Up valley the view extends as far as remote and lonely Fur Tor; while downstream beyond the edge of the moor uncounted miles of North Devon extend into the haze.

DINGER TOR

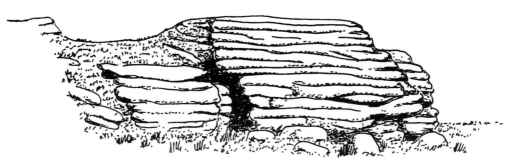

Believe it or not, this low tor in the middle of nowhere is the original home of Devon Cream Teas.

In the dim and misty past there lived here a giant who had four wives. The three oldest were mean and ill tempered, but the youngest had a loving nature and was the giant's favourite. For this reason the other three became very jealous, and decided to make the giant's life a misery until he got rid of her. This they managed to do so well that in the end, in order to make life bearable for himself, the giant took his youngest and dearest down to the coast, where he installed her in a cave. Thus, wearing his seven league boots, he was able to visit her from time to time.

One day a brave action on the girl's part enabled her to prevent a ship from being lured on to the rocks by a gang of wreckers. The captain, by way of thanking her, showed her how to prepare a tea time delicacy so appetizing that, once tasted, no one could resist it.

When next the giant came to see her she baked some scones and made a dish of this wonderful food which she called "clotted cream". So delighted was the giant that he took her back home to Dinger Tor, determined now to overrule the wishes of his other wives.

However they too were so entranced by this new "food of the gods" that their characters quickly changed, and before long all four women were making plans to set up the Moor's first CREAM TEAS cafe. This thrived for many years and the fame of Devon cream teas spread throughout the county.

When the army came to the Moor they laid a track from Okehampton Camp to the tor to make it more easily accessible. They rebuilt the old cottage and labelled it No. 20. It is still there in good repair, though at the time of writing cream teas are no longer being served.

Here is a pleasant place for a rest, either before or after the steep climb up to Steeperton Tor.

The little tin mine whose remains are a hundred yards or so upstream, had only a short life, mostly in the 1870's, but the track and ford had been in use long before that, mainly by peat cutters travelling between Belstone and the Hangingstone Hill area.

At one time there was a clapper bridge here of four arches, but it was washed away soon after the mine closed. Many of its slabs still lie beside the ford, and some have been used, probably by the army, to pave the river bed.

A short walk upstream will take you to the main mine site. The most obvious item is the ruined building on a terrace above the west bank. This was likely to have been a combination of smithy, store, office, and quarters for the miners. Some of these would only return home at weekends.

Between the track and the stream are some much fainter remains. The circular depression quite near the path would have been a buddle. This was used to wash the crushed ore in order to separate the heavy tin bearing particles. The long, narrow, wet looking patch was the wheel pit, which was filled in when the mine was abandoned.

A really wild tor, this one, that looks as if some careless giant had been throwing great piles of granite about.

All these wild flowers grow on the rocks of the tor. The Stonecrop and Bedstraw are white, the Golden Rod yellow.

Whortleberry

English Stonecrop

Golden Rod

Heath Bedstraw

Ling

THE WALLA BROOK

To the northwest of the Walla Brook clapper, the Gallaven Brook, a leat, and the Walla itself all wind through an extensive mire. A plod across this poses time and again a problem similar to the one that Hamlet encountered:

To jump or not to jump: that is the question:
Whether 'tis better for the feet to paddle
Naked through this rush-girt stream
Or to risk a leap, and not succeed,
And fill one tardy boot with peaty water;
Then suffer soggy socks for squelchy hours.
To leap: to fail: to know the indignity
O sprawling, draped across the slith'ry bank
Like washing blown to earth from Monday's line,
One foot submerged, one knee enbedded
'Mong the rushes: 'tis a consummation
Hardly to be wished. To jump: to fall:
To slide: perchance to sink—ay, there's the mud.
To move, or what to move: that's then the question:
Whether 'tis best to press into the mud
One knee, and thereby pull a watery boot
From out its aqueous bed; or whether
To stand more firmly on that riverbed
And slide one muddied leg beside the other . . .
. . . A contemplation not truly to be wished.

To jump or not to jump? Let discretion
Be our tutor. Let's find a bridge.

SCORHILL CIRCLE

This is the finest of the early Bronze Age circles on Dartmoor, for no other one has so many large stones. About two dozen are standing and another eight or more are recumbent. The exact number cannot be stated because of the difficulty of knowing whether some of the smaller boulders are broken stumps or fallen pieces. A study of the gaps in the perimeter suggests that originally there may have been fifty or more stones all told. That would have been an impressive sight.

No restoration has been carried out, only despoliation. It can be plainly seen that two of the larger fallen stones have been drilled to make gateposts. Happily the culprit was caught before he had time to split them and was forced to abandon his project.

Several of the missing stones can be found shoring up the bank of the nearby leat, and doubtless a number of others are now sunken along the leat side.

The tallest stone is over eight feet high. If this has always been the tallest, does it occupy a special position in the circle? If you were to stand in the centre of the circle at about 10 p.m. BST on a midsummer evening you should see the sun setting behind it. But that is only surmise—it is too late at night to be so far from home!

In any photograph of this circle taken from eye level some of the further stones are concealed by the nearer ones. A little artistic licence has therefore been taken in order to include all the standing stones.

GIDLEIGH

A drive through Gidleigh might give the impression that the village consists of two houses, a church, and two more houses. There is indeed very little more than that; but nevertheless a half hour's exploration will reveal all sorts of interesting things.

The oldest building is certainly the castle, which dates from about 1300. It is not certain whether the remaining two floors are actually the keep of the castle or the fortified end of a larger building. They stand in private grounds but can be viewed from the gate.

The church was built in the castle grounds, but only its south wall is likely to be of the same age. The screen is well preserved, though the colours are not original.

Against the outside wall, near the porch, is stacked a row of tombstones, quaintly lettered in 17th century fashion. An unusual feature of the church-yard is the stream that runs through it.

Other items of interest that won't take long to find are one of the church pinnacles in use as a gatepost near the road junction, and the village notice board that has been growing steadily and quietly for a hundred years.

HERE LYETH
THEBODYOFW
ILLM VOGWE
LLTHE ELDE
R BURYED N
OVEMBER TH
E 3ANODONI
1683

*Inscription
on a
tombstone*

Gidleigh Castle

66

HOLY STREET MANOR

The guide book to Chagford says that the curious name of this manor house has no connection with a holy street, but is derived from an Anglo-Saxon term meaning "a tongue of land in a hollow". Be that as it may there is an imposing statue of a bishop in a niche under the gable; while inside there is a chapel dedicated to St Boniface. The core of the building dates from the 15th century, but it was considerably enlarged in the early years of this century. The corn mill in the grounds has also been recently restored.

A walk up the short steep hill (the tongue of land) beyond the manor will reveal in the grassy verge a plant that is very uncommon in Devon.

This is SPRING BEAUTY, which blooms during May and June. The small white flowers can be identified at once because they belong to the only family in England whose flowers have two sepals and five petals. Only two other plants of this family are to be found on Dartmoor: BLINKS, a tiny plant of damp, grassy places (See Square X 12), and PINK PURSLANE, which is often to be found by the side of ditches and in other damp and sometimes shady places. If you have walked here from Chagford you will already have passed quite a lot of it.

Spring Beauty   *Pink Purslane*

CHAGFORD

The square at Chagford is surely the most lively and vehicle crowded town centre in the National Park. On any fine weekday you can stand here for an hour and have sixty minutes of entertainment: and every quarter of an hour you can pop in for refreshment to one of the four inns all within a stone's throw.

Overlooking everything is the "Pepperpot"—more properly called the Market House—with a variety of boutique-like shops beneath its entrancing roof. Another unusual roof is over the nearby bank: few of these conduct their business under thatch.

Well stocked shops reflect the interests of the townsfolk. Most bewitching of all the Chagford shops are the two adjacent ones referred to in the town guide as ironmongers. They both resemble Aladdin's cave rather than a shop. In what other ironmonger's can you buy books, shoes, handkerchiefs, toys, lawn mowers, underwear, newspapers, rucksacks, crayons, chocolate, compasses, maps, seeds, and or course all manner of hardware for kitchen and workshop. In one of these, if you explore for long enough, you will come across a fascinating museum of homely bygones.

DREWSTON

Upper, Middle, and Lower Drewston are the sites of adjacent farmsteads, completely different from each other. Upper Drewston has been considerably redesigned and now presents an appearance of gracious country living.

Middle Drewston retains more of its original character—a typical farmhouse in local tradition. On a lawn beside the road stands a trough which has every appearance of being the base of a small apple crusher. Cider mills were often twice this size, so that the vertical roller which ran round the flanged base could be turned by a horse walking a circular route at the end of a shaft. This one may have been turned by another method. It was perhaps not apples that were crushed but some smaller fruit. The extracted juice clearly escaped over the lip in the rim . . . Or is it, more mundanely, just a pig trough?

Lower Drewston offers the biggest puzzle, and most unusual remains, of them all. Half hidden under sprawling Ivy are the ruins of a huge fireplace with a mighty granite lintel topped by a curved line of stonework. Some yards further down the slope is a massive chimney, and nearby is a covered spring with a beehive-like roof. It has been suggested that the chimney served for smoking joints of meat, and the spring for washing dairy utensils, but no expert assessment has been carried out.

It should be pointed out that these ruins are on private land, are in a dangerous condition, and are protected—especially the canopied spring—by some of the largest Stinging Nettles and most prodigious Brambles you may ever encounter.

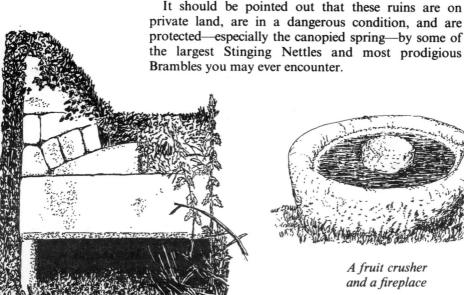

*A fruit crusher
and a fireplace*

CRANBROOK CASTLE

Trigonometrical point on the ramparts

Of the three Iron Age forts above the Teign Gorge this is the easiest to visit, being on land open to the public and not hemmed in by trees. The defences around the southern half of the enclosure are impressive, for they consist of two concentric banks and ditches. It is thought that the inner rampart, which is much higher than the outer one, may have been added later.

A walk round the ramparts (which enclose about ten acres) will show that along the northern sector the bank has almost disappeared. This is largely due to roadmakers in the 18th and 19th centuries who found it a convenient source of supply. Very little in the way of buildings or implements has been found here. This may be because the site was mainly a defensive one and not a permanent settlement.

The two other similar forts in the neighbourhood are Wooston Castle, about a mile and a half to the east, and Prestonbury Castle on the other side of the gorge above Fingle Bridge. To the northwest across the river stands the newest castle in all England—Castle Drogo. (See Square D 16)

The southern defences

It is a rare granite boulder that has a wind vane on its summit. This enormous lump of rock stands at the entrance to Willingstone Farm.

On the other side of the road is a Larch wood.

Larch is by far the most interesting of the conifers in the moorland plantations: it is the only one that has a colour change for each season. Being deciduous its winter aspect is a rather sombre brown, but as soon as spring has gained a foothold its tufts of narrow leaves break out in a pale bright green. By summer their colour has changed to a mid-green; and then in autumn before they fall they turn a warm yellow. In a sunny spell after a wet October the glory of a golden Larch wood across a valley is a match for any of our native trees.

Most large or old Larches belong to the European species, but younger plantations, like this one, are often Japanese Larch—a faster growing tree. The easiest way to tell them apart is by examining a few cones. The scales of a Japanese Larch cone have tips that are bent outwards. In the European species the scale tips remain upright.

However there is also a vigorous hybrid that is becoming widely planted. The cones of these are intermediate in character.

Larch leaves

Japanese Larch cone

European Larch cone

71

MARDON DOWN

The standing stone near the road is marked on the map as "Headless Cross". Since it has no head this would seem to be a good name: on the other hand it probably never did have one, so it is not a cross at all, but more likely a prehistoric menhir. As such it is known as Maximager's Stone. On a dark night when the wind is just right it is said to cry pitifully.

Now Maximager was a giant, and if you take the track uphill to the southwest you will find the Giant's Grave. It can be seen how the inmate pushed up the huge coverstone to escape after he was interred. But why he walked only as far as the road before becoming petrified has never been explained.

Near the grave are the scanty remains of another burial cairn, and also a curved line of seven boulders that suggest an outer circle.

In some years on this downland there is quite a display of the red twining stems of DODDER, a most unusual plant that parasitizes Gorse and Heather and has no need of leaves. It has flowers, however, tiny clusters of pale pink ones that are worth examining closely. The seeds germinate normally, but as soon as the questing stem detects a woody plant it coils round it, inserts suckers into its new support, casts off its own roots, and continues to grow drawing all its nourishment from its host. By late summer some of the Gorse is covered with an intricate and delicate red mat formed by the twining stems of Dodder.

Maximager the Giant

. . . and his grave

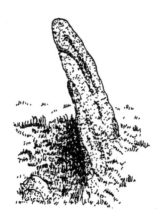

Dodder

ST THOMAS CLEAVE

G.R.795884

This steeply sided, densely wooded valley is not named on the map. It is best reached along the footpath that runs off from the car park above Steps Bridge. The route is clearly marked, and the path is wide, though for a short stretch it is quite steep.

Come here when the spring display of Daffodils along the banks of the Teign is nearly over, in order to see the next show: the Wood Anemones or Windflowers. Few woodland walks will provide a braver show of white flowers dancing in the April breeze.

The plant's name comes from a Greek word meaning 'wind'. Other variations to be heard in Devon are 'Nemony' and 'Emony'.

The number of petals to each flower is variable, but usually from six to eight.

Wood Anemone

The other white spring flower to be found beside the path is Wood Sorrel. This normally has five petals. The shamrock-like leaves fold down at night and in dull weather, giving the plant another of its names, Sleeping Beauty. But its most glorious name is Alleluya, because it flowers at Easter when alleluyas are sung.

The leaves, and the flowers too, contain oxalic acid, like weak lemon juice, and are very pleasant to the taste. Indeed this used to be extracted and sold as 'Salts of Lemon', for use medicinally as well as for removing stains from linen.

Wood Sorrel

The weir

Steps Bridge and Wild Daffodils are inseparably linked. Thousands of people come here every Spring to see the fine show of cream and yellow blossoms that spangle the meadows, the river banks, and open patches of woodland. Such is the attraction that in the past uncaring invaders collected so many armfuls of flowers that the annual display was in danger of disappearing. Much of the woodland now belongs to the National Trust, and a stretch along the north bank is managed by Devon Wildlife Trust. In Daffodil time a warden is always at hand.

Plaques on the bridge show that it was built in 1816, and that the river divides the parishes of Bridford and Dunsford. The stepping stones that give the bridge its name are just a few yards downstream but are no longer usable. A little way upstream is the mediaeval weir, which always provides a picturesque view of white water cascading among its boulders. The water was leated off from the river's left bank, just above the bridge, to turn wheels at two mills not far downstream. The leat still runs, through a new sluice, and one of the mills is still working. The mill wheel can be seen turning beside the road, providing power for making edged and other agricultural tools.

Not far below this mill is a Baptist chapel. The leat runs beneath the floor, in which a trap door gives access to fresh water for use during the Service of Baptism.

DUNSFORD MILL STEPS

A notice on a tree declares that these stepping stones are a **PUBLIC FOOTPATH**, but only in summer or early autumn are they likely to be negotiable. The seventeen stones in the water are so rectangular that they look as if they have been squared up before being carefully settled on the river bed.

This route, connecting the parishes of Dunsford and Bridford, crosses the Teign near an old corn mill. Water to turn the mill wheel came down a leat from just above Steps Bridge. This leat is still in use at another mill about three hundred yards up the road.

Carrying a sack of corn or flour across the stepping stones would have been a risky business. It is likely that carriers used the ford instead, preferring wet feet to a broken leg. The ford was also used when cattle were brought down to the valley meadows after summering on the high moor.

The footbridge a little way downstream is a private one.

In 1990 the millhouse and barns were being converted into holiday accommodation and a hotel.

HIGH DOWN FORD

Here are a ford, a little bridge, some stepping stones, a wide grassy bank, plenty of car parking space, and a stream that babbles over a bed of small flat stones—altogether a pleasant place to spend a sunny day. For three hundred yards in either direction you can find places to picnic, paddle, or build little weirs across the river (The Lyd).

This idyllic place for grandchildren and grandparents (who have some fine tors to look at) lies at the end of a track that comes up from "The Dartmoor Inn" on the A 386, opposite the turning to Lydford.

Although there are no buildings, no icecream vans, no toilets, and no shade this is a popular spot, especially on a summer weekend. Visitors are therefore particularly asked to respect the countryside. The down you drive across or picnic on is sheep grazing land.

You can cross the Lyd by bridge, ford, or stepping stones

GREAT LINKS TOR

The huge masses of rock on this lofty hill make this tor one of Dartmoor's most magnificent. The views extend far across the whole Moor and include numerous other tors. To the west the highest hills in Cornwall can be made out, and if the air is clear the light good you can see the English Channel to the south and the Bristol Channel to the northwest.

On a rocky platform a triangulation pillar stands sentinel, and near the southern end of the outcrops is a fine peat cutters' bond-stone.

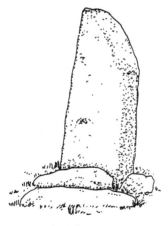

Bond-stone

Golden Rod
grows on ledges of the tor

For a real surprise walk to Bleak House by way of Great Links Tor. From there pass between the two Dunnagoat tors and lo! Just when the expanse of heath and bog begin to look endless there comes a little valley, a gurgling stream, and a cottage. It's hardly habitable now, but in 1879 the West of England Compressed Peat Company considered it a "des.res." for the manager of their recently revived Rattlebrook peatworks.

A railway had been laid down (See Square E 5) to carry the products down to Bridestowe, and some substantial buildings had been constructed at the railhead, about 500 yards upstream.

The acres of stripes on the slope of Amicombe Hill behind the house are the remains of the "peat ties". To cart the peat to the works temporary narrow gauge lines were laid along which trucks could be pushed by hand.

The workshops upstream now have a despondent air about them. They were (more or less) blown up in 1961 so as not to become a hazard.

A search among the white bricks lying about will reveal the full name of MR LEO.

RED GROUSE on AMICOMBE HILL

The great unbroken ridge of Amicombe Hill stretches the best part of four miles from Branscombe's Loaf to Watern Oke. These are long rather monotonous miles of heather, grass, and sedge, perhaps not very appealing to many humans but fine country for Skylarks and Red Grouse.

The usual experience of a Grouse is a sudden whirr of wings lifting a heavy body swiftly away from you. They are by no means common on Dartmoor: those here form a last southern outpost of their main habitat on the northern hills.

The birds may pair up in the autumn and remain more or less in their territory until the following summer. Their food consists largely of Ling, leaves, shoots, and seeds all being eaten; but Whortleberry, the other two heathers, and grass and rush seeds are all taken.

The young feed mainly on caterpillars.

Ling

Nests, eggs, and young birds are all difficult to find, for their colouring provides excellent camouflage.

Whortleberries and a flower

GREAT KNEESET

This hill, high in the inner fastness of the Moor, has two low outcrops on its summit. The southern one, being slightly higher, offers far ranging views through 360 degrees. The great heights of the Northern Moor are all to be seen. In clockwise order High Willhays, Yes Tor, Hangingstone Hill, Cut Hill, Fur Tor, Great Mis Tor, Great Links Tor, Black Tor, all stand out boldly.

Looking north to High Willhays and Yes Tor

Noticeable too is the difficult terrain on the west flank of Black Ridge. The peat hags and dark pools make walking there both strenuous and circuitous.

The sides of Great Kneeset are pockmarked with shell holes. Some of these are just water hollows in the black peat, while others contain glistening boulders of whitish granite that have been tumbled about by the explosive. Many of these boulders are partly rotted where the felspars have become soft and crumbly.

Here is a Dung Bonnet.

This is the larger of two species of toadstool that are frequently found on dung from late summer onward.

OCKERTON COURT

G.R.603868

If it were not for the military tracks in the area this pool would be difficult to find, for the depression it occupies on the long ridge of Okement Hill is such a slight one. After a long dry spell the water may disappear, but the bed of the pool remains firm enough to walk across. It was once probably about an acre in extent, but is usually smaller now.

In the vicinity of the pool are some great peat hags, which show well the difficulties of tramping across the immense blanket bog that stretches away to the south.

A little way to the northwest of the pool is the upper end of one of the Phillpotts peat passes. See square G 8 for information about these. This one does not have any memorial stones. Following it downhill and then turning up the valley of the West Okement probably offers the easiest route to Cranmere from the north.

The pool's name is also commonly spelt "Huggaton". Other variations are "Ockaton" and "Ockment".

Whortleberry

Here is a tor that makes a fine goal for a walk.

The close parallel jointing of the granite adds an unusual dimension to the outcrops that make up the tor.

The "Thirlstone" is the gap between the two northerly piles.

If you move just a few yards one way or another the gap becomes an arch or two arches, or disappears altogether.

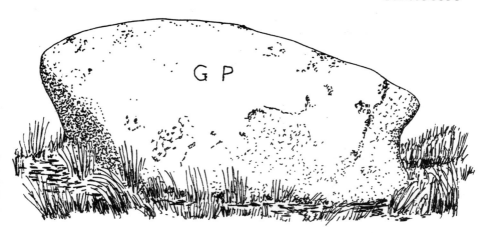

You can sit astride this rock with one leg in the parish of Gidleigh and the other in Lydford, and wonder why historians bother to argue about the boundaries of "The Forest of Dartmoor". Whether Hugh Lake that falls into the Teign just below was the 'Wotesbrokeslake" of the boundary document written in 1240 or not, is of no consequence. On a calm, sunny day the aspect of hills and valleys will fill the mind and surpass such mundane quibbles . . . and if it is cold or wet or windy or misty, and you have to ford the river, then there are more immediate problems to consider: such as whether it would be better to remove boots and socks before doing so, or to keep them on and rush across with long, quick strides. Either solution is likely to be more sensible than trusting yourself to the slippery stepping stones with their handrail of loose barbed wire.

Hugh Lake and stepping stones across the Teign

THE TEIGN TOLMEN

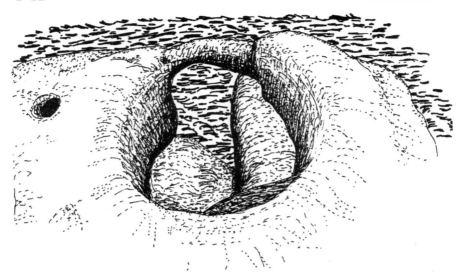

There is no other boulder anything like this on Dartmoor. It lies by the left bank of the Teign opposite the end of the wall that runs down from Batworthy Corner. If you have come from there then cross the Teign-e-ver clapper, turn upstream, cross the Wallabrook clapper, and then go downstream.

The word tolmen means holed stone.

Various writers have hinted, wishfully, that from the twentieth century B.C. to the twentieth century A.D., rites, ceremonies, and faith cures have all been associated with the hole in this stone. Surprisingly, one belief and practice has lasted well beyond the middle of this century, and there is no reason why it should not continue. The belief, which has been around for a long time, is that anyone who carefully slides down through the hole and stands on the ledge beneath will be cured of rheumatism. Several people who have done this declare that since then they have suffered no rheumatic pangs! It is also recounted that the same procedure was once used to cure children of whooping cough. Before you try it yourself it would be wise to consider how you are going to get back.

The accepted explanation of the hole's origin is that at a time when the river was much deeper—perhaps millions of years ago—small stones became trapped in a natural hollow on top of the boulder and were whirled around by the force of the current, gradually deepening the hole until it was worn right through.

KESTOR ROCK

Kes Tor has a lot to recommend it: approach is easy; there is no difficulty in climbing to the top; the views are grand; and almost on the summit is the largest rock basin on Dartmoor.

The basin usually has about two feet of water in it. After a long wet spell it fills until the surface is about five feet across. For the origin of rock basins see Square L 6. At one time this basin was protected by iron railings, to prevent animals from falling in. These have now been removed—modern breeds of sheep are apparently more sensible.

On the open downland of Shovel Down, roughly to the southwest, are half a dozen stone rows, four of them double ones. They run up each side of the ridge towards the crest. The finest stone of all is the ten foot high menhir— another "Longstone".

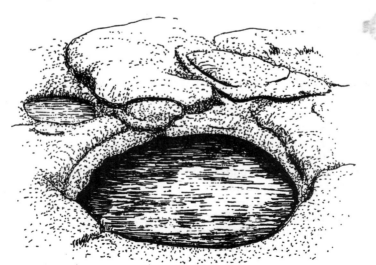

Dartmoor's largest rock basin

HOLE FARM

G.R.685861

In *The Buildings of Devon* Cherry and Pevsner cite this house, together with Higher Shilstone (Square D 12) as representing the "peak of the fully developed longhouse tradition of the 17th century". The long mediaeval wing runs down the slope, with the shippon at the lower end. The shorter wing at the upper end would have been added in the 16th or 17th century for extra accommodation. This is of course a private house so it is only possible to view it from the road, or to look over the gate into the yard at the back.

There is however a typical Dartmoor longhouse that you can visit. See Square O 15 for information.

Among the flowers spangling the roadside banks with colour are Foxgloves. These are, of course, pixies' flowers—the wee folks' gloves—and therefore should not be picked. But if you do have business to conduct with the local piskies then a whole stem of Foxgloves in your hand might well win you the day. If you are wondering what business dealings you could possibly have with pixies there is the possibility that your child might have gathered a handful of Stitchwort from the same bank, and therefore been stolen by the little folk. Rescuing stolen children is no easy matter. Forewarned is forearmed.

Among the many other names for Foxgloves these three are recorded from the southwest: Flop-poppies, Popguns, and Poppies. To understand why, carefully pick a single flower. Now, using two hands, squeeze each end between thumb and forefinger to make the flower airtight. Then sharply snap your fingers together to fire the gun. The reward is a gentle pop.

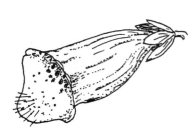

Glove for wee folk

WEEK DOWN

Here are two very old crosses, each with a story attached. They were probably both simple waymarks on the route from Chagford to either North Bovey or Moretonhampstead.

Week Down Cross

Week Down Cross stands on the open hillside, a little way back from the road. Until 1867 it stood, or rather leaned, on the roadside bank. But the bank became unstable and the cross was removed to a safer position a few yards back. Whoever was in charge of the operation had the imagination to have it set up in its new hole leaning at the same angle as before—for after all, it had always leaned like that! An examination of the Maltese cross cut into each face poses an interesting speculation. On one face the incised arms are nearly parallel to those of the leaning cross, but on the other side the small Maltese cross is cut with its arms almost vertical to and parallel with the ground.

From here a few minutes walk southeast along the road brings you to an even older cross which is thought to date well back into Saxon times. Such is its simplicity that it is not easy to make out the cross cut in relief on the lichen covered granite. For a quarter of a century this stone, known as Short Cross, was in use as a sunken platform under a pump at Middlecott Farm further down the hill. In 1900 it was brought back here to its former position.

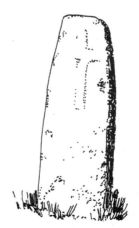

Short Cross

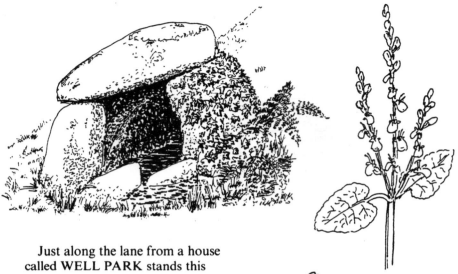

Just along the lane from a house called WELL PARK stands this well, or spring. No water is drawn from it nowadays, but even in the dry summer of 1990 the ground beneath the canopy was decidedly damp.

Opposite the farm near the road junction the pale creamy flowers and wrinkly leaves of Wood Sage decorate the tall hedgebank. The leaves were formerly collected and used to flavour home brewed beer, at times when hops were expensive or in short supply.

Wood Sage

On the other side of the road on a grassy patch grows Musk Mallow. This is not nearly so often encountered as the Common Mallow. Its leaves are dissected into narrow segments. The flowers are rosy pink. Towards the end of a warm day if you crush a few leaves a faint smell of musk can be detected.

Musk Mallow

SLONCOMBE

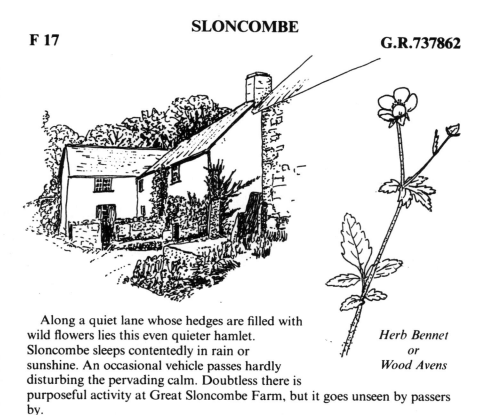

Herb Bennet
or
Wood Avens

Along a quiet lane whose hedges are filled with wild flowers lies this even quieter hamlet. Sloncombe sleeps contentedly in rain or sunshine. An occasional vehicle passes hardly disturbing the pervading calm. Doubtless there is purposeful activity at Great Sloncombe Farm, but it goes unseen by passers by.

Along the hedgebanks the yellow flowers of Herb Bennet are frequent. The name of this plant is simply a corruption of *herba benedicta*, the blessed herb. It was so named long ago because of its many virtues. In particular it was the sweet smelling root that was most used. These were best gathered in spring, then dried and ground. Half an ounce of powdered root was added to a pint of hot water, or better still, wine. This pleasant cordial would cure diseases of the liver, obstructions of the chest, and various stomach upsets. It was also recommended for use in cases of snake bite and stitch. Externally it could be applied to the skin to remove spots, bruises, or freckles. It was such a safe medicine that there was no maximum dose. A glass taken every morning would comfort the heart and ward off the plague.

But this was not all. A whole plant hung up indoors would keep the Devil at bay; and a piece carried in the pocket would protect the wearer from venomous beasts and wicked men.

Of all the uses of Herb Bennet the one that survived longest was to keep a few clean, dry roots in the linen drawer as a moth repellent.

The inhabitants of Sloncombe are indeed lucky to find such a medicine chest growing almost on their doorsteps.

MORETONHAMPSTEAD

Moretonhampstead sits just about in the very centre of Devon, well inside the National Park, and as used to be said, "is about twelve miles from everywhere". If you come from the east heading for the open, uninhabited miles of moorland ahead, this is the last place to stock up with food or fuel. If on the other hand you are arriving from the wild and windy heights then there are cafes and inns for your refreshment. You can even have a light meal in what was for many centuries the most important house in the village, Mearsdon manor. The house, in Cross Street, is easily missed, for it now fits unremarkably into a terrace of other buildings. Here in 1309 the first Lord of the Manor to live in Moreton set up his home. The village had been in existence for at least 500 years before that, but there is nothing now left from its Saxon days.

The most notable building in the town is the row of granite almshouses, built during the reign of Charles I. Nearby is a Copper Beech planted to replace a mighty Elm once known as "The Dancing Tree", because it had been pollarded in such a way as to allow a platform to be built on high, where dancing and other entertainments took place. The cross in the sketch stands below the tree.

The Toll House, also depicted, is to be found along the road to Bovey Tracey, a little way beyond the former railway station.

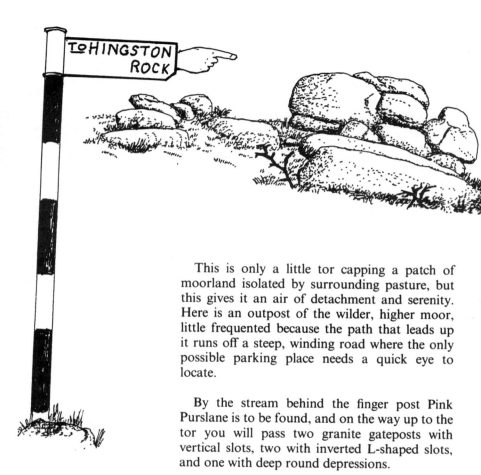

This is only a little tor capping a patch of moorland isolated by surrounding pasture, but this gives it an air of detachment and serenity. Here is an outpost of the wilder, higher moor, little frequented because the path that leads up it runs off a steep, winding road where the only possible parking place needs a quick eye to locate.

By the stream behind the finger post Pink Purslane is to be found, and on the way up to the tor you will pass two granite gateposts with vertical slots, two with inverted L-shaped slots, and one with deep round depressions.

The view from the summit is a fine one. To the south Hay Tor stands boldly on the horizon, and from there round through the west to the north the greater moorland heights rise and fade into the distant haze.

Below lies the town of Moretonhampstead, and below that the old railway yard, now full of lorries.

There is a tendency to drive straight through this village, for it has no inn, no shop, no church, and nowhere to park. But that does not prevent it from being a very pleasant cluster of old houses. Particularly attractive is the long row of thatched granite cottages. The gardens are carefully landscaped and contain a notable collection of trees and flowering shrubs. Come here in Rhododendron time, and choose if you can a sunny day when the tea shop is open. It has its own car park.

"Old Post Office Cottage" is a reminder of the time when it was less easy for the inhabitants to travel to town to do their shopping. Indeed there was also, earlier this century, a small shop and an inn here.

Doccombe is always a colourful place. The gardens are well tended and bright with flowers, and along the walls grow wild Geraniums, Bird's-eyes, and Welsh Poppies.

This last flower is bright yellow, but otherwise has an obvious resemblance to the red Poppies. It grows in shady, rocky places, and although it is a native wild plant, it is usually found not far from human habitations. It is also known as Mountain Poppy, for it is most at home in Wales and the Lake District. See also Square M 13.

Welsh Poppy

This isolated little tor stands like an outpost of the high moor, for there is no sizeable granite outcrop further east than this. Although it is surrounded by farmland there is a public path up to it from a minor road.

A mile away to the southwest lies Blackingstone Rock (G 20). On that page the legend is told of how these two tors came into being.

A short climb round the back of the rock will reveal a surprise. The outcrop is split into two, and the chasm between the parts gives an entrancing view down to the fields below.

Of all the small villages set among the steep hills and narrow lanes of the eastern borderland of the National Park Bridford is perhaps the most delightful. It is not quite at the "end of the road", though if you walk along the main street beyond the one church, one shop and one pub until you come to the Old Rectory (which has some fine Redwoods on the lawn) you might well think so.

On a warm day in spring when Celandines, Primroses, and Wild Daffodils spangle the hedgebanks, and the gardens are glowing with Forsythia, this seems a sleepy and forgotten corner of Devon, basking contentedly in the sunshine. Long may it continue.

The simple granite church, very light inside because the sills of the south windows are so low, has a particularly interesting rood screen. It was constructed early in the 16th century, and among its richly carved decorations are many pomegranites. These were the symbol of Catherine of Aragon, the first wife of Henry VIII. The twenty eight figures along the bottom of the screen are unusual in that they are carved in relief as well as being painted. The colours have survived well. It is only the faces, mutilated by the Puritans, that have suffered from the storms of history. There are similar but larger figures on the pulpit.

The Teign splashes down many falls on its way from the high moor to the sea, but none is more spectacular than this wide, semi-natural weir that swings in a long bow across its confluence with the Sowton Brook. For over five miles this stretch of the river forms the eastern boundary of the National Park, the road alongside offering frequent glimpses of it below tree lined banks.

This weir is just above Bridford Bridge, but it is almost hidden from the road. For the best view go in spring, and scramble down the bank.

Overhanging the leat that runs beside the road is a Hornbeam, a tree that is not nearly as common on this side of the Moor as it is on the Tamar side. Until the distinctive fruits appear in early summer the tree easily passes unnoticed, for its leaves are like those of a Beech, excpet that they are toothed along the margins.

Hornbeam wood is extremely hard, and is used for such implements as mallets, chopping blocks, cartwheel hubs, and the cogs of wooden gearwheels such as were once used in flourmills. It is quite possible that the Hornbeam here owes its presence to the former mill not far downstream.

Hornbeam leaf and fruit

95

LYDFORD VILLAGE

In a village with a stormy history, next to a castle with an evil reputation where once the harsh Stannary laws were meted out, stands the church of St Petrock. In the churchyard near the porch is a tomb on whose flat top is carved this fascinating epitaph.

Here lies in horizontal position
The outside case of
George Routleigh, Watchmaker
Whose abilities in that line were an honour
To his profession.
Integrity was the mainspring
And prudence the regulator
Of all the actions of his life.
Humane, generous and liberal
His hand never stopped
Till he had relieved distress.
So nicely regulated were all his motions
That he never went wrong
Except when set going
By people
Who did not know his key.
Even then he was easily
Set right again.
He had the art of disposing his time
So well
That his hours glided away
In one continual round
Of pleasure and delight
Till an unlucky minute put a period to
His existence.
He departed this life
Nov. 14 . . 1802
Aged 57
Wound up
In hopes of being taken in hand
By his Maker
And of being thoroughly cleaned, repaired
And set agoing
In the world to come.

The Watchmaker's Epitaph

BLACK ROCK

An easy 300 yard stroll downstream from High Down Ford (Square F 4) will bring you to a seat at the foot of Black Rock—a very pleasant place indeed to sit and while away a dreamy half hour on any fine day.

Fixed to the rock above the seat is a plaque in memory of a Dartmoor lover.

IN LOVING MEMORY
CAPTAIN NIGEL DUNCAN RATCLIFFE HUNTER M.C. (AND BAR)
ROYAL ENGINEERS
WHO WAS KILLED IN ACTION AT BIEFVILLIERS,
NEAR BAPAUME ON MARCH 25TH 1918, AGED 25 YEARS.
HE LOVED THE MOORS OF DEVON AND ON HIS LAST VISIT
TO LYDFORD HE WROTE THE FOLLOWING LINES: -

Are we not like this moorland stream
Springing none knows where from,
Tinkling, bubbling, flashing a gleam
Back at the sun: ere long
Gloomy and dull, under a cloud,
Then rushing onwards again:
Dashing at rocks with anger loud,
Roaring and foaming in vain?
Wandering thus for many a mile
Twisting and turning away for a while,
Then of a sudden it's over the fall
And the dark still pool is the end of all.

Is it? I thought as I turned away
And I turned again to the silent moor.
Is it? I said, and my heart said "Nay!"
As I gazed at the cross on Widgery Tor.

Here is a tor that cannot be mistaken for any other. It is the only one that has a large cross on its summit.

Brat Tor is one of the heights that mark the western edge of the high moorland. It is easily accessible from High Down Ford (Square F 4), which lies at the end of a drivable track running up from "The Dartmoor Inn" on the A 386. The climb to the top is rewarded with magnificent views in all directions.

The cross was erected at the expense of William Widgery, a Devon painter, to commemorate the golden jubilee of Queen Victoria in 1887. It is not fashioned from a single mass of granite like the older crosses, but from a number of roughly hewn blocks.

Jubilee celebration

The course of this little valley makes a pleasant exploration. It has seen more activity in the past than most other moorland streams.

Three thousand and more years ago the Bronze Age folk came here to draw water. In mediaeval times tin streamers turned over the topsoil seeking precious metal. In the summer of 1240 a party of knights rode the entire length of the river from "Rakernebrokysfote" to its head, thus fixing for all time part of the western boundary of what became known as the Forest of Dartmoor.

Peatcutters crossed the river on their way to and from the vast peat country to the west.

In later centuries other miners came. They dug pits and gullies (gerts), and constructed leats, workshops and a wheelpit. The remains of all these can be found without difficulty.

Near the head of the valley, between Bleak House and the end of the rail track, the Rattlebrook peatworks (see Square F 6) dominated activities from about 1850 for nearly a hundred years. All are now silenced.

This small stone beside the river is one of a series along the boundary of Willsworthy firing range.

WILDERNESS

Of the 365 square miles
of the National Park
this one is unique—it is the only one
in which, on the map,
there is no named feature.
Stand at the grid reference above
and you will be in its very centre,
somewhere on the southern slope of
Amicombe Hill. True, the hill is named,
and so is the brook along its foot, but
the writing is in another square.
A square mile of empty wilderness?
Look again: there is so much to see.
It will have taken at least an hour's hard
slog to get here, so don't hurry away.

There are many areas on the blanket bog that covers much of northern Dartmoor which are quite impossible to cross on horseback.

So round about the turn of the century a number of passes were cut under the direction of Frank Phillpotts who was a keen hunstman. These passes were dug down through the peat until a hard surface was reached.

Phillpotts was responsible for nine of these routes, and after his death a small memorial was set up at one or both ends of most of them.

This one—the wording is the same on all of them—is at the northern end of the longest pass of all. It runs south across Black Ridge for about a thousand yards.

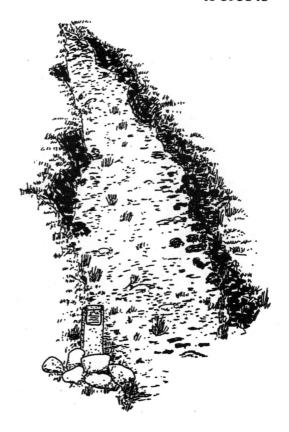

THIS STONE MARKS
A CROSSING THROUGH
THE PEAT, WHICH MAY BE
OF USE TO HUNTING AND
CATTLEMEN: THE CROSSING
WAS MADE BY
FRANK PHILLPOTTS,
WHO DIED OCTOBER 1909.
IT IS KEPT UP IN
HIS MEMORY
BY HIS BROTHER AND SON.

CRANMERE POOL
LETTER BOX

It all started in 1854 when a Dartmoor guide, James Perrott of Chagford, placed a jar here where visitors who were hardy enough to reach the pool could leave a card to prove they had "made it". The game slowly gained momentum, and nowadays this letterbox, one of the only two permanent ones on the Moor, provides a goal for thousands of searchers every year.

On a fine summer weekend the "pool" may be like a moorland Piccadily Circus, but off season or in dismal weather only the spirit of Benjie Gear hovers round, trying to empty the remaining water with his sieve.

REMINDER: The pool lies within the Oakhampton firing range.

GREAT VARRACOMBE

This little stream runs happily down the combe to join the North Teign not far from Teignhead Far.

There is nothing much of unusual interest, though once the tin streamers must have found enough ore here to make it worth their while building the hut close by the brook. Nowadays the herons find the young frogs to their liking.

Tinners' hut

TEIGNHEAD FARM AND CLAPPER

G 11   **G.R.636844**

Here are the ruins of Dartmoor's remotest farm house. It was built in 1780 and inhabited until 1943.

The occupants seem to have had a liking for massive stonework. There are several very large gate posts near the house; and the clapper bridge, built at about the same time, is one of the Moor's finest. It has three sets of imposts (slabs) three abreast. The newtake walls were several miles long, enclosing something like 1,500 acres of good grazing land.

By the river below the copse is a blowing house whose walls almost certainly provided stones for the farm buildings. All that remains of it are two mighty boulders, in one of which are two tin moulds. It is worth a visit to inspect these and to ponder on the fact that an ingot of tin taken from the larger mould would weigh more than a large man. Presumably the miners of Great Varracombe (Square G 10) also made use of it, as well as those who dug in the immediate vicinty.

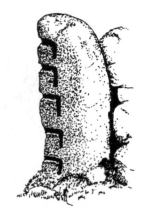

In later days this spot became known as the Blacksmith's Shop.

Gatepost

Scots Pine   *Western Hemlock*   *Douglas Fir*   *Spruce*

IDENTIFYING CONIFERS

NEEDLES: SCOT'S PINE needles grow in pairs.
          WESTERN HEMLOCK leaves vary in length.
          SITKA SPRUCE leaves are very stiff and bluish.

CONES: SCOT'S PINE are hard and woody.
        DOUGLAS FIR cones have 3-pronged scales.
        WESTERN HEMLOCK cones are much smaller
          than the others. (About 1″)
        NORWAY SPRUCE cones are much longer than
          the others. (5″ or more)

Sitka Spruce

For LARCH see Square E 18.

Western Hemlock

Scots Pine   *Douglas Fir*   *Norway Spruce*

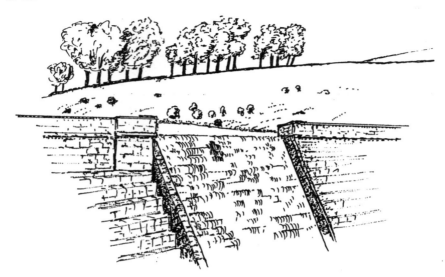

A footpath across the steep sided valley allows a fine view of the dam, and when the wind is whipping surface water over the spillway this can be a fascinating sight. Most of the water is piped down to Trenchford (Square H 21) for treatment. The dam was completed in 1942 and now impounds an area of about 70 acres. When the water level is low several hut circles can be visited between the dam and the fishermen's hut. On display in the hut are some useful charts for bird identification.

About 300 yards from the dam along the north shore is a well preserved kistvaen. It lies a little way back from the path, roughly opposite the fishermen's hut, and is well worth inspecting.

It was not discovered until 1878, when it was carefully excavated. Close by it, under the same cairn, was a smaller one which is now on display in Torquay Museum. The grave here gives an excellent idea of the construction of these chambers, although the site is unusual in that two graves were located under a single mound. Some flint tools were found, but no bones or ashes.

Kistvaen

For those who "collect" old barns
this fine row seen across the walled yard
at Lower Jurston will be a prize item.
There has been a farm here for over six
hundred years. These buildings are not
as old as that, but the six great
doorways must have witnessed a good
many generations of farm folk coming
and going.

On the wall facing the road is a
colony of Rustyback Fern.
See Square L 20 for an illustration.

In the hedge opposite grows Red
Campion. There is no month of the
year when its bright flowers cannot be
found somewhere in Devon. But inland
at these altitudes it is not very likely to
be found during the winter months.
Each Red Campion plant produces
either male or female flowers. They are
easy to tell apart for the male ones have
ten stamens and the female ones five
stigmas.

On the bank and even on the wall the
blue flowered Sheep's-bit is to be found.

Sheep's-bit

Red Campion

The Watching Place and the Watcher

Just here the Moretonhampstead to Tavistock road is crossed by the equally old, and once equally important, Chagford to Ashburton road. In fact within a quarter of a mile of this spot six roads come in. What better place to sit and watch, or hide and watch. Why? Well, at least four explanations can be found. Here are the three most likely.

One is that the Lord of the Manor had a gallows erected here, from which local highwaymen and footpads were hanged. It was their relatives who sat and watched the swinging body until given permission to take it down.

Another is that it was the highwaymen who did the watching, waiting for their "prey" to come by en route to one of the towns mentioned above.

Yet another is that at one time an outbreak of the Plague struck the inhabitants of a nearby house. They were of course confined to their home, but kindly neighbours used to place food for them on a slab of granite near the cross roads, watching all the while to make sure that the plague victims kept their distance while the donors were there. The sufferers too would have watched. . . . until the day came when they were no longer able to fetch the food. As soon as that happened the house was burned down.

Even now there is still a watcher on duty: Beetor Cross, much battered by the vicissitudes of history, stands on a bank opposite the signpost.

This is a remarkably fine cross to find beside such a narrow and little used lane. There is a local tradition that it once belonged to a little chapel down in the woods by the stream, where travellers used to call to offer prayers for a safe journey before setting out westwards across the open moor.

When the chapel fell into disuse the cross was brought up here to the road junction, where it now occupies a commanding position high on the bank. In spring daffodils flower round its base.

Both the cross and the road junction about five hundred yards to the north take their name from the farm on the other side of the road.

The word "hele" occurs as a place name several times on the Moor. It is possible that it is derived from an Anglo-Saxon word meaning "a place of hiding".

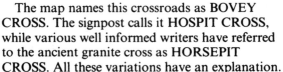

The map names this crossroads as BOVEY
CROSS. The signpost calls it HOSPIT CROSS,
while various well informed writers have referred
to the ancient granite cross as HORSEPIT
CROSS. All these variations have an explanation.

The first name refers to the nearby village of North Bovey.

The second name is derived from the tentative suggestion that there may
once have been a hospice for travellers near the crossroads. The modern word
"hospital" comes from the same Latin root.

Thirdly, the field behind the hedge was known as the Horse Pit.

This is a matter of paying your money and taking your choice.

Long before the present signpost was erected someone turned the old cross
into a waymark by carving a letter into each face, to point the way to
Okehampton, Moretonhampstead, Newton Abbot, and North Bovey. Here
lies a good excuse for not spelling out these places in full!

Later still the map makers came along and cut a bench mark into one face.
A good deal of "vandalism" of this sort was done to wayside crosses during
the last century.

Tucked into the hedge at the road junction is a boundary stone. On one face is clearly cut an M; on the other, hidden by overhanging vegetation and encrusted by lichens, is the curious symbol illustrated here. Since the Moretonhampstead/Lustleigh boundary runs along this lane the M is easily interpreted, but what is the other letter? Push aside the Ivy and Hazel and Vetch and see what you can make of it.

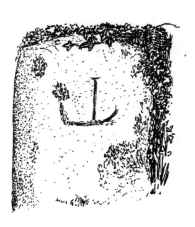

Three hundred yards to the west both parishes abut on North Bovey. There stands another stone, a very much newer one. On one side is cut a single letter and a date. Does this explain anything? The stone is indicated on the map but not labelled.

Along this bank in late summer the deep yellow "buttons" of Tansy make a bright show. The strongly aromatic leaves were once used, either fresh or dried, to flavour cakes, puddings, and omelets, delicacies specially eaten at Easter time.

The leaves had another property too. Nicholas Culpeper, writing in the days of Oliver Cromwell, says: "Dame Venus was minded to pleasure women with child by this herb." The leaves were to be boiled in beer, and the decoction drunk. He continues, "I know of no herb like it . . . Let those women that desire children love this herb: it is their best companion, their husband excepted."

Another use for Tansy was to preserve the roots in honey. Nibbling these was recommended as a cure for gout. Gerard, writing in 1616, stated that the proper dose was "a reasonable quantity every day for a certain space". That should suit most people.

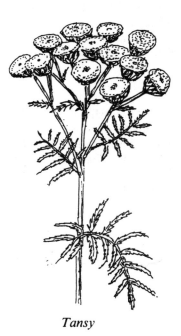

Tansy

WRAY BARTON

The Lustleigh to Moreton line at Wray Barton

The flourishing settlement that was here in late Saxon times is now mostly a scene for the imagination. In the Domesday Book it was recorded that the Lord of the Manor farmed about sixty acres, and the eighteen families on his land about three times as much.

There are still remains of some late mediaeval buildings to be seen, and a fine high barn. Another long low barn-like building has recently been converted into a row of three houses.

On the other side of the road runs the track of the Great Western Railway, along which the last train ran in 1964, almost a hundred years after the line was opened. The story is told locally of how the king once spent a night in a train here, just below the bridge, on his way to visit the prison at Princetown. A charming spot in a rural valley for a quiet night away from the hubbub of Buckingham Palace. In the morning freshly baked bread was brought from the village—perhaps Lustleigh. This story could refer to the royal visit in 1937 when George VI came this way to Moretonhampstead.

BLACKINGSTONE ROCK

This little tor lies by a minor road, like an island of wild granite vegetation surrounded by pasture and forest.

Just a mile away to the northeast is another similarly isolated tor. This is Heltor Rock. The story goes that once upon a time these two hills had no granite outcrop upon them, until one day the Devil took his stand here and began to hurl boulders at King Arthur who was on Heltor Hill. Arthur of course replied in kind, and the two of them kept this up for a while without much effect, though the boulders they cast became bigger and bigger. Finally such was the size of their missiles that neither could carry on. They departed, leaving behind the last shots that landed—and that is how these two tors came into being. Blackingstone Rock was Arthur's parting shot, and Heltor was the last one the Devil threw.

There are several small conifer plantations in the vicinity. On the hill near the tor are Scots Pine, and in the valley below are Larch and Spruce.

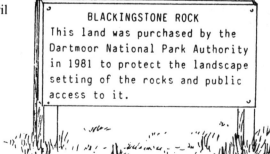

BLACKINGSTONE ROCK
This land was purchased by the Dartmoor National Park Authority in 1981 to protect the landscape setting of the rocks and public access to it.

KENNICK RESERVOIR

This reservoir was constructed during the 1880s when it was found that Tottiford reservoir, which lies immediately below it in the same valley, could not supply enough water for the growing population round Torbay. The dam was built largely of earth and clay, and given a sloping grassy face. The reservoir covers about 50 acres and can hold nearly 200 million gallons of water. This makes it the largest of the three reservoirs in this complex. The other two are described in squares H 21 and H 22.

The public paths which link the reservoirs avoid the shores of this one in order to allow anglers to fish here without disturbance.

The National Park publishes an excellent leaflet which provides a historical background to the area and a good map of the footpaths. These offer varied walking along the shores, across bridges, beside pastures, through conifer and hardwood plantations, and past farm buildings and quarries. The leaflet is usually available at the Trenchford Reservoir car park, as well as at the park information offices.

THREE HOLES

*Part of the nameplate
at Middle Hole*

Higher Hole, Middle Hole, and Lower Hole are three farmsteads set just under the edge of rolling fields of grass on the higher land to the south. The first and last hide shyly behind screens of trees, only smart stabling or high barns being visible from the road. But Middle Hole is more easily admired. The house has recently been renovated and rethatched, and makes an attractive picture against its hillside background.

Two scarecrows in the kitchen garden when this visit was made were so lifelike that for many minutes they were thought to be gardeners attending to a painstaking task.

The cheerful hedgerows abound in wild flowers. One that graces almost every lane through the moorland borders is Greater Stitchwort. By the time it is in full flower Spring is well under way. It has almost a hundred different English names. Many of these refer to snakes, cuckoos, pixies, stars, and the Devil. Its brittle stems are recalled in such names as Snapjacks, and the belief that picking it would bring a thunderstorm about your head in the name of Thunderbolts.

But on Dartmoor this is above all the pixies' flower, so heed well the local advice:

"Doan'ee go pickin they piskie flowers, mind, or yu'll be piskie-led."

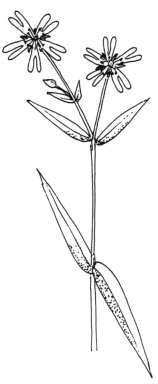

Greater Stitchwort

CHRISTOW

If you should visit this village on Tail-pipe Day keep a good humoured lookout that a youngster does not pin a notice to your coat tail. For Tail-pipe Day is April 1st, and the usual custom that "foolish" pranks must be played before noon is here reversed: it is during the afternoon that these age-old jokes are practised.

In the churchyard are some fine Yews, and on the path outside the porch lies a stone which states that "Heere Dyed XIX Feb 1631 Nicholas Bussell 46 years Clark". History tells that he was shot on this spot for refusing to hand over the church keys to a posse of Roundheads.

There are many typical old farmhouses in the parish.

Hill Farm

An easy one to find is HILL about half a mile to the south. The wing of the house facing the road is the original mediaeval cottage. This consisted on the ground floor of just two rooms separated by a cross passage. This type of home developed from the longhouse, always built on a slight slope, in which the quarters on the lower side of the passage were for animals, and the rest of the house was for humans. The wing at right angles is also very old, and is still thatched on the north side. It would have been added to form a separate kitchen.

LYDFORD GORGE

**G.R.509845
and G.R.502832**

This is the narrowest of all the gorges or cleaves through which a number of Dartmoor rivers escape from the high country. The sides are very steep and densely wooded.

Along one side of the gorge the path runs high above the river, while on the other it keeps fairly close to the river bank. There is a footbridge at each end, so that a "circular" tour can be made.

Among the spectacular sights are the one hundred foot high "White Lady" waterfall at one end of the walk, and as an optional extra "The Devil's Cauldron" at the other. This was once described in a newspaper as "not for the nervous".

The gorge is owned by The National Trust. There are two entrances: one near Lydford village and another at the southwest end about a mile and a half away. Both entrances have a carpark, shop and toilets.

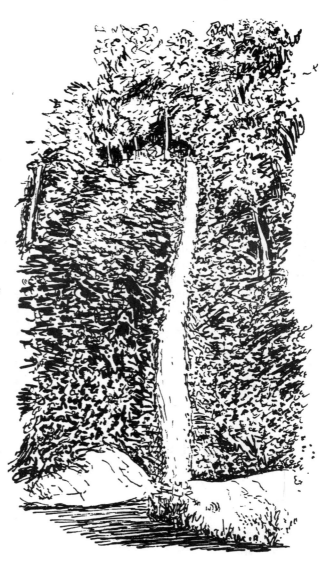

The White Lady

117

Much of this square mile is open, rather featureless downland, on both sides of the main road.

So here is a selection of granite and concrete posts along a quarter-mile stretch of the road just south of the car park.

The information they display must be useful to some one!

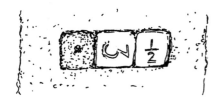

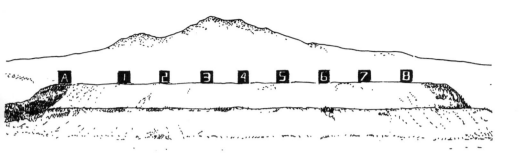

Hare Tor in the background

It cannot be pretended that this is an entrancing view, but the army have been here for a long time and are likely to stay for a long time yet, so we have to accept things as they are. Willsworthy range is at present used more often than the other two larger ranges, but generally there is little firing at weekends and none during the main holidays: at those times you can wander where you will.

Much of this downland looks rather empty and uninteresting, except for the obvious military encumbrances, but two leats still carrying water run across it to provide hydro-electricity for the national grid. At one time they supplied power for three different mines.

The Lych Way also crossed this down, as well as another track that ran from Brentor to Rattlebrook mine. Both of these passed quite close to the army huts.

Rook   *Crow*

Both Rooks and Crows are to be seen in the area. In the adults the Rooks have a bare patch at the base of the beak. The old way of telling them apart still holds good: "If you see a lot of Crows they are Rooks, but a Rook all by itself is a Crow".

This magnificent gorge through the granite is worth a visit at any time of the year. When the Tavy is in spate the water rushes down in wild abandon, hurling itself over the falls, tumbling through the cataracts, and filling the dark pools. After a dry spell the laughing water dances lightly along its rocky bed. You can then wade through the shallows, jump from boulder to boulder, or even sit under a waterfall or two.

The large pool into which the river cascades through a narrow cleft is known as "The Devil's Kitchen".

WATERN OKE

Hare Tor in the distance

This wild, boulder strewn hillside offers a field day for hut circle enthusiasts. For here is a Bronze Age village consisting of over seventy huts—the largest collection on the Moor. The slope is so thickly littered with boulders as to make walking in a straight line impossible for more than a few yards at a time. On careful inspection it is seen that many of the stones once belonged to the tumbled huts. The builders chose the site for obvious reasons: plentiful building material, nearby water, and a southwest aspect.

The settlement was probably occupied for many generations, but the population at any one time cannot really be estimated. Some of the circles are too small to have been homes: they were possibly outhouses. Some were connected by low walls, while in several places a wall runs out from a hut and then stops for no apparent reason.

This village was extensively studied and excavated in 1905. A great deal of charcoal was unearthed, many flint scraps and cooking stones, and some pottery fragments, but nothing really "exciting".

It is worth sitting for a while on one of the fallen walls, and contemplating the scene, peopling it in the imagination with villagers going about their business: repairing roofs, fetching water, driving animals, preparing food . . . .

It is fairly certain that three thousand or more years ago, when the village was occupied, the climate would have been better than it is now.

AMICOMBE BROOK

H 7

Fur Tor is nearer the middle of Northern Dartmoor than any other tor. Only the nearby Cut Hill, which has no tor upon it, can claim a more central position. So from which ever direction you come it's a long slog over rough terrain. If you come from the west then by the time you reach Amicombe Brook there is only one steep climb left.

O.P.15 is a favourite taking off point for those coming from the north.

FURRY TOR

It was never so far to Tipperary

It's a long slog to Furrytory,

It's a long way to go.

It's a long slog to Furrytory,

To the grandest tor I know.

Goodbye Ohpeefifteen, farewell Hangingstone,

It's a long, hard slog to Furrytory,

When I'm all alone.

FUR TOR

This is one of the grandest, and certainly the most remote of all the tors.
Sing this song to the tune of "John Peel" on your way there.

If ye ken Fur Tor on a wintry day,
If ye ken Fur Tor when the skies are grey,
If ye ken Fur Tor when the sun's far away,
  Then you've come a long way since the morning.

CHORUS: For the Queen of the Tors has a mighty head
           Which she lifts on high from her bog moss bed:
           And whether you steered, or were pixy led,
             You have climbed Fur Tor in the morning.

If you came from the West over Amicombe Hill
Through heather and sedge and tormentil,
Then you saved to the end the steepest thrill
  Of the climb to the top in the morning.

CHORUS

If you came from the South by Beardown Man
The going was tough, so you'll change your plan,
And return by another route, if you can,
  When you've climbed Fur Tor in the morning.

CHORUS

The way from the North is all very well,
But swing a bit East, and it's hard to tell
If you're tramping for joy or trudging through Hell
  On your way to Fur Tor in the morning.

CHORUS

Now the long slog back will be five times worse:
Your legs are tired, every fall brings a curse:
You'd be far better off in a motorized hearse,
  When you've climbed Fur Tor in the morning.

CUT HILL

Cut Hill has an aura of bleakness and remoteness that acts like a magnet to those who like to penetrate the innermost recesses of any wilderness. There is no direct route from any road—at least not one that you would take twice.
So try this way—to the tune of *"She'll be coming round the mountain"*.

We'll be trampin' off to Cut Hill when we go,
We'll be trampin' off to Cut Hill when we go,
We'll be trampin' off to Cut Hill,
We'll be trampin' off to Cut Hill,
We'll be trampin' off to Cut Hill when we go.

We'll be headin' out 'cross Black Ridge when we go . . .

We'll be climbin' up from Cut Combe when we go . . .

We'll be sloggin' round by Vur Tor when we go . . .

We'll be jumpin' 'cross the peat hags when we go . . .

We'll be squelchin' through the bogmoss when we go . . .

We'll be ploddin' on in wet socks when we go . . .

We'll be tired an' wet an' hungrey when we're there . . .

But the day is not yet over when we're there . . .

We have still the journey back to do and so . . .

We'll be ploddin' back in wet socks when we go . . .

We'll be squelchin' through the bogmoss when we go . . .

We'll be jumpin' 'cross the peat hags when we go . . .

We'll be sloggin' round by Vur Tor when we go . . .

We'll be climbin' down to Cut Combe when we go . . .

We'll be headin' over Black Ridge when we go . . .

We'll be trampin, back from Cut Hill when we go . . .

Statt's fireplace

Now here's a house with a fine view. Through 360 degrees the fen rolls away to distant horizons. Peat cutters built this shelter two centuries ago as a refuge from tempest and darkness. The floor has risen as thatch and boulders have fallen in, but the fireplace is still there—though smoke from a peat fire would have difficulty in finding its way up the chimney. The opposite end of the little house is rounded, and one can imagine two or three peat cutters sitting here in semi-darkness when weather or fatigue demanded a respite from work. As often as not there may only have been one man here for days at a time. It's a long, rough trudge to the nearest settlement, and precious hours of daylight would have been wasted in journeying to and fro.

The cut slabs of peat might need a month to dry out in summer before being taken away by barrow or cart—no easy task over soft, hummocky ground.

Walking across a landscape turned over by peat cutters is hard work: as William Crossing wrote, "The peat worker found Dartmoor rough, and contrived to make it a little rougher".

A hundred yards to the northwest stands the marker at the upper end of one of Phillpott's Peat Passes. Refer to Square G 8 for information about these. This is one of the easiest to find. A walk down the pass towards the East Dart will show that parts of it have been paved. At the lower end where the pass runs down a ramp on to firmer ground stands another marker.

GREY WETHERS

Walk down from Sittaford Tor imagining the forest unplanted and the walls unbuilt . . . . Here is a site of wonder and speculation. Nowhere else on Dartmoor is there such a pair of stone circles. Nowhere are there any larger ones still standing. No others are so entirely composed of stones chosen with such regard for their geometrical shape and regularity.

In 1909 a careful restoration was carried out to re-erect the many fallen stones in their original holes. There are still a few gaps but the general appearance must be much as the builders intended, perhaps nearly four thousand years ago. But why they planned it like this is another of the Moor's fascinating puzzles. Why two circles? Why is the northern one about four yards smaller in diameter than the southern? Did that one always contain fewer stones? Why . . ? . . . There's no end to the questions . . . . and no answers either.

There is however a legend to explain why so many of the stones had fallen by the beginning of this century. It seems that in order to expiate her sins an erring wife had to perform a number of ritual tests at various localities on the Moor. The last of these was to kneel before a stone in one of these circles and pray for forgiveness. If nothing terrible happened she rose thankfully, but if the Lord of the Rings considered her transgressions unforgivable then the stone fell upon the poor woman. After nearly four thousand years of history about thirty stones had to be re-erected.

FERNWORTHY RESERVOIR (S.W. end)

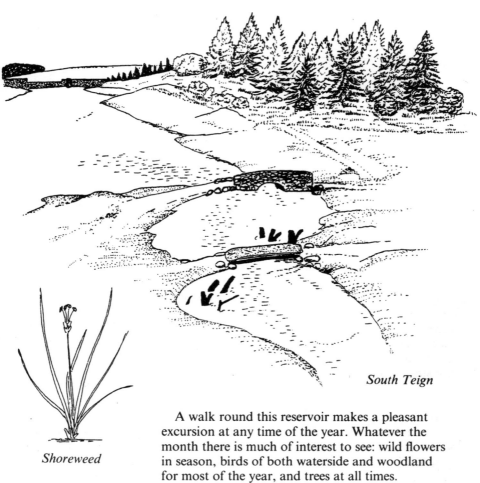

South Teign

Shoreweed

A walk round this reservoir makes a pleasant excursion at any time of the year. Whatever the month there is much of interest to see: wild flowers in season, birds of both waterside and woodland for most of the year, and trees at all times.

Every few years—after a summer drought—the water falls so low that an old track across the valley to Fernworthy Farm on the west bank becomes uncovered. It is then possible to walk across both the little bridge and the much older clapper, both of which spend most of their time under water. The river flowing beneath them is the South Teign.

In summer when the water has receded slightly it is worth searching just a little way down the slope for a small plant that is usually submerged. This is Shoreweed whose flowers seem to consist only of four stamens at the head of a slender stalk.

Some of the stone rows on Dartmoor are disappointing because the stones are small, or fallen, or many may be missing. But here is a row, a double one, that is undoubtedly complete. At the lower end stands a hefty blocking stone, set as usual at right angles to the direction of the row. Then come forty nine pairs of stones, of various sizes, sufficiently equidistant to make it certain that every one is still in place—ninety nine in all. A few are nearly smothered in vegetation, but there is no difficulty in locating them all. At the higher end the last stone on the left is much taller than any of the others.

Immediately beyond the end (or is it really the beginning?) of the row there was once, again as usual, a grave and a cairn. Only a low mound now remains and one or two well embedded boulders.

It is sad that a monument such as this, probably the only complete double row on the Moor, should lack the cairn that was once such an important part of it. For presumably the grave was the reason for setting up the stone avenue.

One can understand despoilers of old dismantling the cairn to rob the grave beneath, but what happened to all the stones? Did they form a handy supply for whoever built the long wall that now encloses Fernworthy Forest?

Small Heath butterfly

A quarter of an hour's stroll upstream from the little car park will bring many rewards to those who like searching for marsh plants. Almost all the way up you can step across the streamlet, though here and there it swells out into boggy patches, and sometimes it disappears underground for several yards.

At the lower end there are plenty of pebbles to delight children who like building dams and weirs. At the upper end, less than half a mile away, the stream emerges from a hidden source into a deep pool. Dragonflies zoom above it, whirligigs and pond skaters play on it, and newts swim lazily within it.

Of the streamside flowers:
BOG ASPHODEL (yellow), BOG PIMPERNEL (pink),
BOG PONDWEED (greenish), and MARSH VIOLET (violet) are
   illustrated below.

LOUSEWORT . . . . is shown in Square K 14
SUNDEW and BUTTERWORT . . . . M 17
MARSH SAINT JOHN'S-WORT and LESSER SPEARWORT . N 3
COTTON-GRASS . . . . S 10
ROUND-LEAVED CROWFOOT and BLINKS . . . . X 12

WATER FORGET-ME-NOT is also common, and quite unmistakable.

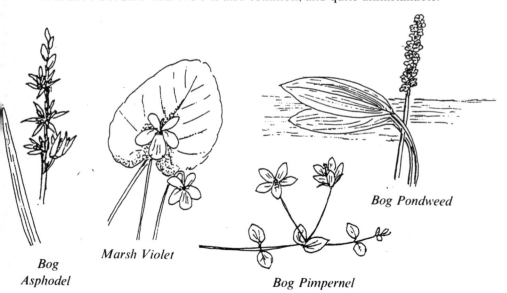

Bog Pondweed

Marsh Violet

*Bog
Asphodel*

Bog Pimpernel

WEST COOMBE

There was a time when sailors who were paid off at either Dartmouth or Bideford and were not able to find another ship in the same port, would walk across Devon to the opposite coast to seek another berth. Their route, partly across eastern Dartmoor, became known as the Mariner's Way. Much of the moorland part of the track is now waymarked, and can easily be followed. Here at West Coombe (or Combe) the path runs not only through the farmyard, but at first sight through the farmhouse as well. For this is a mediaeval longhouse and the path makes use of the passage between the shippon and the living quarters. It is quite likely that the house also served as a hostel for travellers.

The massive blocks of granite used in building both the shippon and the barns on the other side of the yard are worth more than a moment of admiration. The shippon is the only one in Devon to have a rounded doorway in the gable end.

The great toothed wheel behind the house was installed about 1940 to generate electricity.

A very short way down the lane is a stone and turf roofed ash house, one of the best examples to be found. Here the ashes from the peat fire would be placed every night, as an insurance against unwanted fires, and a source of fertilizer for the fields.

The Mariners' Way

This very old longhouse has twice been extended, but still retains some of its original features: for instance, a truly magnificent fireplace and an interior granite staircase, though of course these are not visible from the road.

On the bank near the farm grows a wild flower which at one time was credited with being able to cure or alleviate forty seven of the disorders and misfortunes "which flesh is heir to". This is Betony.

The reddish purple flowers appear in late summer along many a local laneside. In some places the plants may well be descended from cultivated ones, for a clump of Betony on each side of a garden gate was supposed to deter any witch from entering.

The stems, leaves, and flowers were all collected and dried. They were then used as required in "syrup, conserve oil, ointment or plaster". The powdered leaves could be drunk in hot water, milk, wine or honey. Among the ills against which this veritable apothecary's shop was said to be effective were colds, coughs, indigestion, jaundice, convulsions, sores, shrinking sinews, gout, headache, earache, obstruction of the spleen, travel weariness, snake bite, rabies, the pains of childbirth, witchcraft, despair, . . . and that still leaves another thirty.

The occupants of Barramoor Farm hardly need the services of doctor or chemist!

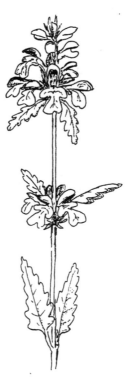

Betony

Here well away from any main road, a little sleepy perhaps in the spring sunshine, is to be found the classic picture of a Devon village. A large green shaded by mature oaks, an old pump, an ancient cross, thatched cottages, a mediaeval church, and an inn whose reputation puts it high on the list of those Dartmoor explorers who like good food, drink and company.

A hundred years ago the population was double its present number, and there used to be a post office, shop, smithy, and school. These have all gone, leaving a slight feeling of emptiness: but thankfully no garage or supermarket has arrived to replace them.

The cross at the edge of the green was rescued from the Bovey Brook in 1829, where for many years it had done duty as a stepping stone. It has been suggested that before that it was a waymark beside another set of stepping stones not far away.

All the objects in the sketch above are to be seen from the village green, but the pump, the cross, and the inn sign have been "relocated" to accommodate them on the page.

132

NEADON

Long before William the Conqueror had ever been heard of there was a farm here. It possibly comprised about 60 acres, for which the "rates" paid to King Edward were fixed at twelve pence a year.

Once William was firmly established on the throne he distributed lands to noblemen and the Church. The Manor of Neadon was one of many given to Baldwin, the High Sheriff of Devon. In 1086 the Domesday Book was compiled. The king's commissioners came here and recorded that the sheriff's tenant had died but that the work of the farm was being carried on by his widow. As well as her own family there were also two smallholders, presumably with their families, and one serf who would have been landless. It was noted that there were 4 acres of meadow, 5 acres of pasture, and enough arable land for one plough to cultivate. Oxen, sheep, and poultry would have been there besides. Such was the success of their farming that the "rates" were increased to five shillings.

In the little hamlet the most noteworthy building by far is UPPER HALL. It is one of only two remaining 15th century houses in Devon built as a "first floor" home. The whole of the ground floor was used as barn and shippon, while the living quarters were above, reached by an outside staircase. There have inevitably been alterations, but the side of the house facing the yard clearly shows the original architecture.

This is not at all a small cross: but it is a large tree: a magnificent Ash.

The cross stands by the road near Sanduck Farm, but probably not exactly in its original position, for this is another waymark that has been unearthed this century. It was discovered among the foundations of the farm house after this was burnt down in 1901. One suggestion is that the cross was hidden, perhaps during Puritan times, and then forgotten.

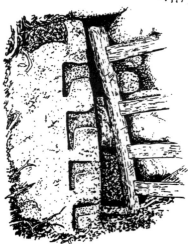

Not far west of the cross another lane comes in from the south. A couple of hundred yards up here on the right stands this fine L-slotted gate post. Its partner, which would have had simple vertical slots is unfortunately missing. It has been replaced by a wooden post, so that the former method of closing the gap with loose poles can no longer be used.

This magnificent Ash stands at the corner of the lane to Lower Elsford.

Ash has always been a valuable tree in the countryside. Its smooth, close-grained, shock resistant timber is particularly suitable for tool handles, poles, oars, and parts of wagons. Of all our native trees it is the only one whose wood will burn equally as well green as seasoned.

Among Devon customs the following have survived into this century:-

As a way of curing a baby of whooping cough an Ash sapling was split longitudinally and wedged open. The baby was then passed through the gap, naked, three times at dawn. The trunk was then bandaged tightly, and as the wound healed so apparently did the child.

Another local custom takes place on Chistmas Eve. A faggot of Ash sticks, tightly bound with nine bands, is burnt either at home or in an inn. As each band bursts the company drink a fresh round of cider.

A decoction of the leaves in either warm water or wine has been recommended in a slimming diet, as a cure for rheumatism, and as an aid to long life.

Finally, if you spot a growing leaf without a terminal leaflet—a so called Even-Ash— keep it. It will bring you good luck.

Ash leaves are similar to those of Rowan (or Mountain Ash), which is widespread on the higher granite areas of the Moor, but the buds are unmistakable: they are coal black, arranged in opposite pairs.

Ash buds

TRENCHFORD RESERVOIR

The dam

Of the three reservoirs in the area this was the last to be constructed, and once again it was necessitated by the still growing population round Torbay.

The building of the dam brought more problems than in the case of the other two (See Squares G 21 and H 22). It had to be much longer, and because of the nature of the underlying rock the foundations had to be much deeper. It was completed in 1907. Yet twenty years later even all three reservoirs could not deliver enough water, and plans for a still larger supply, from higher on the Moor, were put in hand. Finally, in 1942, the Fernworthy reservoir, nine miles away, was completed, and the water from it can be seen flowing into this reservoir between the car park and the dam. The total outflow now reaches something like seven million gallons a day.

This is the best starting place for a leisurely day's exploration of all three reservoirs. For here, near the large car park, are picnic tables, toilets, information and maps.

One of the less commonly planted conifers to be seen along the waterside path is the Weymouth Pine. Look for a pine with long, narrow cones and needles in clusters of five.

This long, narrow reservoir is the oldest in the National Park. The dam, which was finished in 1861, is built mainly of clay and earth. It was constructed to supply Torquay with water; but that town was growing so fast that within eight years the embankment had twice to be heightened. The reservoir now holds about 100 million gallons of water, and covers an area of 31 acres.

About half way along the reservoir a causeway crosses the water. This was built at the same time as the dam in order to provide a screen which would filter out much of the sediment coming down the Kennick Brook. The causeway carries a public footpath which runs from Trenchford reservoir to Kennick reservoir, returning by a different route.

The paths and other facilities are further described on the pages dealing with the other reservoirs in this complex. See Squares G 21 and H 21.

These mine workings are surprisingly close to the Tudor mansion of CANONTEIGN BARTON. This was built early in the 17th century on a typical E-plan, but the road passes so close to its rather plain back that there is only a glimpse of the ends of the wings to give an impression of its grandeur.

The mine is named, not after the seaside town, but in memory of Lord Exmouth who lived at CANONTEIGN HOUSE a short way to the south-west.

Tall as they are the mine buildings are fast becoming overwhelmed by Oak, Beech, and Spruce. But the roofless engine house still has its magnificent oak door, and beside it rises an octagonal chimney faced with granite on all its external angles.

The mine operated from 1845 until 1874 producing mainly lead. The slopes of the spoil heaps running down into the valley are still not overgrown with vegetation. Besides lead smaller quantities of silver, barytes, and fluorspar were also mined.

Engine house door

This is a deceptive village, and a remarkable one too. There is no shop, no post office, no school, and no inn, yet the villagers have three halls in which to meet, all being well used; and in their homes they produce quilts, cushions, ceramics, leatherwork, and a monthly newspaper. The butcher, the baker, the grocer, the cobbler, and the postmaster have all gone. Only the "smith" remains. Linger outside his workshop to study the fascinating display of wheels, pulleys, gates, grilles, tubes, nesting boxes, bird tables, windvanes, anemometers, furnace doors, a guillotine, and his row of discarded briar pipes.

The main line railway station is only a minutes walk away. The canopy over one platform is still in excellent condition, as also is the bold station sign announcing "BRENTOR", and a more discreet one advising GENTLEMEN where they may go. A Southern Railway notice still advertises "Inter City to Europe". But between the main platform and the shelter and seat on the opposite one there is now a well kept lawn with a few apple trees approaching twenty years of age.

Only ghost trains run through BRENTOR these days.

The items in the sketch below are not of course in their correct relative positions, but all are to be found in a five minute stroll through the village.

Stand by triangulation pillar No. 3450 on the summit of the hill for a magnificent panorama of Dartmoor tors. Not only is the whole line of western heights in view, but beyond them if visibility is good the innermost crests of the blanket bog, Black Ridge and Cut Hill, form a grey horizon.

From North to South the prominent tors on the horizon are Sourton Tor, Great Links Tor, Dunnagoat, Sharp Tor, Hare Tor, Fur Tor, Lynch Tor, White Tor, Great Mis Tor, Little Mis Tor, North Hessary Tor, Roos Tor, Great Staple Tor, and Cox Tor.

This hill is so named because there was indeed a gibbet up here, a specially built one that had an iron cage suspended from its arm. In this cage malefactors were imprisoned and left to die. The former road from Tavistock to Okehampton ran over the hill so that passing folk could treat the prisoner to a crust of bread or a feast of invective, as they felt inclined.

Near the triangulation point are some old mining gullies, and about 300 yards to the south are two shafts, now filled in and fenced in. But it is not a good idea to climb the fence to see if the infilling is adequate.

WHEAL BETSY

A walk round this engine house will show the remarkable curvature of the chimney stack.

The various explanations for this pleasing oddity involve: a drunken stone mason, . .
an apprentice who didn't use a plumb line, . .
a workman with curvature of the spine, . .
badly mixed mortar, . .
a rainstorm during building operations, . .
and any others you like to make up for yourself . . .

WHEAL BETSY
THIS ANCIENT SILVER-LEAD MINE WAS RE-
OPENED IN 1806 AND WORKED SUCCESSFULLY
FOR THE NEXT SEVENTY YEARS.THE MINE WAS
WORKED BY WATER POWER UNTIL 1868 WHEN
THIS BUILDING WAS ERECTED TO HOUSE A
CORNISH BEAM PUMPING ENGINE, UNTIL
ITS CLOSURE IN 1877 ALL PUMPING,WINDING
AND CRUSHING OF ORE WAS CARRIED OUT BY
STEAM POWER.
IN 1967 THE RUINED ENGINE HOUSE AND
STACK WERE ACQUIRED AND MADE SAFE BY
THE NATIONAL TRUST AS A MEMORIAL TO THE
MINING INDUSTRY OF DARTMOOR.

WHEAL JEWELL RESERVOIR

G.R.523813

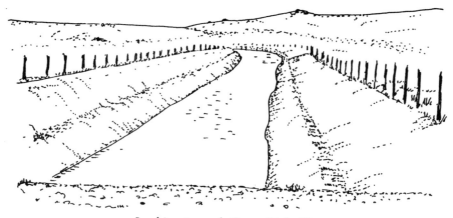

Looking towards Great Links Tor

This reservoir, which has no possible claim to beauty, is surprisingly well hidden in a landscape devoid of hills, trees, hedges, and crops. Two leats run in at the northern end. At one time or another these supplied water to three different mines: Wheal Friendship, an important copper mine, Wheal Betsy (See Square I 3), and Wheal Jewell which was situated just here. Nowadays the water is piped underground to the hydro-electric power station at Mary Tavy.

Here are two similar Dandelion-like flowers that grow along the banks near the green hut.

Cats-ear, which has smooth branched stems bearing a few tiny bracts, is a common plant of waste places everywhere; but the Greater Hawkbit, with hairy and unbranched stems, is not a moorland plant at all. It normally likes a mild or limy soil, so it probably arrived with the ballast and cement imported when the reservoir was built in the 1930's.

Greater Hawkbit

Cat's-ear

CATALOO STEPS

G.R.540812

The Lych Way along which parishioners from Postbridge and Bellever used to carry their dead for burial at Lydford crossed the Tavy, if the water was low enough, by these steps. Today, 700 years later, they still make a safe and easy crossing—but only after a dry spell. If the river is running high they are under water.

The shortest route from those settlements (one only to be undertaken in settled weather) involved a hard slog of a dozen miles over wild and desolate hills and across several streams. In the case of a funeral cortege the body would almost certainly have been slung on a packhorse.

Having crossed the Tavy the worst of the journey was over, and the first habitations would soon be in sight.

So here in Coffin Wood the body was placed in its coffin and the bearers would continue up Corpse Lane, very likely seeking rest or refreshment at Higher Willsworthy Farm.

This part of the way, much of it along sunken tracks, is clearly waymarked, and can easily be followed.

The alternative river crossings would have been upstream at Standon Steps (which is not now a public right of way) or a considerable way down-stream at Hill Bridge. (See Square J 4).

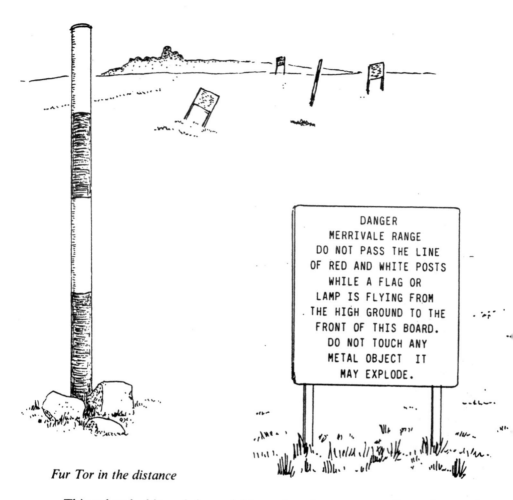

DANGER
MERRIVALE RANGE
DO NOT PASS THE LINE
OF RED AND WHITE POSTS
WHILE A FLAG OR
LAMP IS FLYING FROM
THE HIGH GROUND TO THE
FRONT OF THIS BOARD.
DO NOT TOUCH ANY
METAL OBJECT IT
MAY EXPLODE.

Fur Tor in the distance

   This red and white pole is much bigger than the ones normally used to mark the range boundaries, for this spot is the meeting point of all three ranges.
   You can, in theory, stand safely in front of this pole when red flags are flying in every direction and there seems to be firing all round, for a narrow triangle of open moor also runs up to this point. But one pace to the left will put you inside Willsworthy Range, one pace to the right inside Merrivale Range, and one pace ahead into Okehampton Range, so watch your step.
   One of the three notice boards is illustrated. It is important to remember that the military term "TO THE FRONT" means "BEHIND".

WALKHAM HEAD PEAT PASS

In dreary weather this square mile can be a desolate part of the Moor, but during a dry spell in summer it offers invigorating walking with wide views and distant tors. The ground cover is blanket bog—not dangerous, but splodgy in places. This is an area where a lot of peat cutting has taken place in the past.

The easiest way to find the peat pass is probably to walk along the spur that runs northwest from Walkham Head. This is one of the shorter passes, hardly 200 yards long, but there is a Phillpotts memorial at each end. For more information about these passes see Square G 8.

If from the northern end of the pass you go down northeast towards the Tavy this large boulder fitted with an iron ring is to be found. It lies on the slope between a streamlet and the river. Here is an unexpected sign that men once worked here. The ring was used to tether a horse, the two boulders providing some shelter from the wind.

TAVY HOLE

This defile is the first picturesque stretch of the river. Between the Head and the Hole the Tavy first runs south, then swings west through a wide shallow basin, and finally turns north to tumble down among the boulders in this narrow valley. This drawing was done towards the end of the long, dry summer of 1989, when the usual shining cascades and whirling pools were far from their best.

The Tavy has a reputation as a wild and unpredictable river. It is born high in the oozing peat of the desolate blanket bog, and drops a thousand feet in about seven miles. This makes it the fastest flowing river of Dartmoor, and the second fastest in all the British Isles.

COWFLOP BOTTOM

This little, marshy basin with its lingering stream and numerous tinners' mounds is one of Dartmoor's lost valleys. Neither the stream, nor the one into which it runs, Broada Marsh Stream, is named on the map, and only the tiniest kink in two contour lines gives any indication of its existence. Yet this remote moorland dell has a name—Cowflop Bottom—bestowed upon it in all likelihood by the tinners who worked here.

Cowflops are Foxgloves. At one time the freshly turned up mounds of stones and soil evidently provided a habitat to suit these plants. They are still here, though no longer in enough numbers to have a valley named after them.

Sphagnum, rush, and sedge fill the watery basin, and in summer the woolly heads of Hare's-tail Cottongrass dance in the breeze. One of the commonest of the smaller plants is Star Sedge.

Well up the valley, under the edge of a peat bank on the northern side, stands a Phillpotts Peat Pass memorial. See Square G 8 for more about these. This one is at the eastern end of Johnson's Cut, which leads over towards the East Dart.

Downstream on the left bank, just beyond the confluence with Broada Marsh Stream, a massive boulder with a vertical face has been adapted to form one wall of a tinners' hut, probably a cache for tools.

Star Sedge

Cowflops

Here for half a mile or so the East Dart rushes along a steep and narrow valley, cutting a winding swathe through the open moor. Cascades and rapids abound, and one of the waterfalls is impressive enough to be located on the map.

Except for short spells when the river is in spate there are slabs of rock to sit on beside and above the falls, and at all times the grassy and rocky banks make a pleasant place to dally. In summer there is an added attraction for the hardy—an inviting pool for a swim.

This spot lies about two miles upstream from Postbridge and can be reached along either bank, but the track that sets off up the west side is a shorter one because it is then possible to cut across the hill where the river makes a long loop northwards.

THE SHEEPFOLD

Inside the upper wall

Blocked entrance

There are two traditions about the origin of this enclosure, which with its magnificent walls is unique on the Moor.

One says that it was built, perhaps in the early 19th century, as a factory where starch would be produced from potatoes to be grown in the vicinity. The two brothers who built it intended also to build a mansion—where Stannon Cottage now stands—but that plan came to naught, and the entire project folded up before ever any potatoes were grown.

The other tradition is that the enclosure was built as a sheepfold, and included the now ruinous dwelling which is still evident at one end of the yard. The array of standing stones along the inside walls are the remains of sheep pens, once roofed over. This enterprise is attributed to the Scotsman who introduced Scottish Blackfaced sheep to Dartmoor. It is possible that he merely took over the abandoned site, blocking up the original wide entrance, and adapting the inside architecture to his own purposes.

Whatever the truth, the walls are still there to be admired. The 6 to 8 feet high uprights built at intervals into the downhill face of the two longer walls have long outlasted the hopes of whoever toiled at setting them up.

Outer face of the lower wall   *Inside the lower wall*

WALL'S-END

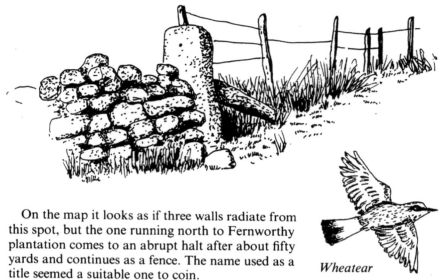

Wheatear

On the map it looks as if three walls radiate from this spot, but the one running north to Fernworthy plantation comes to an abrupt halt after about fifty yards and continues as a fence. The name used as a title seemed a suitable one to coin.

A notice by the stile over the wall says that in the newtake (on the south western side) experiments in heather management are being conducted. Since from the wall top there appears to be very little heather on that side the work done is obviously either very successful or a dismal failure—depending on whether the object of the exercise is to eliminate or to encourage heather. This is not explained.

The wall that runs southwards from here is an excellent example of a cornditch still in good shape. These were walls built with a ditch on the outside to prevent Red Deer from leaping in. However should one somehow get in to the enclosure then the ramp on the inside of the wall made it easy for the animal to jump out again. Red Deer were exterminated on the Moor in the 1780's, so no cornditches were built after that. Very occasionally Red Deer are still seen on the Moor, but these are single animals that have made the journey from Exmoor.

A walk along the wall may send a Wheatear flitting ahead of you from post to post. Wheatears (or White Arses as our ancestors called them) are migrants that spend the winter in Africa. They are back on Dartmoor by about the middle of March, and stay until late October. They frequent rocky places, building their nests deep among the boulders.

Here is a well known story about this lonely inn,
Sing it to the tune of "Away in a manger".

Away on the moorland
As darkness set in
A trav'ler arrived at
The Warren House Inn.
The weather was bitter—
Deep snow on the ground—
His faltering footsteps
Made never a sound.

Mine host bade his welcome,
"Good evening", he said,
And set to preparing
A meal and a bed.
"We've not had a guest here
Ten days in a row,
For no one could get here
Because of the snow."

Salt mutton for supper
And freshly baked bread
Soon meant that the trav'ler
Was ready for bed.
A cheery "Goodnight", and
He went up the stairs;
Then knelt by the bedside
To say a few prayers.

He noticed a coffer
With half opened lid,
And sleepily wondered
What in it was hid.
He lifted it higher
And held up the light—
Inside was a body
All glistening white.

The whole of that long night
He ne'er shut an eye;
He dared not relax as
The hours crept by.
But nobody entered
With cudgel or knife,
To claim one more victim,
Or threaten his life.

Next morning at breakfast,
—Salt bacon and toast—
"I hope you slept well", said
His jovial host.
The bleary-eyed trav'ler,
Not sure what to think
Admitted with candour
He'd not slept a wink.

"I looked in that coffer,
—You know what lies there—
A white, naked body
with glistening hair.
The weather's so bad that
I had to stay here,
But I was determined
To sell my life dear."

"Forgive me, I pray you,"
The landlord replied,
" 'Twas two weeks ago now
That grandfather died.
The snow lies so deep that
We're cut off from town,
So upstairs we laid him
And salted him down."

THE FOUR ACES

These four curiously shaped little fields are on the lower slopes of Birch Tor. The traditional story of how they got there is here told in Coleridgian fashion. The central figure is Jan Reynolds of Widecombe, and the date is 1638.

It is perchance Old Nick himself
Who stoppeth foolish Jan.
"By thy cloven feet and horny head
What wantest thou, my man?

"I have no cash to give to you
Or other begging folk."
"The boot is on the other foot".
Quoth Nick, "It's you that's broke.

"You've lost the lot by playing cards
And now you're into debt.
Perhaps you'd like a hefty loan,
And pay no interest yet?"

The gold was paid, the bargain made
With little rigmarole.
"That's fine", the Devil said, "One day
I'll come to get your soul."

The months went by. October came.
At Poundsgate on the hill
Mine hostess took a golden coin
And put it in the till.

'Twas paid her by a handsome guy
Well dressed beyond belief:
That same Old Nick, who played a trick
And changed it to a leaf.

Then off he rode to Widecombe,
And hitched up to the tower,
Inside the village folk had met:
It was the Vespers hour.

O. Jan. have care, the Devil's here,
He's come to take his due.
But Jan was thinking of his cards
Beside him on the pew.

A flash, a crash, a rending sound,
And Nick was by his side.
"The time has come to keep your pledge
You'll come with me and ride."

Jan grabbed his cards. They rose aloft.
A corner stone fell in,
Which killed four people down below—
The price of one man's sin.

Then through the sky, in haste, on high,
Poor Jan was borne away;
But all unplanned, from out his hand
Four aces dropped astray.

Canst see them on the western slope.
Below the tor named Birch?
Then mark them well, for Jan's in Hell,
Who took his cards to church.

The Ace fields

GRIMSPOUND

Gateway into Grimspound and the pound wall behind

Of the large prehistoric pounds on the Moor this is the most frequently visited, for it is easily accessible and comparatively well preserved. It probably dates back to the early Bronze Age, say three thousand years ago.

The outer wall is about 500 yards in circumference and encloses about four acres of downland. Because there are no walls of more recent date in the vicinity it is likely that most of the stones used in building the pound and huts are still there. It has been estimated that the impounding wall would originally have been about nine feet wide, but only five feet high. This was clearly not a defensive site to keep out human enemies, but an enclosure in which to keep animals safe from such marauders as wolves. The nature of the magnificent entrance bears this out. It was paved to prevent it from becoming a quagmire due to the frequent treading of livestock. There are also traces of stock pens against the inside of the western walls. Water was of course no problem, as a stream flows through the site.

In 1894 an extended exploration of the site was made, and one of the living huts was partly rebuilt in order to give a better idea of its original appearance. The hut walls could not have been more than about four feet high, though the doorway might have been a little higher, having a lintel across the top. A central pole probably supported a thatched roof.

Apart from some charcoal in a number of the huts, very little else was found to give any clues to the lives of the inhabitants, just a few scraps of plain pottery and some flint scrapers.

One of the hut circles, showing the entrance

THE HEATHERCOMBE FISHES

G.R.725808
718811
717808

The three map references are to three tall stones each having three fishes carved in relief on them. They were set up between 1969 and 1976 round the boundary of the Heathercombe estate. All the stones are of a similar elegant shape, and each bears a simple inscription, though the wording on the second and third stones is not as recorded by either Eric Hemery or Harry Starkey.

The first stone, "THINE IS THE POWER", stands at a road junction. There is space to park a car off the road a short way along the lane to Heathercombe. The rest of the route must be followed on foot. The second stone, inscribed "AND THE KINGDOM", also stands by the roadside, at a steep bend beyond the two houses.

To find the third stone continue up the lane, and just past Heathercombe Adventure Centre (once a Silver Fox farm) take the steep bridle path to the left. Follow the wall round the plantation, down into Heathercombe, and up the other side. Near the brow of the hill there is a gate in the wall. The last stone, "AND THE GLORY", stands just inside. It can be seen that it was once a gatepost.

While crossing Heathercombe you will come to the conclusion that a better name for it would be Brackencombe, for there is precious little heather in it. A better spelling, the one often used by the estate itself, is Hethercombe, because this shows that the name is derived from the words Higher Combe, the manor's earlier name.

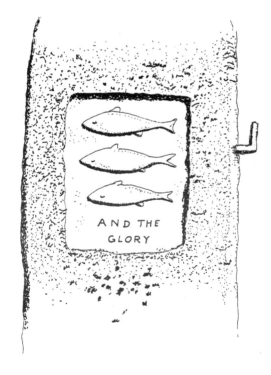

WHOOPING ROCK

This open hill stands in isolation from any other, for it is encircled by a garland of lanes—lanes that wander happily round fields and behind high hedges, now and again visiting a farm, but not really sure where they are going, or why. The most surprising one of all runs from Barracott to Easdon Farm. It starts off with what was once a tarmac surface, though this is now pockmarked by frost and channelled by rushing rivulets. Then suddenly the jigsaw of pieces of tarmac stops and the way continues as a typical moorland track of grass, granite, and growan. This route is a good deal more direct than the road down the hill, so what happened? Did the supply of tarmac run out? Or did a machine break down? Or was the way too rough? Or . . . .? Inventing possible reasons is an entertaining pastime.

Just below the triangulation pillar on the hill stands Whooping Rock, looking as if a mighty shove would send it sliding down into the valley. Two explanations have been given for its name. One, that the wind makes a whooping noise as it rushes through the aperture beneath the boulder perched on top; and two, that people once brought children suffering from whooping cough up here so that they could rest awhile among the sheep that often sheltered by the rock. It seems there was a belief that the presence of sheep could alleviate the distress caused by prolonged coughing.

Another local name for this outcrop is Piggy Rock.

Manaton village is curiously separated into two clusters. The church, the Rectory, the old school, and a former inn all flank the delightful green with its avenue of Limes, while the post office, the shop, and the present inn are half a mile away to the southeast.

If you stand outside the church porch you can see to the southwest the stack of granite known as Bowerman's Nose (Square J 17). It is just coincidence that Bowerman's eldest daughter is said to have been called Winifred, and that the church was later dedicated to St Winifred.

Just inside the western gate to the churchyard stands a crudely carved and obviously very old cross which has an unusual story. It was once the custom at a funeral for the coffin to be carried round the cross three times before being taken into church. In 1841 a new rector came to the parish. He objected to this custom, but was not able to persuade his parishioners to give it up. He therefore arranged for the cross to "disappear". No amount of searching could find it, and before long the rector moved on. However in 1908 a workman noticed, built into the foot of a wall across a local stream, what was obviously a cross. With rejoicing the ancient monument was re-erected in the still empty socket in the churchyard. However it was soon realized that this was not the cross that had come out of the socket. It didn't fit, and it was much too roughly carved ever to have been a churchyard cross. It was almost certainly an ancient waymark, probably from some local crossroads. So the real church cross is still missing, . . . and coffins nowadays are taken straight in to the church.

LUSTLEIGH CLEAVE

Round Lustleigh Cleave and village there are several scenic walks along well signposted footpaths. The cleave is a deep, steep valley containing a good deal of natural woodland, and the River Bovey rushes enthusiastically through it, much of its course being hidden by the canopy of trees.

A round tour might take you up from the village, along the eastern rim of the cleave past Sharpitor, Raven's Tor, and Hunter's Tor, and then down to the river to follow its bank as it picks its headlong way beneath overhanging Oaks.

A path runs from this stout log bridge back to the village, and further downstream another one goes up from Hisley weir.

A Springtime walk, before the trees are in full leaf, may be rewarded with drifts of Snowdrops, Daffodils, Wood Aemones, or Bluebells.

This is a cheerful and busy village which has had a long history. Within the parish bounds are Bronze Age hut circles, an Iron Age fort, and an inscribed Saxon memorial (in the church). In the Domesday Book is a record of honey production by the villagers. Even mid-twentieth century life is remembered, by wartime evacuees, in their description of the village as a place of " 'orrible 'ills and 'ellish 'ush".

Down in the Town Orchard on top of a huge boulder is cemented a stony seat. This is the throne on which the May Queen is installed and crowned on the first Saturday of every May.

The names of all the queens from 1954 onwards are engraved on the face of the boulder.

BULLATON FARM

Rick stands

The farmhouse is late mediaeval with a Tudor wing, but a new slate roof and cement rendering of the outside walls have camouflaged its origin. The house and the fine row of old barns—some newly roofed, some unroofed—are all tucked into the steep side of a combe to take advantage of slope, aspect, shelter, and spring water. Near the entrance gate, on the left, is an ash house.

A public bridle path skirts round above the cluster of buildings. A walk along it, and a peep over the walls, reveals a fascinating collection of discarded machinery—a horse drawn plough or two, harrows, rakes, a corn drill . . .

In a small field above the house are the two stone-faced rick stands illustrated above. The projecting rims would have made it difficult, though probably not impossible, for rats to gain entrance to the ricks.

GREAT ROCK MINE

This was the last mine on Dartmoor to stop working. Digging was begun in the area during the 19th century, and work continued until 1969. The mineral obtained was micaceous haematite, a speckly form of iron oxide. The ore was crushed and the haematite separated out in water in a similar way to tin ore, but in this case there was no need for smelting. It was used raw in the manufacture of anti-corrosion paint. All that was required was a highly concentrated product.

A walk uphill from Beaden Bridge (towards Christow) will take you past several adits in the hillside on the left. They are hidden from the road but are only a few yards away, behind spoil tips or the remains of ore chutes. The mined rock was loaded on to carts here and taken to the dressing floors over the hill to the west.

WARNING: IT IS NOT SAFE TO ENTER THESE ADITS.

CANONTEIGN FALLS

To get the best view of these spectacular falls it is necessary to come early in the season before the trees are in leaf, or even in winter. From Easter until the end of October the park is open every day, but from November until Easter only on Sundays.

There is a charge for entry, but this includes a great many things. The 400 foot climb up one side of the falls and down the other is steep and rough in places, but the souvenir guide presented to everyone provides a minute by minute commentary on everything to be seen. Natural history and industrial archaeology are inextricably interwoven in explaining the landscape. This guide sets an excellent standard of how such things can be done.

In addition to the leaping water there are quiet pools, water fowl, picnic and barbecue areas, a superb commando assault course for children, toilets, a restaurant and souvenir shop, and a growing collection of old farm machinery and wagons.

This is not a place
to visit in a hurry.

Lady Exmouth Waterfall

BRENT TOR

The legend of the founding of the church on Brentor is here retold.
It should be sung to the tune "While shepherds watched . . ."

While sailors watched the waves one night
All standing round the deck
The captain of the ship announced
It soon would be a wreck.

"I fear", said he, "this mighty storm
Will drive us hard aground.
Prepare yourselves to swim, my lads,
We'll not make Plymouth Sound."

But Hugh the merchant raised his voice
And prayed with upstretched hand,
"St Michael, save us, we implore,
And bring us safe to land."

Thus spake good Hugh, and promise made
That if they came ashore
He'd build a little church for Mike
Upon a Dartmoor tor.

St Michael saw the upraised hands
And heard the merchant's plea.
He took compassion on the ship
And calmed the raging sea.

They steered a course for Plymouth Hoe
And entered Dev'nport dock,
Where Hugh espied some miles inland
A likely looking rock.

Forthwith he hurried, Northward bent,
To keep the vow he'd made.
At Brentor rock he set to work
With hammer, pick, and spade.

For fourteen days his pile of stones
Upon the summit grew.
"Tomorrow morn, if all goes well,
I'll start to build", quoth Hugh.

But Satan came that very night.
Said he, "A trick I'll play."
He lifted up the pile of stones
And flung them far away.

It took poor Hugh the whole next day
To carry back the stones.
When evening came he went to bed
To rest his weary bones.

But once again the Devil came
And played his dirty trick.
Old Hugh took back the stones, and prayed,
"O help me, please, St Mick."

The third night when the Devil came
He got a big surprise:
St Michael hurled a rock at him
And hit him 'tween the eyes.

No more attempts the Devil made
To hinder valiant Hugh,
Who went ahead with building ops
And saw the project through.

Now if you climb up Brentor hill
To see the glorious view,
Remember there to pause and give
Your thanks to Mike and Hugh.

GORSE

When gorse is in blossom
Kissings' in fashion.

. . . . . which means, as everyone knows, that there is never a day when a kiss would be out of season. This is not because Gorse (or Furze or Whin) is such a remarkable plant that it blooms throughout the year, but because there are two species which have different flowering periods. The taller European (or Common) Gorse blooms roughly from December to June, while Western Gorse, a lower more compact shrub, is normally in flower from July to November. The species can therefore be identified by consulting a calendar, or perhaps your watch. Here beside the road both kinds are to be found. In some seasons there may be a slight overlap so occasionally it is possible to find at least a few flowers of each species at the same time. The stature of the bush and the number of new buds or dead flowers will usually sort them out. If not then examine the tiny bract at the base of any flower. (See illustration). If it is at least 2 mm wide and also wider than the flower stalk then the species will be European Gorse.

Difficult as it is to handle, Gorse has been an extremely useful plant to countryfolk. As fodder for horses or cattle it is very nutritious, though of course it has to be well pounded first. This could be done with a mallet or in an apple crusher. It was even sown as a crop for this purpose.

Gorse burns well even when green, and it was once a popular fuel for bread ovens. The ashes contain a good deal of alkali, and can be used as a substitute for soap. Then there was wine and a yellow dye to be made from the flowers, and walking sticks from the stems.

If you are passing a Gorse bush in late summer and hear clicks and snaps you are listening to the ripe seed pods splitting open.

In August Grayling butterflies are to be found on this common. They are not easy to spot where they rest in the grass with retracted and camouflaged wings.

Grayling

THE ELEPHANT'S NEST

This delightful old inn dates back to the time of the first Queen Elizabeth. Even in those days there was a considerable amount of mining in the area, at first for tin ore and later for other minerals.

It is probable that the main cottages that make up the inn were built for miners, but at some time one of them became a small farmhouse, and later a dairy was added. There is still good pastureland round here.

At an unknown date the building became "THE NEW INN", perhaps during the burst of mining activity in the nineteenth century.

Just after World War II the actual bar was much smaller than it is now, hardly more than a large alcove, in the centre of which sat the publican, everything within reach. It seems he was an unusually large man—a figure of 28 stone has been suggested—and one day somebody described him as "like an elephant sitting in its nest". The description had appeal and it stuck, and about 1950 the name of the inn was officially changed.

"The Elephant's Nest" now makes a pleasing port of call, either for a drink or a light meal. In summer there is a well tended garden to sit in, and in winter a log fire blazes in front of your knees, while overhead the ceiling is papered with banknotes.

HILL BRIDGE

Many of the small settlements in this area have been in occupation for up to nine hundred years, so the twisting lanes, fords and bridges connecting them have a long history.

The Tavy can be violent and unpredictable. It is said to have the second fastest current of any British river, falling about a thousand feet in seven miles. A cloudburst on the high moor can result in a six or seven foot rise in the water level down here in only an hour or so. If you visit this delightful spot at the end of a summer drought this will be hard to believe.

The present bridge replaces one that was washed away in the last century. The oblong openings in the parapets are designed to allow water to pass through when the river is running higher than the road level.

The set of pools concreted into the river bed is a fish ladder built to help salmon on their upstream journey to spawn.

You can climb down an iron ladder to the footpath along the leat. The water taken off here was originally used as a power source for a number of mines, but nowadays it provides hydro-electricity for the national grid. The power station is near Mary Tavy.

BAGGA TOR

Here is a satisfying little tor, a good one for beginners, or toddlers, or those who like a short gentle climb rewarded with pleasing views without having to penetrate deep into the high Moor.

There is room to park a few cars just inside the moorgate, and then it is only five minutes up the slope to the top. The summit platform is a grassy one where Tormentil, Stonecrop, and Bedstraw blossom in summer. If the wind is in the southwest there is shelter for a picnic, looking up at the great slope of Standon Hill and down on to Baggator Farm among the valley trees.

There was a farm there 800 years ago, and if in those days you had stood on this height you would occasionally have seen coming down the moorland track a bit to the right of the circular plantation a slow moving procession. It would have passed in front of the gate at the end of the road, and then on down the hill towards the river. A closer look would have shown you that this was a funeral cortege: for the track is part of the Lych Way, along which the dead were carried on their journey to Lydford.

At the river are Cataloo Steps. These stepping stones are pictured in Square I 5, where there is more information about the Lych Way.

Tormentil
(yellow)

English Stonecrop
(white)

Heath Bedstraw
(white)

LIMSBORO' CAIRN

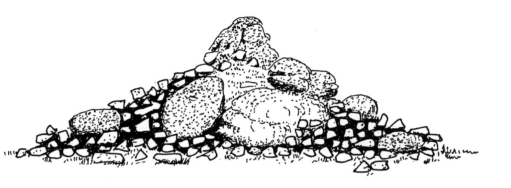

This interesting summit is formed by the remains of a Bronze age cairn built up round an outcrop. Many of the cairn boulders are of a deep pink granite. The military flagpole is no ornament and has been omitted from the drawing. It is a pity it could not have been placed on Lynch Tor which is only a hundred yards or so away. The weekly published programme of firing on the Merrivale range states that the pole is on Lynch Tor: perhaps the army are not keen to publicize their despoliation of a historic monument. They presumably consider this spot to be merely the highest point of Lynch Tor (which it undoubtedly is) and ignore the works of our ancestors.

The cairn was chosen in the year 1240 to be one of the markers when Henry III despatched a party of knights to ride round and record the boundaries of the royal Forest of Dartmoor. This done he gave the forest to his brother. About a century later it was transferred to the king's eldest son, the Black Prince. It has remained part of the Duchy of Cornwall ever since.

Since 1608 Lynch Tor has replaced Limsboro' Cairn as the named point on the Forest boundary. But the map clearly distinguishes one from the other, and equally clearly shows the boundary running through the cairn. To the west is the parish of Peter Tavy, and to the east is Lydford which very roughly corresponds to the "Forest".

There are fine views from here, encompassing much of the great northern morass of the Moor. Great Links Tor, Fur Tor, Cut Hill, and Great Mis Tor show up clearly when visibility is good.

UPPER WALKHAM VALLEY

The upper reaches of the valley
have much of interest—even rivalling
"*The Quartermaster's Store*".

I'm soaking wet, I cannot see,
I have not brought my mac with me,
I have not brought my mac with me.

There is rain, rain,
Lashing down again,
On the Moor, on the Moor.
There is rain, rain,
Lashing down again,
On my way 'cross Dartymoor.

I'm soaking wet . . .

There are bogs, bogs,
Full of froshus frogs,
. . .

And the frogs, frogs,
Are fierce as flamin' dogs,
. . .

There are slugs, slugs,
Big as cider mugs,
. . .

There are snakes, snakes,
Vipers in the lakes,
. . .

There are ants, ants,
Creepin' in my pants,
. . .

There are clegs, clegs,
Crawlin' up my legs,
. . .
There are bats, bats,
More like flyin' rats,
. . .

There are stones, stones,
Shakin' up my bones,
. . .

There are rocks, rocks,
Stuck inside my socks,
. . .

There are roots, roots,
Tangled round my boots,
. . .

There is peat, peat,
Clingin' to my feet,
. . .

There is rain, rain,
Lashing down again,
. . .

I am cold, cold,
I must be gettin' old,
I am tired, tired,
I wish I was expired,
I am wet, wet,
. . . But my heart is singing yet!
. . .On my way 'cross Dartymoor.

I'm soaking wet, I cannot see,
I have not brought my mac with me,
I have not brought my mac with me.

168

BEARDOWN MAN

Devil's Tor and Beardown Man

*Edge on view
of the menhir*

Its splendid isolation makes this menhir one of the most impressive on the Moor. Most of the other tall standing stones are associated with a row or circle or tomb or prehistoric pound, but Beardown Man stands aloof and alone, in desolate surroundings. It is over eleven feet high, and seen edge on is incredibly thin. There is no explanation of its siting here. The only other nearby feature is the rather insignificant outcrop known as Devil's Tor.

This spot is a last firm outpost for those walking from the south. To the north rise some of Dartmoor's highest tors and loneliest hills, and five miles of blanket bog.

BROWN'S HOUSE

Poor Mrs Brown. It is said that Brown was an unsociable and jealous man who had somehow managed to win a pretty wife. To prevent her from associating with other men and to avoid, in the words of Sabine Baring-Gould, "the danger such proximity might bring to his connubial happiness" he built his home in this remote place of desolation. This happened perhaps in the early years of the 19th century: yet the house had fallen into ruin long before that century came to an end.

Of all the remote homes on the Moor this one seems the most forlorn. A few peat cutters' huts may be more distant from any road (for example, Statt's House in Square H 10), but these were not permanent homes.

How long the Browns lived here is not known, but for the young wife it must have been too long. The dreary expanse of Wildbanks Hill (un-named on the map) rises behind the ruins, while below a wide marshy basin extends from the West Dart to the Cherry Brook. Even crossing the latter stream on the way to Postbridge is difficult, for the slight valley between the house and Rowter Down, from where there is a passable track, is very miry.

Near this mire there is a small colony of Heath Spotted-orchids. The flowers are usually white or pale pink with a pattern of reddish dots.

Heath Spotted-orchid

This tract of moorland is not named on the map. Its crest lies just north of the long wall that comes up from the East Dart. On the breezy summit are several low outcrops. At the northern one some fine "feather beds" of granite lie in the turf. The sketch shows the rocks on the western side, looking like piles of plates stacked upside down.

If you've been tramping across the fenny wastes of the northern moor this is a grand spot for a last rest before going on down to Postbridge. The views across the central valley are magnificent, and from here on it is downhill all the way.

The delicate and attractive Wavy Hair-grass (illustrated in Square S 10) dances on the rock ledges in the slightest breeze.

Green-ribbed Sedge

The other tall plant that stands well above the turf shaking its catkins in the wind is Green-ribbed Sedge. There will be a male catkin at the tip of the stem, and usually two or three fatter female ones well spaced out below.

The smaller bluish-green grass-like leaves in the turf are those of Carnation Sedge.

Carnation Sedge

Holly

Rowan

Memorial

Willow

How to find the memorial

At midday on 21st November 1913 William Donaghy left the school in Warrington where he taught science and disappeared. Just three months later his body was found beside this stone. The weather had been stormy for some days and he certainly died here of exposure to extreme cold and rain.

IN MEMORY OF
WILLIAM DONAGHY
OF LIVERPOOL
WHO DIED BESIDE THIS STONE
FEBRUARY 1914

Among his scanty possessions were a guide book, a page of notes suggesting a cross-moorland route from Exeter to Plymouth, twenty pounds in gold coins, and a cloakroom ticket from an Exeter railway station dated February 4th. When this was redeemed by the police it was found to refer to a bag (deposited under a false name) which contained some personal belongings as well as a revolver and ammunition.

The mystery of why William Donaghy left home and work, and what he was doing in this wild place has never been explained.

MERRIPIT HILL

The pigs you might come across on Merripit Hill are far from ordinary ones, especially if it is growing dark, and misty into the bargain.

For up here lives a legendary sow and her litter of piglets. Food is scarce and the little ones are hungry.

"We're starvin' ", they cry.

The old sow hears of a dead horse lying near Cator Gate, so the family set off eagerly to look for it.

Down the hill they trot, and across the road towards Runnage Farm; on along the lane to Widecombe, crossing the Walla Brook at Runnage Bridge; and then over the common by the bridle path to Cator Gate.

Arrived there they find the horse, but they are too late. Other hungry bellies have forestalled them.

"It's all skin an' bone", they cry piteously.

They are two miles from home and desperately hungry. Sadly the old sow has no choice but to take them back again. It is a long uphill trot, and the piglets get thinner and thinner as they struggle on. Finally, almost worn to a shadow they disappear back into the mist on Merripit Hill.

But next time that mist and darkness descend on the hill you may with luck see them once again acting out their phantom journey of hope and misery.

GOLDEN DAGGER MINE

G.R.685800

The heyday of this tin mine was from about 1860 until 1914. Old photographs show that there were then—and until much later—no trees in the valley. The plantations on the western side now hide almost all the mine workings, but alongside the track near the stream, the Redwater, several evocative remains are still to be seen.

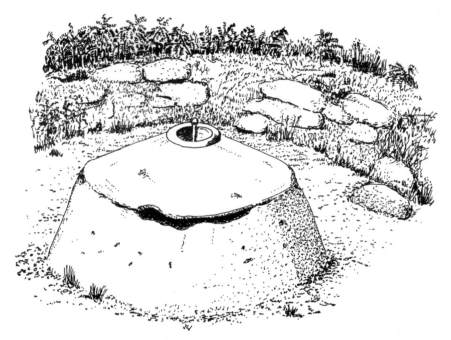

This large circular trough with a conical concrete boss in the middle is a buddle. The finely crushed ore was washed down a chute on to the dome, from where it spread out across the basin. The heavy tin particles would sink first and the lighter sandy material further out. While it was settling a set of horizontal vanes revolved above the surface. These were hung with strips of sacking to smooth and distribute the deposit. When about ten inches of material had built up evenly across the bed of the buddle, the water was drained off and the tin shovelled out, care being taken to keep the rich "heads" near the centre separate from the poorer tailings near the circumference.

About a hundred and fifty yards up the track from the buddle is a ruined building known as Dinah's House. It is worth clambering down to get a view of it from below. Further on still, near the junction of two paths is a large wheelpit.

THE LEGEND OF CHAW GULLY

G.R.687808

Edgar Allan Poe might have told the story this way.

Once upon a Winter Friday when I started out to tidy
Dusty shelves containing ancient volumes of Westcountry lore,
While I nodded, gently browsing, almost to the point of drowsing,
Suddenly a legend, rousing thoughts of gold galore,
Told of treasure long abandoned 'neath a gully near Birch Tor.
   —Dreams of wealth for evermore.

Sleepily I sat there thinking, and my thoughts were busy linking
Tales of tin and gold dug out and hoarded in the days of yore.
Avidly I read the story, learned the details *con amore,*
Revelled in the golden glory that was lying 'neath a tor,
Vowed, with dreams of endless wealth, I would not leave the golden store
    Lying there for evermore.

On the morrow in the morning, taking care to give no warning,
Stealthily I picked my way with torch and rope across the moor.
Eastward now the sky was glowing, but although the day was growing,
Night still filled the gully, throwing shadows on its rocky floor.
Shades to hide a plunge into an unseen pit along the floor—
    To be lost for evermore.

Boldly now my passage wending to the venture fast impending,
Soon I reached the ragged shaft that opened like a gaping door,
When a coal-black raven fluttered to a beetling crag and muttered,
As it were, a warning, uttered croaking hoarsely, to deplore
Such violation of his golden secret 'neath the moor,
    He thought was his for evermore.

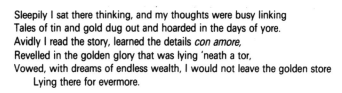

But neither threat nor pleading would have swayed me into heeding
Word or sign that menaced my intention to explore.
Down the gully mists were swirling, writhing round the rope unfurling,
Well belayed, then thrown uncurling, down for fifty feet or more.
Quickly then I slithered down, and as I touched the stony floor
    The raven croaked once more.

Torch in hand I paused there standing, when the thud of something landing
Just behind me made me turn and throw the beam across the floor,
Till the dull light dimly streaming found a skull whose mouth was screaming,
And whose eyes were faintly gleaming on my rope upon the floor—
Fifty feet of rope that I would madly grasp from off the floor—
    In my hands for evermore.

In the valley to the east lies Natsworthy, a manor that has existed since Saxon times. During the 1850s the Lord of the Manor, the 11th Duke of Somerset, had the boundaries of his land marked with named and dated stones. The western series of these runs up on to Hamel Down and then southwestward along the ridge. Five are to be found in this square and two more in Square K 15.

In this set one already existing stone—the much battered Hamel Down Cross—was used instead of a specially cut boundstone. All are inscribed with the date 1854 and the initials D.S., standing for Duke of Somerset.

Along the eastern boundary of the manor, across Haytor Down, runs another series of stones, dated 1853. These are featured in Square K 19 in quite a different way.

JAY'S GRAVE

J 16   G.R.732799

The story of Kitty Jay is often told. By way of a change sing this song,
sadly, to the tune of "Billy Boy".

"Where have you been all the night, Kitty Jay, Kitty Jay?
"Where have you been all the night, O Kitty Jay?"
"I've been tucked up nice and warm
With young Harry at the farm,
    And young Harry promised to marry
    Me, his charming Kitty Jay".

"Oh, don't put your trust in men, Kitty Jay, Kitty Jay,
Oh, don't put your trust in men, dear Kitty Jay.
For he's changed his mind since then
And you'll not see him again,
    So young Harry never will marry
    You, my charming Kitty Jay".

What a dastard to betray Kitty Jay, Kitty Jay,
What a dastard to betray poor Kitty Jay.
Now this fills her with dismay
'Cos she's in the family way,
    And young Harry never will marry
    Her, O wretched Kitty Jay.

"You've been taken for a ride, Kitty Jay, Kitty Jay,
You've been taken for a ride, poor Kitty Jay".
"Since I'm not to be a bride
I'll resort to suicide,
    'Cos young Harry never will marry
    Me, his lovesick Kitty Jay".

She was buried on the hill, Kitty Jay, Kitty Jay,
She is buried on the hill, is Kitty Jay.
She lies sleeping on the hill
    'mong the flowers that blossom still,
    So take pity now upon Kitty,
    Young and foolish Kitty Jay.

BOWERMAN'S NOSE

G.R.742804

The story of Bowerman the Hunter should be sung to the tune of
"The Mermaid" (One Friday morn as we set sail)

One Friday morn as Bow'rman's eyes
O'er the rock-strewn landscape scanned
He there did espy an old, ugly crone
With a broom and a stick in her hand, her hand, her hand,
   With a stick and a broom in her hand.

CHORUS   O, the moorland mists came down,
           And the Autumn winds did blow,
           But Bowerman the Hunter heeded not the skies
           Nor the foul witches lurking down below, below, below,
             Nor the foul witches lurking down below.

Then off rode Bow'rman to hunt the witches down.
Quoth he, "I'll cause mayhem".
He rode right through the middle of the coven
Which was scheduled as an A.G.M. gee em, gee em,
   Which was scheduled as an A.G.M.

CHORUS . . .

The witches vowed to take their revenge
And punish bold Bowerman.
Then up spake the oldest, "I'll tell you what", she said,
"I can turn into a hare, O, I can, I can, I can,
   I can turn into a hare, O, I can".

CHORUS . . .

The next day came, and Bow'rman rode out,
And soon found a hare all alone;
But the hare was a witch and it led a merry chase,
And ended up by turning him to stone, to stone, to stone,
   And ended up by turning him to stone.

     CHORUS   O, the moorland mists came down,
              And the Autumn winds did blow,
              But Bowerman the Hunter heeded not the skies
              Nor the foul witches lurking down below, below, below,
                Nor the foul witches lurking down below.

BECKA FALLS

A visit to "Becky" Falls is a visit to one of Dartmoor's "honeypots". On any fine day in the summer holiday period there are likely to be too many people and not enough water, so choose if you can some other time between Easter and the end of October, and allow a couple of hours or so to explore the paths that meander through the woodlands.

The present Becka Brook is clearly not powerful enough to have brought down the large boulders that make up the falls. It is supposed that they were tumbled down from higher on the Moor during a great melt at the end of one of the Ice Ages. The little valley is thickly wooded and supports a particularly rich community of mosses, liverworts, and lichens. For this reason the estate has been designated as a Site of Special Scientific Interest.

Two well illustrated booklets are available giving information about the history, geology, natural history, and nature trails round the falls and woodlands. One of the books also describes some longer walks to the villages of Lustleigh and Manaton.

TRENDLEBERE DOWN

From the viewpoint marked on the map this down looks rather monotonous, a great open sweep of heather and bracken that rises steadily to the southwest for a thousand feet in just over a mile. But the view is certainly worth a pause, for below runs the densely wooded valley of the Bovey, and beyond are the rocky heights on the far side of Lustleigh Cleave.

Beside the road at the eastern end of the down are some mature Birches, and several spots where a car can be parked and a picnic enjoyed.

The "Lady of the Woods" is perhaps the most elegant of our native trees, casting only a light shade even in summer. In winter the reddish brown of its branches distinguishes it from afar from all other trees. The silvery bark is at all times a joy to behold. Peal off the outer skin and admire the smoothness of the inner layer. In spite of its delicate appearance the Birch is a hardy tree: its range extends far north into the snowy wastes of Scandinavia.

The timber from large trees makes excellent plywood. Besoms for sweeping and birches for beating were traditionally made from Birch twigs. In the Highlands the wood is used to make small items of furniture, table ware, carts, and fences; the finer branches are employed in thatching, smoking herring, and distilling whisky; and the sap produces a wine.

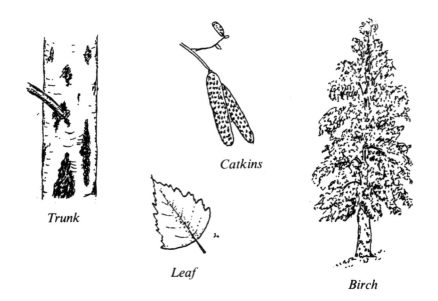

Trunk

Catkins

Leaf

Birch

This little bridge spanning the Bovey is as picturesque as you could wish. Go there in Snowdrop time or Primrose time or Bluebell time, when the sun has a chance to strike through the woodland canopy and add a sparkle to the water and dappled light to the banks and paths.

There is also a ford and a weir here, but it is the mediaeval packhorse bridge that delights the mind. It once linked the village of Lustleigh to the Manaton to Bovey Tracey track, which still runs along the valley on the west side of the river.

At the end of one parapet stands an interesting granite gate post. The five vertical slots were cut to receive loose planks whose other ends would be dropped into L-shaped slots in the opposite post. (See Square H 19). Later on two iron pivots were drilled into the post for a hanging gate. But what about the five depressions carefully cut into another face of the post? How were they used? Where could the other gatepost have been?

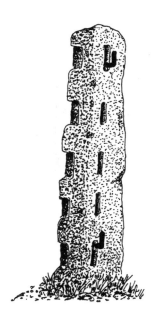

FERNS

Along the high roadside banks between this giant milestone and Mary Tavy three of our largest and commonest ferns grow in abundance.

At a glance they all look similar, but close examination will reveal differences that are not difficult to spot.

Note first the shape of the smallest leaflets along each side stalk. Those on the Male Fern and the Lady Fern are simpler and less indented than those on the Broad Buckler.

Then turn these leaflets over to look at the brownish spore patches that are to be found on the undersides for most of the summer and autumn. On the Lady Fern these patches are banana shaped, but on the other two they are circular or kidney shaped.

The names "Male" and "Lady" have nothing to do with the sex of the plants. Mediaeval imagination has been at work!

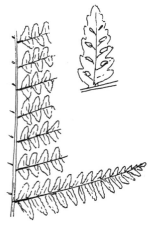
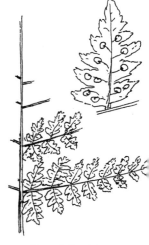

Male Fern   *Lady Fern*   *Broad Buckler*

The older part of the village lies well back from the main road.

The village cross, just inside the churchyard gate has suffered severely over the years. The fine pedestal is probably the original one, but a close look at the shaft will show that this is made from a different type of stone, and though undoubtedly old it may well be a replacement. Part of the original head lies on a step of the pedestal, the one on high being comparatively modern.

Inside the church porch are the village stocks, an unusually long set built to accommodate four people at a time. Those Devon miners must have been a wild bunch!

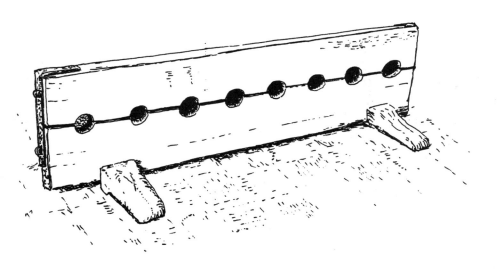

STEPHEN'S GRAVE

Scottish Blackface

A lonely place to be buried—but back in the eighteenth century suicides were never interred in a churchyard: an unhallowed site was chosen, often as far from the village church as possible.

John Stephens, who lived in Peter Tavy, was in love with a local girl. The story goes that she spurned him, or was unfaithful to him, or was refused her parents' blessing—there are several versions—and in despair the young man took poison.

Several authors in writing of the burial, which probably took place in October 1762, say that the body was buried "in the usual barbarous fashion". Referring to suicides, this seems to mean choosing a spot at the farthest bound of the parish, sometimes at a crossroads in order to confuse the spirit of the deceased should it feel like wandering; and occasionally of driving a stake through the corpse to keep it down. Perhaps that is why the ghost of John Stephens has mostly been seen sitting on the grave—but only after dark.

The small rough pillar of black stone was re-erected and set on a base in the 1930s. Just an "S" was engraved on the plinth.

THE LANGSTONE

G.R.550787

This is one of the half dozen mightiest menhirs that dot the moorland landscape. The peat track coming up from Peter Tavy past Stephen's Grave (Square K 4) runs close by it and then on down to the Walkham; and another track branching off the Lych Way also heads here. Evidently peat cutters and other travellers found this "long stone" a useful waymark.

Like some of the other great menhirs this one also stands at the end of a stone row. The row runs away north for about a hundred yards, but its stones are few and small and easily passed unnoticed.

As always at a site like this a pause for reflection induces feelings of wonder and puzzlement. Why was this particular spot chosen? Was the huge monolith lying here all ready, just waiting to be set up by our Early Bronze Age ancestors, or did they drag it down from the tor? Were they the same people who raised the stone circle half a mile away to the southeast? And did they inhabit the settlement just out of sight beyond that? (See Square K 6).

If the menhir (and row) and the circle did have some connection then why choose a hilltop that has a nasty mire in between the two? But perhaps the mire was not there then? . . . And when was "then"?

A close examination of the giant stone's surface will show a number of pock marks. These testify to the accuracy of American machine gunners who were practising here in 1944.

This drawing of the Langstone does not look like the usual photographs found in other books. This is because the stone is here seen edgeways on.

LANGSTONE MOOR

**G.R.556779
and 556782**

The prehistoric remains on Langstone Moor make an intriguing puzzle. To find the answer you would need to return here, perhaps once or twice, some when between three and four thousand years ago.

Hut circles

If you climb up from the Walkham you first come to Langstone Village, a collection of Bronze Age buildings, mostly hut circles, scattered over an acre or so of turf, with pleasant views down and across the river. Some circles have smaller huts adjoining them; others are close to the walls of a pound.

Langstone Circle

Climb higher to the brow of the hill and you come to Langstone Circle. This was once a fine monument in a glorious situation. But alas, troop training during the last war resulted in the demolition and damaging of about ten stones, and now only six remain upright, perhaps a quarter of the original complement. Nevertheless this is a good place to pose the problem. Look N.W. across the down: half a mile away, to the right of White Tor, stands a mighty menhir—the Langstone itself. (This is featured in Square K 5).

Is there a connection between the menhir, the circle and the village? Which came first? If the people came first why did they build the circle just out of sight? Or did they arrive long after the circle had been abandoned, and so had no knowledge of its purpose? What was its purpose, anyway? The only apparent link between the circle and the menhir is their proximity, yet a thousand years may have passed between the erection of the one and the other.

Questions . . . questions . . . .

186

TWO TRACKS

Two old tracks, both easy to follow, run roughly southeast to northwest across this square. The northern one is the Lych Way and the other, half a mile or more to the south, is a peat cutters' path once used by workers from Peter Tavy.

Between the two tracks waves a sea of grass and sedge, spangled with sheep pretending to be white horses riding the wind blown rollers of Purple Moor Grass.

This guide stone stands beside the Lych Way on Conies Down.
Beardown Tors on the horizon

Both tracks cross the Walkham and also now the Prison Leat, which here runs almost parallel to it. The river crossings are not named on the map, although both have a name. The Lych Way ford is called (like several others) Sandy Ford, while the other one is Shallow Ford.

TRAVELLERS' FORD

Where Conies Down Water runs into the Cowsic is a small meadow-like area known as Broad Hole. Just to the north of the confluence is Travellers' Ford by which the Lych Way crosses the main stream. On the steep east side of the valley the track, coming down from near Lydford Tor, is deeply cut into the hillside. The slope here abouts makes a pleasant place to rest: it offers views across the ford and up and down the valleys of the two streams.

A few hundred yards further downstream the steep defile gives way to a much broader valley, where the Cowsic twists and turns for a mile or more along a flood plain.

After the year 1260 the Lych Way was no longer used to carry the dead to Lydford from the hamlets around Postbridge, for the parishioners there were allowed to attend Widecombe church instead. But a good deal of traffic still came this way: for at Lydford were castle, prison, market, and the Forest Courts.

Here is a tor that, given a good push, seems ready to slide down the hill.

Under the overhang is one of the Moor's long established letterboxes. The "stamp" is shown below.

On the platform above grows the wild Golden Rod, as well as a number of commoner flowering plants.

Golden Rod

Letterbox, visitors' book, and "stamp"

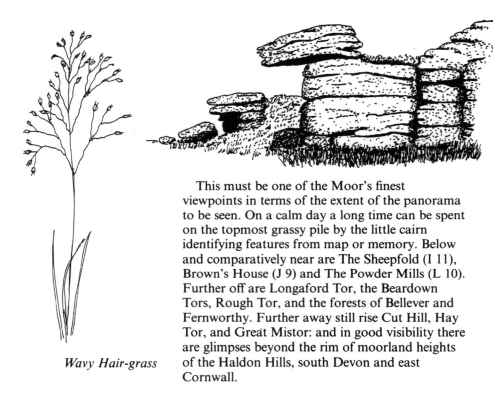

Wavy Hair-grass

This must be one of the Moor's finest viewpoints in terms of the extent of the panorama to be seen. On a calm day a long time can be spent on the topmost grassy pile by the little cairn identifying features from map or memory. Below and comparatively near are The Sheepfold (I 11), Brown's House (J 9) and The Powder Mills (L 10). Further off are Longaford Tor, the Beardown Tors, Rough Tor, and the forests of Bellever and Fernworthy. Further away still rise Cut Hill, Hay Tor, and Great Mistor: and in good visibility there are glimpses beyond the rim of moorland heights of the Haldon Hills, south Devon and east Cornwall.

Whichever way the wind blows there is shelter to be found and a picnic spot with a view.

On the little summit plateau Whortleberry and Heath Bedstraw grow. Among the grasses to be found are these three.

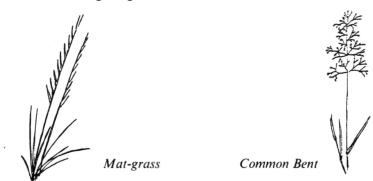

Mat-grass   *Common Bent*

THE HAIRY HANDS
K 11

The stretch of road for about a mile and a half to the southwest of Postbridge has since 1920 been the scene of a number of road accidents and horrifying experiences all associated with The Hairy Hands.

In view of this the following Kiplingesque advice is offered to Girl Guides who may be camping in the vicinity.

If you wake at midnight when camping on the Moor,
  And hear a snuffling sound that's just outside the door,
Don't go peeping out to find out what and why:
  Just stay inside, my darling, while the Hairy Hands go by!

  Long and hairy fingers
  Probing through the night,
  Seeking flesh to grapple,
  —Searching left and right—
  Feeling for a handhold
  On a maiden's thigh.

  So stay inside, my darling, while the Hairy Hands go by!

Don't creep out to arm yourself with saucepan or a stick;
  If you left the tent flap open make haste to close it quick!
Wait inside, in terror, till the snuffles die away.
  Sleep then—if you can—until the coming of the day.

  Long and hairy fingers
  Probing through the night,
  Seeking flesh to grapple,
  —Searching left and right—
  Feeling for a handhold
  On a maiden's thigh.

Don't give way to panic;
Don't even bat an eye.
Just stay inside, my darling,
While the Hairy Hands go by!

Of the many clapper bridges on the Moor this is the largest complete one that remains. It has been here for something like 500 years. It must also be the one most often photographed.

The central opening is spanned by two slabs. Of these the upstream one was once deliberately thrown down as the beginning of an attempt to prevent a local man's ducks from swimming too far downstream. However when it was seen that the slab was completely immersed the project was abandoned. The clapper has been back in position for over a hundred years now. Some invisible repair work has recently been done to the piers to ensure the continued safety of the bridge, for in flood times the swirling waters reach nearly up to the clappers.

The "modern" bridge dates from the building of the turnpike road from Moretonhampstead to Tavistock about 1790. The actual turnpike and toll-house used to be near the petrol pump.

EPHRAIM'S PINCH

G.R.677785

Epraim's Pinch
is the short steep hill
at the southern end of Soussons Plantation.
It owes its curious name to the following history.

The story has several versions. The one told here is adapted from an account by Jonas Coaker who lived near Postbridge during the 19th century, though the actual incident may have taken place much earlier.

Ephraim was a young man of Widecombe, well respected for his strength. "Volks said he was strong as a hoss." One day among a group of villagers a bet was made that he couldn't carry a sack of corn from Widecombe to Postbridge without putting it down on the way. This would have been the best part of six miles by the shortest practicable route, but nevertheless in a fit of bravado Ephraim accepted the bet.

A sack of corn was obtained from the mill and "pon his back he fling'n purty smart". Off he set up Church Path and the long climb over Rowden Hill. Then down to Blackaton Bridge, and up and down again to cross the West Webburn. This was over half way, but by now he was tiring fast, and the "pinch" (a short steep hill) proved too much for him. In despair he flung his load to the ground.

Jonas Coaker concludes his story:

"He wad'n a man to flinch,
so from that the place have long been known
by the name of Ephraim's Pinch."

*The Cator Boundary
stone stands on the
right hand verge.*

193

Along the eastern side of the lane runs a marshy stretch that sports a wealth of bog loving plants. Several of them, often shy to flower, bloom in greater profusion here than in many other places where they may also be found. A sunny spell in summer encourages especially the Round-leaved Sundew to throw up a miniature forest of flowering stems.

Easy to find, because they are both frequent and colourful, are:

Greater Bird's Foot Trefoil	(yellow)	on this page
Lousewort	(purple)	on this page
Bog Pimpernel	(pink)	see Square H 14
Bog Asphodel	(yellow)	H 14
Ivy-leaved Bellflower	(pale blue)	M 14
Round-leaved Sundew	(white)	M 17
Marsh Saint John's-Wort	(yellow)	N 3
Lesser Spearwort	(yellow)	N 3 and T 12
Bogbean	(pink & white)	P 8

Greater Bird's-foot Trefoil

The large dragonfly with a pale blue body that haunts this marsh is the male
BROAD-BODIED LIBELLULA.

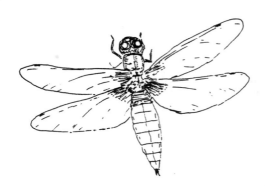

Lousewort

HAMELDOWN BEACON

This commentary follows on from Square J 15.

It can be seen from the sketch that the Duke of Somerset's stone mason had his own ideas about spelling. The history of these boundary stones is explained in Square J 15. This one stands on top of a prehistoric cairn, as also does the next stone to the north. The smaller of the two cairns at Two Barrows possibly suffered a reduction in size when the wall builders used it as a turning point for their construction work.

Feeding on the heather along this ridge can be found in summer the large green caterpillars of the Emperor Moth. They have tufts of black bristles rising from transverse rows of yellow warts. The moths have wings patterned in grey and white, with four large eye spots.

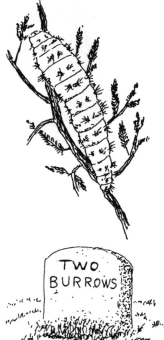

MIOLSTONE

This entertaining milestone is just one miol from the village in the wide combe, along the lane to Natsworthy.

It was possibly put there at a time when Napoleonic prisoners of war were quartered in Widecombe, to show them the furthest point to which they were allowed to walk when on parole. The prisoners, presumably French officers, would doubtless have been well enough educated to understand the inscription.

This tor and Great Staple Tor (Square L 5) are probably the two that contain the most fascinating displays of fantastic granite shapes. When the stacks are seen in silhouette against a stormy sky there is no end to the number of giants, animals, caricatures, fiends, and gargoyles that can be imagined. Some writers have experienced an aura of fear surrounding this mighty pile of rocks, but in fine weather it is a popular tor with visitors, for there is now a handy car park.

*Sillhouettes
traced from photographs
taken against the light*

The tramway once served five quarries on Haytor down. It now provides about two miles of easy downland walking. The line, the first railway in Devon, was opened in 1820 to transport the quarried stone to the canal at Teigngrace about seven and a half miles away. Except for about a quarter of a mile coming up from Holwell quarry the whole journey for laden trucks would have been gently downhill.

The wagon wheels had no flanges: they simply ran along the outer edge of the granite rail. At some of the junctions a hole is to be seen at the tip of the V: it may be that a toggle was pivoted here to direct the wheels along the required track.

The best quarry to visit is in Square L 18. Another section of the tramway is shown in Square K 20, in Yarner Wood.

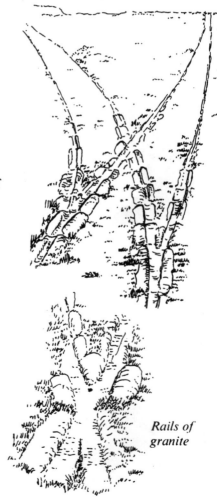

Rails of granite

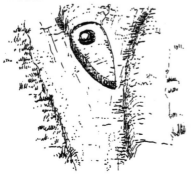

198

BOUND STONES on HAYTOR DOWN

These named boundstones run for over a mile across Haytor Down.

You might pass them all on your way to "WIDECOMBE FAIR".

Bound stones, bound stones, across Haytor Down,
 Up along, down along, out along lee,
The grass may be green or the bracken be brown,
 There's John Moorstone, Prince Albert, Will Stony,
 Old Jacko, Vic Torrier, Prince Waley,
 And Owlacombe Burrow and all . . . and Owlacombe Burrow and all.

The old Duke of Somerset had them put there,
 Up along, down along, out along, lee,
They dance in a line like the Ballet Rambert,
 Do John Moorstone, Prince Albert, Will Stony,
 Old Jacko, Vic Torrier, Prince Waley,
 And Owlacombe Burrow and all . . . and Owlacombe Burrow and all.

They show where his boundary went over the hill,
 Up along, down along, out along, lee,
The Duke may be gone, but his stones are there still,
 Are John Moorstone, Prince Albert, Will Stony,
 Old Jacko, Vic Torrier, Prince Waley,
 And Owlacombe Burrow and all . . . and Owlacombe Burrow and all.

They've weathered a century of fair wear and tear,
 Up along, down along, out along, lee,
Now some of them look like a piece of Gruyère,
 Do John Moorstone, Prince Albert, Will Stony,
 Old Jacko, Vic Torrier, Prince Waley,
 And Owlacombe Burrow and all . . . and Owlacombe Burrow and all.

When us be all dead and under the grass,
 Up along, down along, out along, lee,
Those stones will be there to watch the clouds pass,
 Will John Moorstone, Prince Albert, Will Stony,
 Old Jacko, Vic Torrier, Prince Waley,
 And Owlacombe Burrow and all . . . and Owlacombe Burrow and all.

Then we'll be the ones who have rattling bones,
 Up along, down along, out along, lee,
While they'll be on duty as boundary stones,
 Will John Moorstone, Prince Albert, Will Stony,
 Old Jacko, Vic Torrier, Prince Waley,
 And Owlacombe Burrow and all . . . and Owlacombe Burrow and all.

YARNER WOOD

Yarner Wood is a National Nature Reserve of about 375 acres. There is a nature trail of about a mile and a half and a woodland walk of wider interest about twice as long. Excellent booklets for the trails are available at the car park. The terrain is hilly, and the wild woodland is primarily of Oak, but Ash, Alder, Birch, Beech, Rowan, Sycamore, Pine, and a few planted conifers add variety. A long list of birds and butterflies has been recorded.

Both native species of Oak can be seen in the wood. The dominant one is Sessile Oak, so called because the acorns are sessile (stalkless) on the twigs. The other species, referred to in books as Pedunculate Oak, has long-stalked acorns. This is more often called English or Common

The Haytor Granite Tramway runs through the wood

Oak. It is the only species to be found on the upland granite areas of the Moor. The leaves of the two species also differ: look at the drawings and then at the leaf bases. Unless you find a hybrid they are fairly easy to tell apart.

The waymarked walk takes you past a copper mine that once employed fifty men, and also along a stretch of the Haytor Granite Railway. (See square K 18). The beech trees along the track were probably planted when the rails were laid down, about 1820.

Sessile Oak

Pedunculate or Common Oak

EVERGREEN ALKANET
at WILMINSTONE

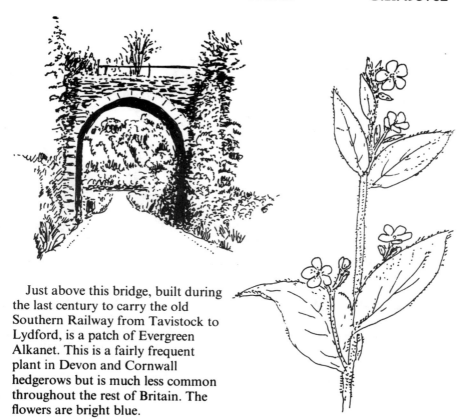

Just above this bridge, built during the last century to carry the old Southern Railway from Tavistock to Lydford, is a patch of Evergreen Alkanet. This is a fairly frequent plant in Devon and Cornwall hedgerows but is much less common throughout the rest of Britain. The flowers are bright blue.

This Alkanet is seldom seen very far from villages: it is possible that in the Middle Ages it was grown as a substitute for the True Alkanet which was not so hardy. It was cultivated for the red dye which could be extracted from the roots. This was used to colour butter, jellies, wine and face powder.

The herbalists of Tudor and Stuart times ascribed many medicinal virtues to Alkanet. An ointment made from it was recommended as an antiseptic for wounds, while a decoction drunk with wine would ease backache. A less credible but more entertaining use was claimed for it in classical Greece: just chew a little in the mouth, then spit at any passing snake. If your aim was good the snake would immediately die!

Well . . . Alkanet and Adders are both to be found on sunny banks in Devon in late Spring!

This seems at first sight an odd place to find what was once a fine cross. It is set up at the base of a high bank along the lane from Headlands Farm to Coxtor Farm.

A look at the back of the cross will reveal an iron spike. This is the remains of a hinge on which for many years a gate hung. When the gate was renewed the cross was removed a few yards to its present position.

It is not known where the cross originally stood, but one possible not too distant site might have been on the old Peter Tavy to Plymouth road, perhaps somewhere near the two stones described in square M 3. The cross is much older than either of these stones. It obviously suited some farmer to remove and adapt it to his own use.

In the opposite hedgebank Earthnut, or Pignut, flowers in spring. It might be mistaken for the much commoner Cow Parsley, but its more delicate leaves with narrower segments clearly distinguish it.

The "earth nut" can be found at the base of the stem, like a bulb. It is edible but not really worth the trouble of digging it out—an operation which in any case is illegal.

Earthnut

COX TOR

G.R.531762

This tor, easily accessible from the road, is well worth climbing for the sake of the magnificent views which stretch far across both North and South Dartmoor. The summit was once encircled by a cairn. This has been despoiled to the extent that its centre is now grassy. Another cairn is to be seen about a hundred yards to the north.

From whichever direction you climb to the top thousands of tiny hillocks like these will certainly be noticed. No other grassy hilltop on the Moor has such a huge collection. They are not molehills or anthills or buried boulders. Therein lies their fascination. The vegetation covering them is quite ordinary, mostly Common Bent Grass interspersed with a lichen called *Cladonia impexa*.

If you would like three explanations of their growth then ask three geomorphologists and take your choice.

These common little toadstools are called Dung Roundheads.

They are smaller than Dung Bonnets, which are illustrated in Square F 8.

This is one of the Moor's half dozen most spectacular tors. Prominent from a distance are two "steeples" (which give the tor its name) weathered to look as if they have been built by piling one boulder on top of another. Huge tumbled blocks rest uneasily at all angles, making caves, arches, and tunnels. If you choose the right one to crawl through it will cure you of rheumatism. There is also a logan stone, best discovered by walking across it.

These silhouettes were traced from photographs taken on a misty autumn day.

A grand tor this, one that rears up as notable landmark from a multitude of far off hills in every direction.

In the year 1240 it was listed as one of the boundary marks of the "Forest of Dartmoor". When these were revised in 1609 the reference was even more specific—to Mistor Pan. This is the fine rock basin more popularly known as "The Devil's Frying Pan". A bit of climbing is needed to find it, for it is scooped out on the summit of a rock pile towards the northern end of the main mass. The Devil, it is related, used to fry his breakfast in it after one of his nights out on the Moor.

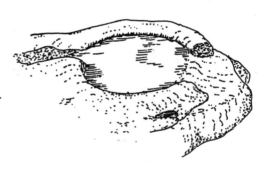

The Devil's Frying Pan

Rock basins—of which there are many on the Moor—are the result of the natural action of rain, frost, wind, and sun. A small water filled hollow in a horizontal surface is gradually enlarged as successive frosts lever out tiny specks of rock. This one is three feet across and six to eight inches deep. It must have taken untold thousands of years to grow to this size.

BLACK DUNGHILL

G.R.581774

There is nothing spectacular about this hill that has such a discouraging name, but neither is there anything dark or unsavoury about it. Once upon a time a good deal of peat cutting was carried out in the area, and on several slopes the faint parallel lines of former peat ties can still be made out. But the bare black peatscape has disappeared.

An old peat cutters' track to Peter Tavy descends the northwest slope of the hill. A walk along it will soon prove that in spite of its twists and turns it offers the best way of crossing both the Black Brook and the Walkham.

In a late summer breeze the hill top rolls like a yellow sea formed by the ripening stems of Deergrass: for this plant makes up an unusually high proportion of the vegetation. Purple Moor Grass, Ling and Cross-leaved Heath add splashes of other colours, but it is the golden tipped Deergrass which draws the eye.

Deergrass

Ling

Bell Heather

Cross-leaved Heath

206

The long straight track running north from the B 3357 west of Two Bridges is a perfectly good road for cars, and on days when the Merrivale Range is open there is ample parking space at the far end. This approach saves a mile of rather dull walking if you want to explore the upper reaches of the Cowsic.

When the red flag is flying on Beardown Tor camouflaged soldiers may sometimes be seen playing Hide-and-seek among the tufts of Purple Moor Grass on Holming Beam.

On the left of the track, behind the fence, are prison lands. These continue north as far as the fence corner, where this boundary stone is situated. D.C.P. stands for Directors of Convict Prisons, the authority to whom the land was originally leased by the Duchy of Cornwall.

The two species of Rush illustrated below are both to be found here.

Soft Rush is extremely common in wet patches—indeed it is quite the commonest rush on Dartmoor.
Heath Rush is not nearly so conspicuous. It grows among the grasses on drier heathland.

Soft Rush

Heath Rush
The right hand specimen
is in fruit.

"The whole world cannot boast, probably, a greater curiosity in sylvan archaeology than this solitary grove in the Devonshire wilderness. The ancient storm-stricken oaks of Wistman are without recorded parallel." That quotation, dated 1848, might now be considered to overstate the case, but nevertheless this is still a remarkable wood.

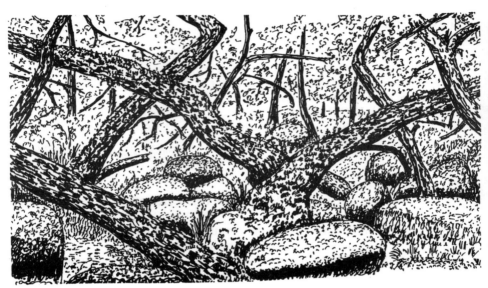

Although no single tree in this tangled mass is likely to be much more than 300 years old, the wood as a whole is far older than that. The oaks were able to grow up among the boulders, protected from wind and animals, until they were mature enough to withstand both the climate and occasional grazing. But wind, weather, and altitude (between 1,200 and 1,400 feet) combined to affect their subsequent growth. The branches sprawled nearly horizontally across the boulders, and the leafy canopy kept the air below moist so that every surface became thickly clothed with a rich layer of mosses, liverworts and ferns. Even small Rowans may be found growing among the branches of the Oaks.

During the last hundred years the wood has increased in extent and the trees have grown taller. This may be due to an imperceptible amelioration of the climate. At the southern end of the wood an area was fenced off in 1965 in order to exclude both animals and people. The difference in the ground vegetation there is now quite marked.

The wood is the reputed haunt of the Devil and his Wisht Hounds, but if you encounter them do not run—or you risk a twisted ankle.

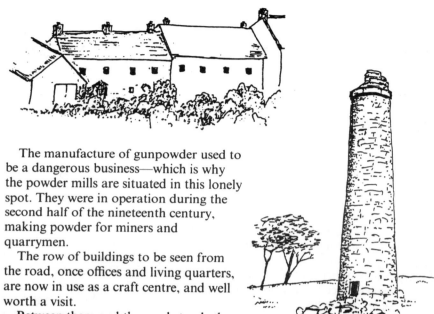

The manufacture of gunpowder used to be a dangerous business—which is why the powder mills are situated in this lonely spot. They were in operation during the second half of the nineteenth century, making powder for miners and quarrymen.

The row of buildings to be seen from the road, once offices and living quarters, are now in use as a craft centre, and well worth a visit.

Between them and the road stands the mortar. This was used to test the quality of the powder by measuring the distance it would throw a cannonball.

Chimneys, leats, and the ruined workshops of the mill are still to be seen in the background, forming fascinating relics of a bygone industry.

Proving mortar

Just round the corner of the summit outcrop in the illustration, below the triangulation pillar, is a grassy dell enclosed on three sides by the rocks of the tor. On a windy day it makes a comfortable place to rest and conjure up the story of Tom White who lived at Postbridge in the days before anyone had conceived the idea of surrounding this grand tor with conifers.

Tom was a conscientious farm worker who had succumbed to the charms of the dairy maid at Huccaby Farm near Hexworthy. The farm was, and still is, well over four miles from Tom's home—a long walk after a hard day's work; but nevertheless Tom did it several times a week, to make sure that his sweetheart did not foresake him in favour of any of her several other suitors in Hexworthy. One summer evening Tom lingered later than usual at the dairy door, and it was past midnight before he set out on his return journey. A waning moon gave him enough light to stride briskly over the open moor, up past Huccaby Ring. The menhir near Laughter Tor guided him up the slope, and soon the rocks of Bellever Tor came in sight. He was picking his way among the dark boulders when suddenly he realized that it was not only his joyful heart that was singing to him, but also a host of small voices, shouting, laughing, and making music. Cautiously he peered round a boulder into a grassy glade, and there he saw half a hundred pixies making merry in the moonlight, dancing all the while in a great circle. He was about to withdraw when a lookout spotted him. Immediately he was dragged into the clearing surrounded by hordes of the little people, and forced to join the dance. For two hours he was pulled and pushed round and round in mad circles until his senses whirled and he knew not what he was doing. But when the sky above Hamel Down took up a yellow tinge the pixies, at a sudden signal, ceased their merriment and disappeared among the boulders, leaving Tom dizzy on the ground. Shakily he rose. Unsteadily he made his way down hill: he still had a mile and a half to go, and there would be little time for rest before another day's labour had to begin.

The story has a sad ending:
It was all too much for Tom White.
He never went to Huccaby Farm again.

BELLEVER BRIDGE

First a ford, then stepping stones, then a fine clapper, and finally early in the 19th century a substantial road bridge. This crossing place of the East Dart has clearly been an important one for the last thousand years. The Lych Way, along which mourners once bore their dead to Lydford, began among the settlements on the eastern side of the valley and crossed the river here. Depending on the state of the numerous other streams they had to cross there would have been another ten to fifteen miles to plod before they reached their journey's end. After the year 1260 parishioners in these parts were permitted to use the church at Widecombe instead. But at Lydford there were law courts, castle, prison, and market, so the route continued in use for several centuries more.

Floods have washed away some of the clapper slabs but it can be clearly seen that the older bridge was two slabs wide. The widest gap however (second from the left looking downstream) may never have borne granite imposts. An inspection will show three notches cut into the top stone of each pier—notches which may possibly have seated baulks of timber.

The hamlet of Bellever lies a few hundred yards to the west. But gone are the two longhouses that stood there for six hundred years before the coming of the conifers.

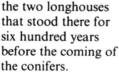

NEW WALLS FOR OLD
near CATOR

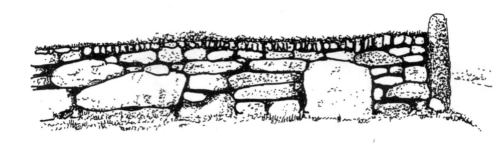

Half way between Middle Cator and Lower Cator a fine old wall that crosses the road has recently been repaired. The work is part of the National Park's Upland Management Project, and the rebuilding has been done by a local craftsman.

The repaired wall is well worth a moment or two of admiration, as indeed is any well built drystone wall on the Moor. If the builder worked single handed then the admiration is enhanced by a sense of wonder as well. Even the great boulders at the wall's base—"grounders" or "shiners" in different parts of Devon—can be edged into position with the help of a few implements. A strong tripod and chain hoist may be used nowadays, but the wall builders of earlier generations had to rely on just a few hefty levers.

John Bishop (see Square O 11), a much respected waller of the last century, used nothing but a lever or two. Some of his best work still stands as sturdy as ever. An easily seen example is the wall along the north side of the road between Prince Hall and Two Bridges. The larger stones of that wall have been lightly dressed to give extra stability and improve the appearance.

Here at Cator, on the south side of the road, the new wall and a length of the old wall have been fitted together like a jigsaw puzzle. It is only the different appearance of weathered and unweathered surfaces that shows where the join has been made.

LOWER CATOR BRIDGE

This pleasing clapper of one mighty slab is not marked on the map because the track that once used it to cross the West Webburn has been rerouted over a newer bridge.

In a shallow streamlet beside the road grows Brooklime, which has bright blue flowers and dark shiny leaves. These may be eaten in a similar way to Watercress, though they are more pungent to the taste.

Valerian

In the damp ground nearby grows the true Valerian. The flower heads are usually white, though sometimes tinged with palest purple, and rise two or three feet above ground level.

Valerian still has a place in modern pharmacy as a sedative. It is mainly the roots that are used, though a tea made from the dried leaves is also effective. The dried roots do have a rather unpleasant smell, but it is one that cats find particularly attractive. It is still cultivated in some parts of Britain and Europe. The roots are dug up in autumn, then dried and pressed to produce Oil of Valerian.

Brooklime

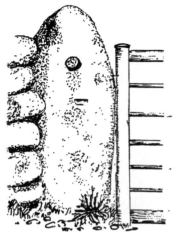

This gatepost at the farm entrance has a bowl shaped hollow cut into one face. The post may therefore once have been the top horizontal support for a gate. The swivelling upright might be pivoted on an iron spike at the bottom, while its top end would turn in the hollow underneath the capstone.

This lane carries a great deal of traffic in the tourist season, so any excuse to wander off it into a handy field is a good one. A little way along you can find in a neglected corner all three common species of thistle in flower at the same time.

There is no mistaking the SPEAR THISTLE. Its heads are much larger than either of the others, and the spear tip of each leaf is much longer and firmer.

Of the other two plants MARSH THISTLE flowers are normally much darker in colour, and the stems are armed with spiny wings nearly all the way down.

Under the pale purple flowers of CREEPING THISTLE the stems themselves are not really spiny.

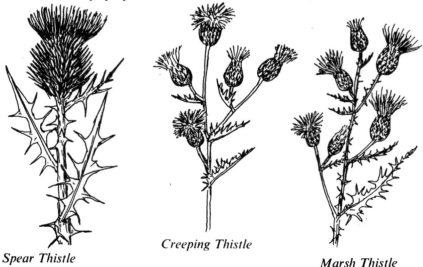

Spear Thistle

Creeping Thistle

Marsh Thistle

214

Many people might
pass this notice
without noticing
that . . . .

There is more to be found here than meets the eye at first sight. On the grassy bank near the road junction is a waymark that has been standing there for at least a century and a half before the present signpost was erected. It still bears all the information that folk in those days needed to take the right road to Ashburton, Bovey Tracey, Manaton, or Moretonhampstead.

Before the cattle grid was set into the road there used to be a gate across it. The two gateposts have only been moved a few yards. One lies on the turf by the roadside and the other has recently been built into the wall. The hinge bolts and latch catch are still in place.

Half hidden in a wall corner a very short way along the Ashburton lane is Stittleford's Cross. This is a boundary stone of Dunstone Manor, to the west. R.M. refers to Rawlin Mallock who was a lord of the manor during the 18th century.

Gatepost

Stittleford's Cross

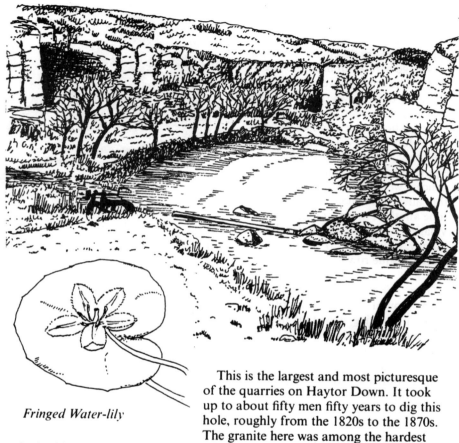

Fringed Water-lily

This is the largest and most picturesque of the quarries on Haytor Down. It took up to about fifty men fifty years to dig this hole, roughly from the 1820s to the 1870s. The granite here was among the hardest obtainable anywhere in Britain. It was used in the building of The British Museum and London Bridge—the one now in Arizona.

An exploration of the quarry floor and sides will reveal all sorts of relics. The old winch always excites interest; and nearby lies part of a derrick, last used perhaps in 1919 when some granite for Exeter War Memorial was extracted.

In the shallow water live the larvae of Whirligigs and the nymphs of dragon-flies. At one time there were also goldfish! On the surface float the leaves of both the White Water-lily and the Fringed Water-lily. This is a much smaller plant than the commoner Yellow Water-lily.

The granite tramway along which the stone was removed features in Square K 18.

The row of cottages and the inn are quite obviously the centre of life of this small community. But appearances are deceptive: there was no village here at all until the late 1820s. The cottages were built expressly to house the workers at the newly opened quarries on Haytor Down. There were originally homes for 24 families. Two rooms facing the road cost the mathematical equivalent of seven and a half new pence a week. The inn was built at the same time. There was also at that time another, more temporary,

Fireplace at the Rock

village for the workers under the shadow of the great spoil heap by the largest quarry, (Square L 18). Those cottages disappeared, whereas these turned into a picturesque row of "olde worlde residences".

The "Rock Inn" is an excellent hostelry with two great fireplaces in the bar, a fine reputation, and a row of parked cars outside at any holiday time.

An interesting item that hides itself from the eyes of most visitors is the entrance under a dark cliff to Haytor Iron Mine. Between the 1850s and about 1910 many thousands of tons of iron ore were taken from this mine. In its most productive years it employed over eighty workers. The adit will be found after a short walk along the path that runs down the combe, just before a fork and a turnstile.

Entrance to Haytor iron mine

ILSINGTON

This is a very satisfying village to stroll round, for so much of the picturesque part is contained beside the road that runs in an oblong round the village centre. From this road five others radiate, and within its bounds stand the church and a number of other old buildings.

The fine lych-gate and the room above it are comparatively modern replacements of earlier ones which had to be dismantled. The statue in the niche is of St George.

In the churchyard are several interesting tombstones dating from the time of Charles II.

The lady who does not want her bones disturbed lies near the path.

By the southeast corner of the church, on another tomb, is a horizontal slab which bears an inscription cut in such a way that if you write down all the capital letters (some of which appear in the middle of a word), and add up in any order the value of each one in the Roman numeral system, you will arrive at the date when the body beneath was interred. Remembering who sat on the throne of England will help point you to the correct answer.

St George

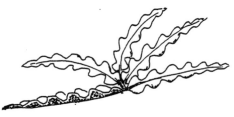

Rustyback

This little fern, found on some of the village walls, is called Rustyback. It really belongs in limestone country, but survives here among the granite because it is rooted in the mortar between the stones.

It was desired by her who lyeth here interred untill the Resurrection that her bones should not be moved

The narrow lanes here run between high banks that are colourful with wild flowers and fruits almost all the year round. Here on a cottage wall are two pink flowered members of the Geranium family.

The smaller Shining Crane's-bill is the earlier of the two to come into flower. A glance at the leaves will show how it got its name. The taller Herb Robert may be in flower from mid spring right through until autumn, the whole plant often turning red towards the end of summer. It is one of Britain's most widespread wild flowers, a fact which is reflected in the record number of English names it bears. Geoffrey Grigson has recorded one hundred and nine local names for this same plant. Many of them incorporate the word Robert or Robin, but no-one can be sure just who was meant when the name was given. A possible suggestion is Robin Goodfellow, that goblin who was wont to play unpleasant tricks unless he was well treated by householders. There is an obvious connection here with the pixies of Dartmoor.

Here are just a few other names for HERB ROBERT, all of them from Devon.

BISCUITS
CANDLESTICKS
CRY BABIES
DOLLY'S SHOES
HEDGE LOVERS
KISS-ME-QUICK
LITTLE JACK
POOR ROBERT
ROBIN HOOD
SOLDIERS

Shining Crane's-bill   *Herb Robert*

The lane running from Mary Tavy to Horrabridge must once have been of greater importance. It was possibly one of the main north–south routes between Lydford and Plymouth, by-passing Tavistock, for it has been suggested that two mediaeval crosses (which are now elsewhere) once marked the stretch between Mary Tavy and Moorshop.

Here, by the track that goes off to Collaton, are two other stones. Both are almost obliterated by vegetation and easily passed without being noticed.

The milestone stands by a gate on the west side of the road, well camouflaged by a covering of moss and lichen, but if you run your finger carefully along the well cut grooves you can certainly make out how far it is to Plymouth.

The boundary stone is set well in to the opposite bank. It stands at the junction of three parishes. Two faces are visible but only one letter is legible. The "T" stands for Tavistock Hamlets to the west. The other two parishes, which here abut each other along the east side of the lane, are Peter Tavy and Whitchurch.

This massive stone is a surprising relic to be found beside a leat, for it is clearly not a millstone abandoned as faulty. The clue to its presence here lies in the scattered heap of boulders not far up the slope. There during the 1870s and 80s was a smithy, and this stone was almost certainly used by the wheelwright when making iron rims for cart wheels.

During those years there was a great deal of activity on the slopes of both Pew Tor to the south and Staple Tor across the road to the northeast. (See M 5) The stonecutters working there would have had frequent recourse to a blacksmith for the tools of their trade, and the carters hauling the granite setts away would doubtless have suffered many broken wheels.

Here is an imaginary reconstruction of the smithy.

SETT MAKERS' BANKERS

Roughly between 1870 and 1880 there was a demand in the larger towns of the Southwest for kerbstones and small blocks of granite for paving town streets. The small squarish blocks were known as setts, and it was here on the southern and eastern slopes of the Staple Tors that much of the paving for Plymouth's streets was manufactured.

First of all boulders of moorstone were drilled and split. The rows of semi-cylindrical holes are still to be seen in many places. These were then laboriously split again into shorter lengths and trundled to the benches, or "bankers" at which the sett makers worked. These may be found either singly or in groups. They consisted simply of a flat boulder mounted at a slight angle on two stout supports and set well in to the slope. Here the sett makers would stand or perhaps kneel. With hammer and chisel the blocks would be cut and squared to the required size. A worker might produce about forty during a day's toil. The finished stones were loaded on to carts and then taken to the railway station at Tavistock.

Near some of the bankers are the ruins of small huts—places to eat the midday meal or shelter from the worst of the weather.

Although a few of these bankers have been discovered elsewhere there is nowhere such a concentration of them as on these slopes.

There is so much to see here that only a few of the antiquities can be mentioned, and then only briefly. The most unusual monument, unique on Dartmoor, is the pair of nearly parallel double stone rows. These are about thirty yards apart, the southern one extending beyond the other at each end. Most of the stones are small, but a single large blocking stone stands at the east end of each double row, and at the western end of the southern row is a large pair of stones. Another unique feature is the stone circle, which may once have contained a grave, half way along the latter row. A third much shorter row runs off southwest, starting just west of this circle.

Lying a very short distance to the south of the rows is a large kistvaen. The cover stone was a huge one until a nineteenth century farmer decided to take a slice out of it to make himself a gatepost.

The most magnificent monument here is certainly the menhir which rises about ten and a half feet above ground level.

Between the menhir and the rows is a circle of eleven stones, from the centre of which it is said the sun can be seen to sink below the horizon in the notch of Middle Staple Tor on Midsummer Day.

There are still more stones on this downland that may well be former menhirs, but the relationship between all these remains, and their true purpose, is still a mystery. This is a fascinating place to pose unanswerable questions.

Kistvaen

*View westward
along the southern row*

Menhir

FICE'S WELL

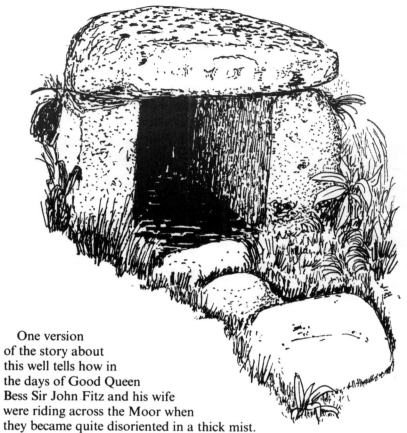

One version of the story about this well tells how in the days of Good Queen Bess Sir John Fitz and his wife were riding across the Moor when they became quite disoriented in a thick mist. They were tired, hungry and thirsty when they came across a spring of clear water. They dismounted to have a drink. As soon as they had quenched their thirst the mist cleared. They recognized their surroundings, and were able to head towards home—Fitzford House, near Tavistock.

In gratitude Sir John later returned and had the spring walled and covered as you see it now. On the front edge of the canopy are his initials, I.F., and the date 1568, though four and a quarter centuries of weathering have made the lettering almost illegible. The outer wall was built later to protect the well from cattle.

There is another well also named after Sir John near Okehampton. That one is known as Fitz's Well. It is described in square A 8.

This entertaining fountain wells up at the point where the branch of the Devonport leat that comes from the West Dart joins the other branch taken off the Cowsic.

The Dart branch of the leat runs down through Beardown plantation, and then near the farm disappears underground in order to cross the valley on a substantial viaduct. A hundred yards further on up the hillside it suddenly reappears like this, adding its waters to those coming from the Cowsic.

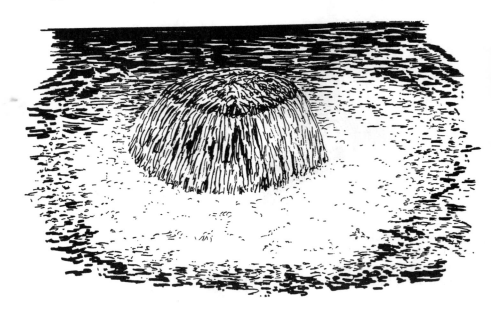

The fountain is enclosed by iron railings which have been omitted from the drawing. They are necessary, but not attractive.

On the route from Moretonhampstead or Chagford to Tavistock there was once only one bridge hereabouts. Now there are three. Nevertheless the scene depicted above is always known as Two Bridges, a name which is said to be a corruption of a term which simply meant "at the bridge".

The long clapper bridge, of five spans, could well be four hundred years old. It is to be found by following the footpath up the right bank of the river for about 600 yards.

In the 1780s and '90s the turnpike road was laid out along the more southerly route and the second bridge built. This lasted until well into the twentieth century, when it became necessary to replace it with a structure more suited to modern traffic.

Beardown clapper across the Cowsic

CROCKERN TOR

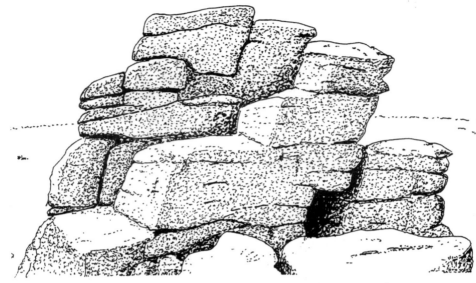

Parliament Rock

For the best part of four hundred years the Great Court (or Parliament) of the Stannaries used to meet here at irregular intervals to review operations, dispense justice, and make laws. The Lord Warden would convene the court, summoning twenty four representatives from each stannary district. These were based at Tavistock, Chagford, Ashburton, and Plympton. At any meeting therefore over a hundred men might have been present. Tradition has it that the Lord Warden had his seat on one of the great steps up the side of Parliament Rock, and that clerks and stannators would sit in session below, either on the greensward or on some of the huge slabs which still remain propped up on smaller boulders. These, and the other slabs since removed, served as seats, tables and canopies for the officials. One of them is to be seen at Dunnabridge Pound (in Square M 11). Eric Hemery wrote that he personally tested the acoustics of the place and found them quite adequate.

It is assumed that this place was chosen because of its central position on Dartmoor. Sessions were not very frequent, and surviving written records are even less so. The laws the Parliament made tended to be harsh and selfish, though towards the end, as tin production and the stannary system declined during the 18th century, some regard had to be paid towards the well being of the rest of the world. The last meeting for which records exist was in 1703. Among the more famous of the Lords Warden was Sir Walter Raleigh, who presided here in the year 1600.

DUNNABRIDGE POUND

Canopied seat inside the pound

This was once the most important of the animal pounds on Dartmoor. A walk round inside the perimeter will show that the walls have been reinforced to double thickness for much of their course. The pound may originally have been a prehistoric one, and any huts inside cleared away during the Middle Ages in order to put the enclosure to a new use.

Several times a year, with minimum warning, The Duchy of Cornwall used to organize drifts, during which all stray animals—that is, those that were illegally grazing on Duchy lands—were rounded up and driven to the pound. There the owners would have to pay a fine to retrieve their property. Up to three weeks might be allowed for this. Stock not claimed by then would be sold by auction. As two or three hundred animals, mainly horses and cattle, might be involved, together with the moormen who had driven them in and no doubt a large number of resentful owners, the occasion must have been quite a spectacle. There is even a suggestion that stocks were installed to "impound" owners as well,—those who were tempted to "rescue" their property without payment.

Just inside the gate is a seat canopied by a huge slab of granite. There is a tradition that this slab was hauled down from Crockern Tor where it had previously been used as a table at meetings of the Stannary Parliament.
See also Square M 10.

Finger posts at each end of the
stepping stones point the way across
the East Dart. The steps form a useful

Dipper

crossing, for they are noticeably rectangular, closely set, and well embedded in
the river. Although some of them may look as though they have been trimmed
there were apparently many similar stones on the hillside up valley readily
available before the conifers were planted. The crossing is not named on the
map, but this is Win Ford.

Have a go at counting the steps from each bank in turn. It takes careful
observation to arrive at the same total each time!

Here is a pleasant place to linger and watch the wild life of the riverside.
Dippers and Dragonflies and Damselflies are all active on a summer day.

The dark winged Demoiselle Agrion
may have irridescent purplish wings if it is
a male, or brownish ones if it is a female.
This species is often to be seen by swiftly
flowing rivers. The young nymphs spend
nearly two years on the gravelly bottom
before emerging as adults.

Here is an example of an insect where
the Latin name for the species, *Agrion
virgo*, is easier to handle than the clumsy
English one, which is after all only a part
translation.

Demoiselle Agrion

The spelling on the signpost gives a guide to pronunciation, but the name is derived from Shere well, a spring that still supplies water to Sherwell Farm. The farmhouse is reckoned to be seven centuries old, and even then it is a replacement of an earlier one on the same site. On the lawn in front of the house can be seen the granite base of a cider mill.

The picturesque thatched cottage on the other side of the road is said to be called "Hornets Castle"—a fitting companion to "Rogues' Roost" a short way up the lane. That name is supposed to have begun as a nickname bestowed upon the house by near neighbours in reference to questionable "goings on" there. That was a long time ago, but the name stuck, and now it is even marked on the map.

An easy stroll up the lane will take you in ten minutes to Babeny, an even older farmstead than Sherwell, though this is not readily apparent from the track that passes through the farmyard.

On the roadside walls at Sherwell Welsh Poppies have been growing for many years. There is more about these flowers in Square F 20.

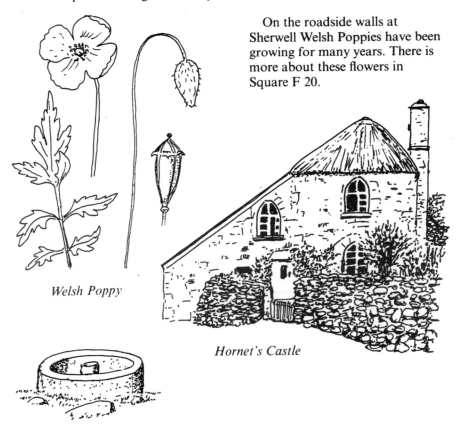

Welsh Poppy

Hornet's Castle

The two farms of West and East Shallowford lie on either side of the West Webburn. Not a great deal of them is to be seen from the road, but if you come this way in high summer stop just above West Shallowford to examine a small, wet patch of waste ground by the roadside. Here are fine displays of two wild flowers particularly worth an inspection.

The more obvious is a clump of Blood-drop Emlets. These are large showy yellow flowers very similar to Monkey Flower, illustrated in Square O 16, except that the lower petals have a number of large reddish blotches on them. Another difference is that the flower stalks are hairless and rather longer. These plants are native to Chile, and must originally have come to this country as either garden plants or as seeds mixed with some other product. They have "gone wild" in several places in Devon. As they also hybridize with the much commoner Monkey Flower the plants here could well be hybrids.

The other plant worth searching for is the small Ivy-leaved Bellflower. This is native in Devon. A grassy mound by the streamlet is festooned with its thin creeping stems, tiny Ivy-shaped leaves and small pale blue flowers. It is closely related to the Campanulas.

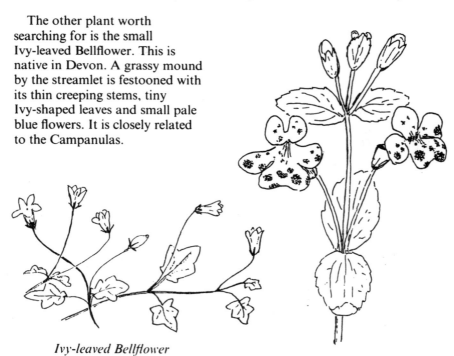

Ivy-leaved Bellflower

Blood-drop Emlets

Jordan Manor House

Here is a haven of delight
to be found by surprise as you round
a bend across the little valley. The public
way runs through what was once the farmyard, and there is a gate at each end.
Even though you are on the Queen's highway to stand within the gates is like
intruding into a private garden. On one side stands the long thatched manor
house, and on the other a barn that has been converted into a home. Both are
picturesque. A magnificient porch and bright
flower beds front the Manor, while on the
other side of the road the lawns of Jordan Barn
are enlivened by a stream and eight staddle
stones.

Not far up the hill to the north, at a road
junction, stands an old wayside cross. A tiny
niche is cut into its face. Nothing seems to be
known about the cross's origin. At one time its
head was built into a nearby wall. Then it was
discarded for some years until an old shaft was
found elsewhere in Devon which made a
suitable match. The two were united, and the
cross stands once again as a waymark, perhaps
not far from its original position by the path to
Widecombe Church.

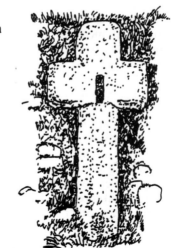

Drywell Cross

On the miniscule village green here there are two objects of interest. The first is the Dun Stone, a large boulder pock marked with what look like tiny rock basins. Long ago the annual courts were held beside this stone, and it was the custom for the lord's tenants to deposit their rent—if it was in the form of coins rather than produce or livestock—in one of the small hollows on the rock.

The stone then also became known as the Rent Stone. It is said that in times of plague the hollows were first filled with vinegar: this was thought to kill any infection that might be clinging to the coins.

On the third of the three boulders on the green stands Dunstone Cross. The plaque beneath it tells part of its history. It appears that the cross fell down about the middle of the last century, and was "rescued" by the vicar of Widecombe and set up in the vicarage garden.

Dunston Manor is just opposite. The coat of arms above the gate is that of the Hamlyn family. The motto is difficult to decipher. It possibly has some such meaning as "You may break me but you will not bend me". There has been a manor house here—though not the present building—since before the time of William the Conqueror.

A look at the name of one of the cottages by the green will show that it was once a school. This is quite surprising in what seems to be such a tiny hamlet, seeing that in Widecombe, not much more than half a mile away, there was another school.

BLACKSLADE MANOR

The map reference refers to the sketch which shows the entrance to the grounds of Newhouse Inn, once a welcome resting place for travellers between Ashburton and Chagford, two important centres of both the tin and woollen industries.

The mire behind the greensward and line of leaning Willows is the home of all three insectivorous plants that grow on Dartmoor. The flowering stems of all of them are only a few centimetres tall. But beware, they grow in real stuggy places!

The two Sundews have leaves covered with reddish, sticky glands, capable of trapping small insects unlucky enough to fall on them. The Round-leaved Sundew is common over much of the Moor, although the white flowers only open in fine summer weather. Intermediate Sundew, which has a much more restricted distribution, is often found in muddy rather than mossy places.

Pale Butterwort entraps its prey by curling over the edges of its sticky leaves. It is not easy to spot, but is such a delightful little plant that a close view is worth a pair of wet knees. The flowers are pale violet.

Pale Butterwort

Intermediate Sundew

Round-leaved Sundew

235

You may be involved in a disappearing trick if you climb up here, for even the triangulation pillar once disappeared. One explanation was that the Bronze Age chieftain buried beneath rose up in wrath because his grave had been disturbed by those who had removed boulders in order to find bedrock on which to cement the pillar. He piled the boulders up again and buried it. Since there are two more prehistoric cairns on the hilltop he possibly had help from friends.

Other objects to search for on the higher slopes, on the sides facing the roads, are a recumbent cross and three abandoned millstones. The cross is the only one on the Moor to be cut in relief on the bedrock. It was presumably not intended to be set erect. Its purpose is unknown: a memorial perhaps? Or a shield against the angry spirits buried under the summit cairns? It is almost certainly many hundred of years old.

The largest of the millstones has some grooves cut into its upper surface. A cheese press has been suggested.

Cheese press?

If you do not find all these things, never mind. For best of all is the view from the summit. On a clear day this stretches from the English Channel to the distant ridge of Exmoor, with many a fine hilltop in between.

A cross of mystery

BAGTOR MILL

Here is as picturesque a mill as you could wish to see; though seeing it is not easy, for it stands in an almost woodland setting, and when the trees are in leaf the great wheel that partly obscures even the upstairs window will be hard to spot. The leat is taken off the River Lemon and runs under the road. There is a small disused reservoir at the roadside and a pond below the mill.

Along the damp, shaded banks thrive two unmistakable ferns.

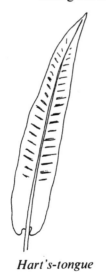

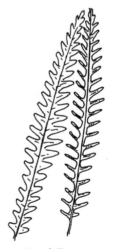

HARD FERN is the only common British fern to have two types of frond. The reproductive ones, carrying spores on the underside, have much narrower lobes than the vegetative ones. Look for both types in late summer.

On the HART'S-TONGUE the spore cases are arranged in parallel lines along the back of the frond.

In the woods above the road a carpet of Pink Purslane has spread out in recent years. This is illustrated in Square E 14.

Hart's-tongue

Hard Fern

FIVE CROSS

The four roads radiating from this triangle of grass are labelled on the older waymark as leading to MANATON, BOVEY, NEWTON, and ASHBURTON. The new one indicates in the same order Haytor, Lounston, Bickington, and Sigford. But what of the fifth way? It goes to Ilsington: but a moment's glance will show that if you have a car you will not choose that route to get there.

Just near the letter box, at the edge of the grass, grows an albino form of Dove's-foot Crane's-bill. Normally the flowers are purplish, but here—at least in 1990—they were quite white. The plant is an annual so it will be interesting to see in future years if the white form recurs.

The leaves of Dove's-foot are among the most softly hairy of all our plants,—a delight to feel. The Crane's-bill part of its name is derived from the shape of the seed pods.

The herbalist Gerard, writing in the time of Charles I, describes an interesting use for this plant, which he says "myselfe have often proved".

As a cure for rupture a half spoonful of the dried and powdered roots should be taken in a glass of red wine at bed time each night for three weeks. This would not be at all an unpleasant medicine, but he adds that in the case of aged persons an extra powder should be stirred in—that of nine red slugs dried in an oven. He gives an assurance that the remedy never fails "as myselfe have likewise proved".

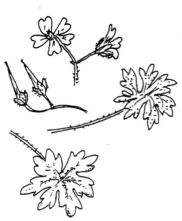

Dove's-foot Crane's-bill

LOOK AND WEEP

This is the name on the map—a name that sets the imagination working to conjure up an explanation of its origin. The name board in the hedgerow where the track leads off to the farm has condensed it to LOOKWEEP FARM.

In the roadside ditch here grows a fine stand of HEMLOCK WATER-DROPWORT. Its great heads of flowers show clearly that it belongs to the Parsley family. But it is not a plant for the kitchen. Although its leaves resemble Wild Celery and its roots are like Parsnips, both are highly poisonous. There are many records of people who have died through mistakenly eating them. Horses and cattle can also be poisoned, but it is said that goats are immune. Country people once used the roots as a bait for rats and mice.

The plants are here growing in a typical habitat—a wet ditch. The species is very common in such situations, as well as along river banks.

Its botanical name is *Oenanthe crocata*.

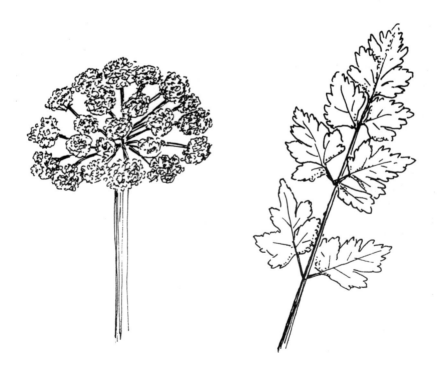

Hemlock Water-dropwort

PIXIES' CROSS

This huge, rugged cross is one of the few undamaged ones still marking the old Abbots' Way from Buckfast to Tavistock. Before the golf course invaded this once lonely stretch of the Moor it would have made an impressive and welcome waymark to travellers coming from the East. There was only one more cross to pass before Tavistock came in sight.

The reason for its name is not known, for the locality is not specially renowned for pixies, but there is nevertheless a delightful story connected with it.

Back in the days when Oliver Cromwell ruled the land a local vicar with extremely puritanical views wished to have the cross destroyed. As no one would do this for him he took the law into his own hands, and one day set about digging it out.

However it was not long before he became aware of a large and obviously angry bull making a beeline towards him.

There was only one place of safety within reach, and he was able to shin up to the cross-piece before the bull arrived. The animal was thwarted but not at all impatient. For the rest of the day and all through the night it grazed and watched contentedly within a few yards of the cross, and all that time the vicar sat on high.

It was well after dawn before a group of villagers "rescued" their parson, but not until he had made a firm promise . . . and that's why Pixies' Cross still stands on a patch of rough ground just off the fairway.

As far as the map is concerned this is an unnamed
bridge across an unnamed stream along a minor road
that does not seem to have much reason to exist.
Nevertheless there is room to park a few cars, a grassy
slope, a ford, and a babbling brook in which to paddle
on a hot day.

In damp patches on the further side of the stream
Lesser Spearwort thrusts up boldly into the light, Marsh
Pennywort hides its tiny clusters of minute flowers under
its leaves, and Marsh St John's-wort waits for sunshine
before opening.

Lesser Spearwort

(both yellow)

Marsh Pennywort

Marsh St John's-wort

This fine seven foot cross with an octagonal shaft is probably more recent than many others marking ancient tracks across the Moor, but nevertheless it must have been standing here for not much less than 500 years. Former tracks from Tavistock to Chagford, Ashburton, and Buckfast all passed this way.

Within a short stone's throw of the cross is another item of interest—an "inch hole" or "bull's-eye" drilled through the rectangular boulder which blocks the leat. This allows a fixed amount of water to be supplied to a farm. The main branch of the leat runs off to the right, and about 150 yards further on another bull's-eye stone can be found.

VIXEN TOR

Associated with this remarkable tor and the nasty mire below it is a legend about an even nastier witch.

In this version the hero is the younger brother of h.awatha.

Should you ask me, "Whence these stories?"
I should answer, I should tell you.
"From the misty moors of Devon,
From the torrents, woods, and hillsides
Where the Dipper and the Wheatear
Make their home among the boulders."

There was born my Lowawatha;
Spent his childhood, grew to manhood,
Learned to love the tors and rivers.

Once a piskie by the Walkham
Fell into the rushing water.
Lowawatha entered boldly,
Plucked him from the swirling current,
Rescued him from being carried
To the shores of Gitchie Gumee.
To the white-waved Big Sea Water.
For this deed of noble valour,
"I will give you," said the piskie,
"Power to see through mist and darkness.
Use it well to travel safely,
Helping others out of danger."

Lowawatha thanked the piskie,
Journeyed on across the moorland
Till he came to Merrivallee
Where he tarried in the hostel.
There he heard the story spoken,
Heard the tale of foul Vixana,
Hideous witch of Vixentoree,
She who watched from Vixen's summit
Waiting for a lonely trav'ler
Coming down from Windiposta
To the mire of Beckamooree.
Conjured mists across the
    pathway,
Cackled as the hapless trav'ler
Stumbled into quaking bogland,
Sank beneath the em'rald
    Sphagnum.

Thither then strode Lowawatha,
Took the path to Samfordspinee,
Took the path he knew would lead him
Through the mire of Beckamooree,
Past the beetling, craggy rock-pile,
Past the home of vile Vixana.

When Vixana saw him striding
Through the Asphodel and Bogmoss
She with magic brought a mist down,
Hid the mire and path across it.

Lowawatha, nothing hindered,
Quickly gained the rocky hillside,
Reached the summit from the hindside.
Saw Vixana peering downward
Waiting for his cries of anguish
From the wat'ry bog beneath them.

"Hi!" said Lowawatha softly,
Waited till she turned towards him,
Hurled her off with mighty effort,
Heard her shriek as down she hurtled,
Plunged beneath the floating Sphagnum
There to bide for ever after.

Vixen Tor

The main quarry is at the end of a deep, narrow, water logged cutting that dives into the southern face of Swell Tor. Outside are the remains of buildings, platforms, walls, stanchions, rails, concrete bases for machinery, spoil heaps, and a squadron of wooden sleepers lying across the siding that runs gently downhill to join the "main line" a few hundred yards away to the northwest. That line was once the G.W.R. connecting Princetown and Plymouth.

A stroll from the quarry entrance along the siding will take you past some of the abandoned "leftovers" cut from great blocks of granite during the quarry's working life—mainly in the late nineteenth and early twentieth centuries. These objects afford fascinating speculation as to their intended purpose. Why did they get so near to the railway, only to be abandoned?

The shallow trough appears to be in good condition, but what is the purpose of such a large container only a few inches deep? The bollard is certainly damaged, but surely it would not have been carried down here if it had not at the time been in good condition.

The most impressive of the leftovers are the twelve corbels cut in 1903 for the widening of London Bridge. Why were they surplus? Why is one longer than the others? This is the bridge that now stands in the semi desert of Arizona. At least one of these spare corbels was collected when the bridge was moved to the New World in the 1960s.

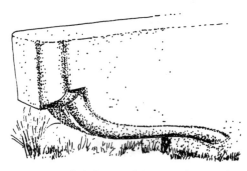

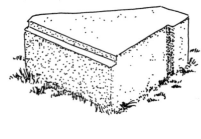

A corbel destined for London Bridge

DEVIL'S ELBOW

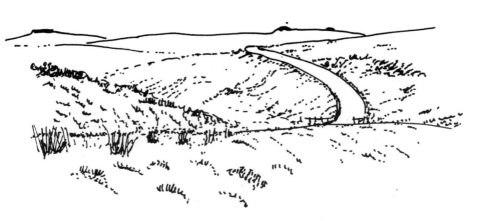

Here Devil's Bridge spans the infant Meavy. Once there was a dangerous double bend at the dip, but as can be seen from the two sketches the road has been considerably straightened. The drawing that includes the bearded devil is adapted from the sign of "The Devil's Elbow" inn at Princetown. The pimple on the skyline is Leather Tor. It is romantic to think of Satan sitting here watching cars hurtling down the dip: perhaps a real sight of him would have a salutary effect on the drivers. But alas, that is not how the story goes. Authority tells us that the man who built the original bridge was a local character said to have been "a bit of a devil".

Devil's-bit Scabious has purplish blue flowers.

OCKERY BRIDGE

The story associated with this bridge is one of the few Dartmoor folk tales that varies little in the telling. Perhaps that shows there is some truth in it. No date can be ascribed to the story, so perhaps the bridge referred to is the clapper that spans the Blackabrook just a few yards below the road bridge.

One day at dusk a countrywoman making her way homeward was walking down the slope towards the river when a pixy appeared in front of her, dancing and gesticulating as he pranced ahead of her on to the bridge. Being wise in the ways of the little folk the woman knew how to avoid being pixy-led. She turned her pockets inside out, reversed the shawl she was wearing, and stepped forward with determination. On the very bridge itself the pixy, still leaping wildly about, landed right in front of her feet. Quick as lightning the bold woman bent down, snatched him up, and without more ado stuffed him into her half empty basket and fastened the lid down.

For a while the pixy talked loudly and fast, but in a language the woman could make nothing of. So on she strode, pondering perhaps the wisdom of taking such a captive into her home. But presently the chattering stopped. Curiosity overcame her. Carefully she raised the lid and peered inside. The pixy had vanished. She felt both disappointed and puzzled, but just a little relieved: her problem had been resolved. But how the pixy, which she afterwards described as about eighteen inches tall, got out of the basket she never discovered.

It seems that the pixy's experience taught it a lesson, for it has not been seen since the present bridge was rebuilt in 1901. But you never know. Go down one evening . . . . .

THE CROCK OF GOLD

The vicinity of Royal Hill was a popular burial area with our Bronze Age forefathers. There are at least ten other kistvaens within a mile of this one. Three of them, by the Blackbrook, are within twelve yards of each other. The Crock of Gold is one of several on Dartmoor that have individual names.

It is an interesting exercise to sit in any of these stone chests that you come across and write your thoughts. Christopher Bobbin might have put his like this:

There are prehistoric circles and mighty stones in rows,
And logan stones that wobble with every wind that blows.
There are heaps of hills and tors and rivers to explore,
   But I read a book in a kistvaen when I go out on the Moor.

There are wipses and wopses and woopses, and 'normous bugs with wings,
And masses of flies and skeeters, and hordes of buzzy things.
You can 'scape them all if you stand in the breeze on a windy tor.
   But I have a rest in a kistvaen when I go out on the Moor.

There are woolly bears a-prowling, and dragons that can fly,
And tiger moths and el'phant hawks zooming through the sky;
And down in Tavy Cleave you can hear the brimstones roar.
   But I take a nap in a kistvaen when I go out on the Moor.

PRINCE HALL BRIDGE

This is a surprisingly fine bridge to find on a track that leads only to a farm. It was built in the 1780s at about the same time as the Georgian mansion seen through the arch. There was until then a ford here on the track between the ancient tenements of Prince Hall and Sherbeton. These two farms would have been within the Forest of Dartmoor when its boundary was officially drawn in 1240. The track later connected up with Swincombe Farm and the Tavistock to Ashburton route which crossed the River Swincombe nearby. Nowadays the bridge principally serves Moorlands Farm on the hillside to the south: and of course it also has considerable use by students of all ages at the adjacent Dartmoor Training Centre.

Although the gate at the Moorlands end of the bridge says PRIVATE access to the two routes beyond it is permitted to walkers.

Prince Hall—which has no connection with the prince who gave his name to Princetown—is now a hotel. The ancient farmstead once there has disappeared, as also has the lodge at the road end of the long avenue of Beeches. These were planted in the 1790s.

The site of the 19th century workings is fairly evident. One of the gerts has been adapted to carry a water pipe from the Swincombe to Venford reservoir. It has a fine granite portal.

Nearby were adits, shafts, underground levels, workshops, dressing floors, cottages, and two 24 foot diameter wheels, one for pumping and one for crushing.

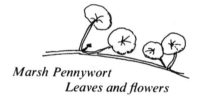

Marsh Pennywort
Leaves and flowers

A little further up the valley, just below the track where it curves round the shoulder of the slope, are the remains of a very much older tin works. This is a blowing house which might easily be missed, but which is well worth inspection. It is the only one on Dartmoor that still contains both the upper and lower stones of a crazing mill, used for grinding tin ore. The upper stone would have had pegs inserted into its four sockets, and was probably turned by horses. The ore, which would already have had its preliminary crushing in a mortar stone (see Square Q 6) would be fed between the millstones and ground to the consistency of coarse sand. It would then be smelted. There are several mortar stones lying about.

There is also a mould stone here which has two small "sample moulds" cut into it. Even these tiny moulds would contain about a pound (in weight) of tin. An ingot from the large one could have weighed up to 180 pounds.

The leat supplying water power can be followed without difficulty all the way to the river.

Upper millstone

Lower millstone

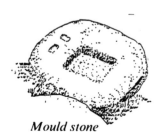

Mould stone

It was once the custom that any man who could in one day enclose a piece of land, build a home upon it, and have a fire on the hearth by nightfall, should be entitled to own it for ever. In this village Tom and Sally Satterly were eager to build a little house. Though they had plenty of helpful neighbours these did not include the tenement holders, who were more inclined to be obstructive. However plans were made, and one day, probably in June 1835, when all the farmers had departed to the fair, a score of willing hands assembled. Within a small enclosure the cottage walls were raised, leaving gaps for door and windows. A timber roof was added and roughly thatched with rye straw. By the time the farmers returned a fire was burning on the hearth.

The first occupants were Sally's parents. Later Tom and his wife moved in. Then their children, and their grandchildren, and their great grandchildren.

Early this century a second storey was added, somewhat altering the appearance of the house, but the name on the gate has not changed—the name of the last house in Devon to be built in a day.

THE COFFIN STONE

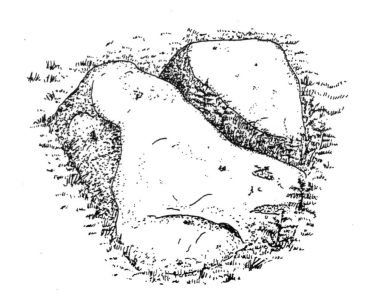

In the Middle Ages wheeled vehicles were almost unknown on the high moor for there were no tracks that could be negotiated by cart or carriage. Heavy loads had to be carried by packhorse. But there was one special kind of load that was never transported in this way: a coffin (containing a body) was always carried on men's shoulders.

One route used by settlers in the Dart valley on their way to Widecombe church led from the clapper at Dartmeet up the steep hill now climbed by a winding metalled road. About half way up—inside the wide bend on the road—lies this stone, a convenient resting place for a coffin while the bearers took a breather. After the cortege had continued up the hill it seems to have been the custom to engrave a cross, or the dead person's initials, on the stone. About seven small crosses and four sets of initials can still be made out, as well as a number of uncertain letters.

The explanation for the splitting of the stone into two pieces is that it was struck by lightning after the body of a particularly wicked character had rested there on its last earthly journey.

Milkwort
has blue, purple or white flowers

THE MONEY PIT

The pit is easy to find—it lies on the other side of the road from the memorial cross—but the amount of money to be found in it is likely to be disappointing. The cairn that once covered this kistvaen has of course gone, but about a dozen of the encircling stones are still in place.

The story goes that "in the long ago" when the cairn was still heaped up over the cover stone a farmer living near Poundsgate dreamed that a considerable sum of money lay hidden in the grave. So one night, without a word to anyone, he set off, presumably carrying a crow bar, to rob the grave. The loose boulders were heaved aside and with great effort the cover stone was levered off the upright slabs beneath. Of course the acid nature of the soil had long since eaten away any trace of bones or ashes. Only a small piece of flint, in the shape of a heart, was to be found. Thoroughly annoyed the farmer pocketed this and in a bad temper tramped back home. He put the flint on a high shelf and returned to bed.

From that day on his friendly and generous nature changed. He became morose and ill tempered. His wife and young son suffered most, but he would also vent his churlishness on neighbours who had formerly been his friends. No explanation for this sudden change in his character could be offered.

A year passed. One day his son, who had now grown tall enough to reach the top shelf in the kitchen, found the little stone and took it for a plaything. Almost at once he lost it, somewhere out on the moor.

Immediately, and again without explanation, the farmer's former good nature returned, and he became once more the warm hearted man that everyone admired. But even he was at a loss to account for the change, until a few days later, on looking for something else on the top shelf, he discovered that his "heart of flint" had gone.

PONSWORTHY

This view of the "splash" and cottages at Ponsworthy has appeared in published photographs for over a hundred years. The earliest one known is dated 1891, and is reprinted in "Dartmoor in the Old Days". In all that time the scene has not changed very much.

The rest of the hamlet lies a minute's walk down the hill to where the road crosses the West Webburn. A stone built into the bridge parapet bears two dates, 1666 and 1911, recording the original construction and a major improvement.

Scars along the inner side of the parapet bear witness to the passing of wide vehicles, but a horseman who came this way on the afternoon of Sunday, 21st October, 1638 left impressions of a different sort. For this was Satan, who had quaffed a tankard of ale at the "Tavistock Inn" at Poundsgate, and was now on his way to Widecombe. There in a thunderstorm which did great damage to the church he seized Jan Reynolds from his seat in the back pew, and carried him off to settle a bargain that foolish young man had once made with him.

Satan was in a hurry that afternoon, and as his coal-black horse galloped across this bridge the animal, according to a quotation by William Crossing, "struck vire wi he's hoofs, an' didn' mun make a clatter whain he waint auver the bridge."

The story of Jan Reynolds and his pact with the Devil is told under the heading THE FOUR ACES in Square I 14.

This photogenic cluster of cottages must have appeared on more picture postcards and chocolate boxes, and in more magazines and brochures than any other rural hamlet in Devon. So when you pass by do so on foot, and take time to appreciate why.

The streamlet that tumbles down under the bridge is Ruddycleave Water, whose source is near Blackslade Mire. (See Square M 17.)

There is no village shop or post office, but a five minute walk up the hill to the west will bring you to the church. This too has a pleasing setting, the view across the valley of the Webburn to Leusdon being particularly attractive. It is surprising to see another church so near, but that one is not mediaeval, like St Peter's here.

The two finest treasures in the church are the 12th century font and the 15th century screen, which is almost complete. On the altar side of the screen are some larger figures in grey and black that look like caricatures.

The often photographed clock in the tower was installed in 1930.

The clock "numbers" read
MY DEAR MOTHER

BUCKLAND BEACON

Here, from a small tor gained without a strenuous climb, is one of Dartmoor's finest views. Below winds the thickly wooded valley of the Double Dart, beyond which the South Hams stretch paling into the distance; and beyond them on a clear day can be seen the glint of the English Channel. In the opposite direction, and especially to the Northwest, the Moor's high and lonely hills ride the horizon.

It is said that a fire was lit on this beacon to signal the sighting of the Spanish Armada in 1588, and certainly there was another one here during the Silver Jubilee celebrations of 1935. An inscription on the tor records that on that occasion everyone shouted "God save the king!"

At the foot of the rocks are to be found the two TABLETS OF THE LAW. These boulders were dressed and engraved during the summer of 1928 by order of the Lord of the Manor of Buckland. It took an Exmouth stone mason about ten weeks to complete the work.

Close to the nearby wall stands an old boundary stone. Although it bears no inscription it does have a name—The Grey Mare. The wall marks the boundary between the parishes of Ashburton, on the other side, and Buckland-in-the-Moor on this side.

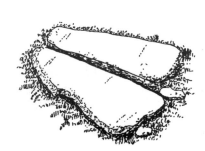

The tablets of the law

The Grey Mare

This monstrous construction, as high as two houses, must be quite the most unbelievable building in the National Park. Except that it is built of good old fashioned brick it might be taken for some hideous bunker housing weapons of horror in a work of science fiction. But no, it is merely the "receiving end" of a rifle range, just over a mile to the southeast of Rippon Tor.

Behind it lies the machinery, still partly intact, for raising and lowering the targets, and beyond that, spaced out nearly as far as the road, are four great mounds, once used as firing positions.

It was all set up at the beginning of the Second World War, and used on and off for a quarter of a century. When the red flag was flying 800 acres of Dartmoor were out of bounds to the public. That at least no longer happens, but the likelihood of the army demolishing this hideous thing is not very great.

Target hoist

This little plant with small flowers of the palest blue grows on dry banks and walls in the village. It used to be cultivated in gardens as a salad plant, but is truly wild nevertheless. It can be sown from late summer to early spring to produce a succession of leaves. The younger they are the better they taste.

Its other common name is Corn Salad. Look for it in flower during May.

Lamb's Lettuce

The second plant here is much commoner and more obvious. It is also known as Queen Anne's Lace, but its book name is Cow Parsley.

This is the first of the common white umbellifers to come into flower in spring along the roadside banks. No other similar flower of this rather confusing family will be out in such masses during May.

It is relished by cattle—hence its name—and also by rabbits, often being gathered as food for domestic ones. Indeed, in parts of Devon it is called Rabbits' Meat.

A bright green dye can be obtained from the leaves, and a yellow one from the flowers.

Lady's Lace

A track leads up here from the road near Combe Farm, and the short walk is rewarded by pleasing views from the hilltop, especially northwest across a pattern of small fields rising up to a skyline shaped by Rippon Tor, Saddle Tor, and Hay Tor.

In the scrub near the road thrives a colony of LORDS AND LADIES. It is not surprising that such a distinctive and common plant should have received many local names. Well over a hundred are recorded in Britain, ranging from BULLS in Dorset to KITTY-COME-DOWN-THE-LANE-JUMP-UP-AND-KISS-ME in Kent.

In Elizabethan time the roots of this plant were used to make a starch for keeping the ruffs of the wealthy in good shape. The roots were also grated and well washed to produce a flour. This used to be called Portland Sago because so much of it was manufactured in that part of Dorset.

The pollination mechanism is a strange one. Inside the bulge at the foot of the spreading spathe is a ring of downward pointing hairs; below these are the stamens and then the ovules. On a spring evening small flies, attracted by the smell of the projecting club, fall or climb down into the warm interior. They become trapped by the hairs, and while crawling around may transfer any pollen they may have picked up from another flower the previous night to the female stigmas on the ovules of this plant. In the morning the hairs above droop down allowing the flies to escape . . . The next evening . . . Cross pollination is assured because in any one plant the pollen is never available at the time when the stigmas are receptive.

It is interesting to break open one of the spathes to see all this. But do not lick your fingers afterwards because the juice of the plant is poisonous.

By autumn the spathes will have died away and the berries will have swollen and become bright red.

Lords and Ladies

This tunnel lies under the main Plymouth to Tavistock road. The railway was built during the 1830s, and included two other tunnels and six viaducts. One of these is featured in Square P 2. This was the South Devon and Tavistock Railway, which later was absorbed into the Great Western. The line closed in 1962.

The sketch shows the northern portal which is just outside the National Park: the other end of the tunnel, 374 straight yards away, is inside the Park. But do not be tempted to walk through: the way is treacherous.

About a hundred yards back from this entrance stands a marker stone engraved S D & T R.

This handsome milestone stands a good hundred yards away from the road, beside the leat that runs across Plaster Down. There is no sign of the road having been moved so presumably the milestone has. Perhaps the builders of the military camp that occupied so much of this downland during the last war (and right up to the 1970s) could supply an explanation.

Quite a number of branch leats are taken off this one higher up in its course, reducing considerably the volume of water flowing along this stretch; and further on the leat divides again to deliver water to the manors of Grimstone and Sortridge, and formerly also to a local copper mine.

What little water remains after that flows back into the Walkham, the river from which it was drawn some six or seven miles higher up.

SAMPFORD SPINEY

A church, a manor house, a school, an ancient cross on the green, a farm, . . . but where is the village?

Well, there is not one. No pupils attend the school, and the green where they once played is more likely to have chicken than children running across it. But this is certainly not a deserted or a ghost village. The school has become a private home, the church is in regular use, and the Tudor manor house dozes peacefully and well cherished behind its garden wall.

The church is small and simple, but it would be hard to imagine one more fitting for its site. A bird bath near the porch adds a romantic touch to a peaceful scene.

The fine cross on the green was moved here from a nearby hedgerow. It too probably dates back to Tudor times.

The parish of Sampford Spiney is one of the smaller ones round the borders of the high moor, though it extends northward up to Pew Tor. A few farms and a cluster or two of houses are all it contains in the way of dwellings.

WARD BRIDGE

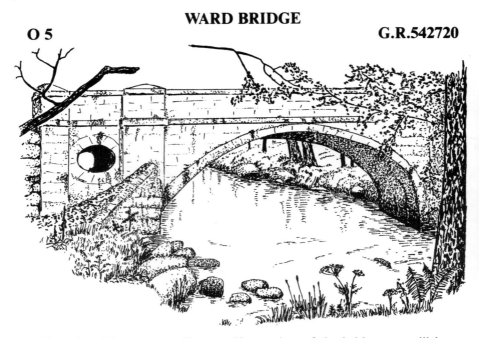

To enjoy this unexpectedly magnificent view of the bridge you will have to scramble down into the meadow on the river's eastern bank. From the narrow lane that here crosses the Walkham there is no clue to the bridge's architecture. In a single wide span it leaps across the river, but to prevent a build up of water when the current is in spate two tunnels have been incorporated into the buttresses. These are about six feet above normal water level, and indicate the height to which the river may rise after prolonged rain on the high moor. Something like twenty times the normal flow may be expected after heavy storms.

In summer it may be gloomy down here even on a bright day, for overhanging the bridge parapet are Oak, Ash, Alder, Willow, Sycamore, Beech, and Hazel. The little meadow is spangled with Earthnut (see Square L 3) that dances in the breeze.

Along the river Grey Wagtails flit from stone to stone. At all times of the year they have at least some yellow on their underparts.

Grey Wagtail

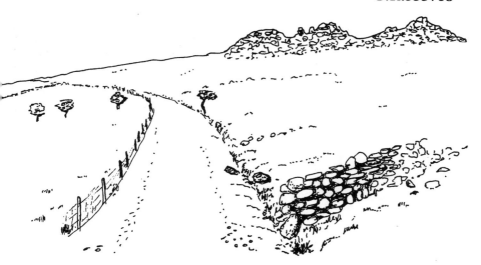

The first railway to come along this track was the Plymouth and Dartmoor Railway built in the 1820s, mainly to haul granite (by horse) from the quarries at Ingra Tor, Swell Tor, and Foggin Tor. By the 1880s profits were so poor that the route was sold to the Great Western Railway, and a new track was laid. But that line too became unprofitable. The last passenger service ran in March 1956, and the rails were removed soon after. The route now makes easy, though stony, walking—the stretch from the B 3212 near Peek Hill right into Princetown offering six miles of scenic pleasure. If, on approaching the Swell Tor quarries, you cut across to Foggin Tor (there is a good track) the walk will be a mile and a half shorter.

Beyond the bend in the sketch the line curves to the right, passing the entrance to Ingra Tor quarry, where there used to be a scheduled halt. It is just possible to imagine where the old platform must have been. Two gateposts nearby are made of discarded rails.

Another half mile will bring you to this fine bridge. It has no discernible track crossing it.

Something to puzzle about.

BLACK TOR FALLS

There can be few more delightful spots to come upon without warning, on the Moor, than here. For the surprise is kept until almost the last moment, especially if your approach is downstream. The young Meavy throws itself laughing over the low falls, subsides briefly into a smiling pool, and then chatters on down the valley. On both sides are grassy banks that beckon a walker to sit and muse . . . and it would be a pity not to do so.

On each side of the falls is the ruin of a blowing house, the one on the left bank being the more rewarding to explore. The leat and wheelpit can be distinguished, on the floor lies a mortar stone, and on the outside of the door lintel XIII is engraved, perhaps a registration number of some kind.

Blowing house on left bank

Wall Pennywort grows on the blowing house on the right bank

A prehistoric reave runs in a dead straight line from Nun's Cross up to this tor, and then on to North Hessary.

The same line was used again in 1240 when by royal command twelve knights made a perambulation to fix and record the boundaries of the Forest of Dartmoor. In 1337 the "Forest" was given to the Duke of Cornwall, and it still belongs to him. See also Square G 6.

About the middle of the nineteenth century several of the Forest boundary features were surmounted by an iron spike. This had a flattened head bearing the letters FB (Forest Bound). Only two of these are now left, this one on the top of South Hessary Tor being the easier to find.

If therefore you grasp the spike—known as "Excalibur" to enthusiasts—your finger tips could be in the parish of Walkhampton and your knuckles in the royal Forest of Dartmoor.

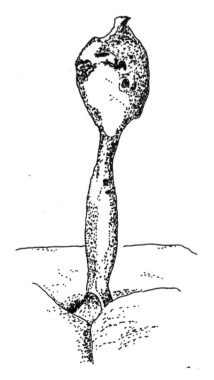

"Excalibur"

DEVONPORT LEAT

O 9

Because of its sinuous nature in following the contours the Devonport Leat
runs for about a mile and a half through this square. It is wide and deep, so
here is some moor advice from Christopher Bobbin.

Whenever you jump 'cross a Dartmoor leat
Be ever so careful to watch your feet:
   'Cos you'll learn how it feels
   If you slip on your heels
On mud that is sloping down into the ooze.
If all you are wearing is bare legs and shoes
   Then smother your squeals
   And enjoy how it feels
To sit among pondweed and tadpoles and eels.

But should you be thinking you don't care two hoots
—Because you are wearing green Wellington boots—
And then you slide deep in a watery leat.
You'll suffer much more than just cold clammy feet:
   Your boots will be filled
   With water well chilled:
Your socks and your trousers, your toes and your heels
Will tell you for hours how uncomfy it feels
To wallow in places more suited to seals.

So whenever you jump 'cross a Dartmoor leat
   Be ever so careful
     to watch your feet.

266

SWINCOMBE RESERVOIR

This little reservoir is very different from the much larger and better known ones that contain millions of gallons of water impounded behind gigantic dams. It fits unobtrusively into the landscape, for the dam is hardly higher than a weir, and retains only an acre or so of shallow water. This is piped down valley as far as Gobbet Mine, (see Square N 11) where an old adit is made use of to tunnel the water into Venford Reservoir, a further two and a half miles to the east. The little building by the dam has two solar panels on its roof.

On the slope to the northwest can be seen Dartmoor's shortest stone row, consisting of just three closely spaced stones. They are fine specimens but there is no sign of any continuation of the row in either direction. Perhaps they once formed a wall of a little building. On the valley face of the centre stone there is a suspicion of a letter, perhaps an H, cut lightly into the surface.

The shortest stone row

JOHN BISHOP AND DOLLY TREBBLE
G.R.641725 and 643725

John Bishop's house

This intriguing ruin dates from the early 19th century. One of its tenants, John Bishop, became well known and respected as a ditch maker and wall builder, so that the cottage is always known as John Bishop's House. A number of walls in the locality, as well as part of the house, bear witness to his skill. The original thatched roof was later replaced by a slate one, which was still partly in place at least up to 1971.

The setting is a romantic one, enhanced by a frame of trees on the approach from the river. The window and door frames, the fireplace, and particularly the magnificent porch, are all worth more than a glance.

The nearby track coming up from the ford is part of the former Ashburton to Tavistock road.

Dolly Trebble's house, of the late 18th century, stands on the brow of the hill opposite, though little but the substantial fireplace now remains.

Dolly, about whom a wealth of unlikely stories is told, moved there is 1850 with three of her six children. But this was by no means the only home of the family. They had previously lived at "Dolly's Cot" beside the East Dart, at Sherwell, and at Hexworthy; and later on at Prince Hall Lodge. She died in 1879 at the home of her son at Foggintor, aged well over eighty.

It seems that the story linking her name with the Prince Regent is pure fantasy.

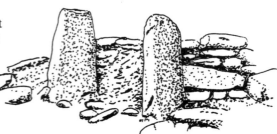

The fireplace at Dolly Trebble's house

*Imaginary reconstruction
of the two blowing houses*

For blowing house enthusiasts there is no better site on the Moor. Nowhere else are there two so close together, or so near a layby on a minor road that itself is full of interest.

The lower building is known as Beara House and the upper one as The Mill. Whether both were in operation at the same time is not known. It is possible that one was once so badly damaged that it was easier to build another rather than reconstruct the damaged one.

The wheelpit in the upper house is a deep one, so the wheel may well have been larger than usual. The furnace was probably in the alcove in the upper wall. In or beside each house are half a dozen well used mortar stones, while in the lower one there is also a mould stone. An ingot of tin that filled this would have weighed nearly 190 pounds.

It is curious that the wheelpits are on opposite sides of the two buildings. After turning the wheel on the right hand side of the upper house the water was leated over to the left to the lower wheel.

The nearest extensive mounds of tinners' debris lie a little way upstream on the opposite side of the O Brook.

The sketches are of course imaginary, but there still remain enough stones, walls, and pits to make a kind of mental reconstruction.

There is more information about how blowing houses operated in Square Q 6.

*The wheelpit of The Mill
might have looked like this.*

The deep gert here was the work of tin miners, probably in the early part of the 19th century. Its name derives from a tragedy that occurred round about 1820. A moorman who had been to a fair at South Brent was riding home late at night. During the long journey he pondered a transaction he had made at the fair: he had exchanged his horse for the one he was now riding plus a small sum of money. By the time he reached this spot he realized that he had most certainly got the worst of the bargain, and not wishing to face the ridicule of his wife is dismounted here, and by means of the horse's halter hanged himself from a Rowan tree. That particular tree has now gone, but the moorman's name, as well as that of the farmer who found him, are both recorded.

Just along the road stands COMBESTONE TOR.

A pleasant way to reach it from here is to follow the Holn Moor Leat (which crosses the gully) upstream for about a quarter of a mile, and then strike uphill across the dry Wheal Emma Leat to the tor.

Combestone Tor

This rock pile holds the record for being, of all Dartmoor's tors, the one nearest to a car park. It is easy to climb and is well worth exploring.

Look northward across the Dart valley, and there on the open hill, provided that both the sun and the Bracken are low, can be seen a crisscross pattern of faint lines. These are reaves, or low walls, that date back to beyond 1,000 B.C. Clearly the land was more worth cultivating then than it is today.

There are several small rock basins on the tor, some in the very earliest stages of growth. Near the western end of the rocks is a fallen block which has a basin now in its vertical face. Uncountable thousands of years are needed to form these hollows. There is more information about them in Square L 6. The largest rock basin on the Moor is featured in Square F 13.

JAN COO OF ROWBROOK FARM

The present farmhouse was built during the early years of this century, but to the left of the farmyard gate there stands a much earlier longhouse. In 1990 this was being completely re-roofed. It must have been here that the lad Jan Coo lived, of whom is told the following story.

Jan was an orphan apprenticed at Rowbrook Farm. One winter evening he came in at dusk to say that he had heard a voice calling from the river. The men left the warmth of the fire and took lanterns to search the river bank. Presently they too heard a voice calling, "Jan Coo! Jan Coo!" But their search revealed nothing and presently all was silent again, except for the sound of the Dart as it swirled along its rocky course through the great valley.

A few nights later, just before the evening meal, Jan again rushed in to say the voice was calling him again. Once more a search was made in the gathering darkness, but when the men answered the call it stopped, and they returned to the house convinced that pixies, who were said to live on the opposite bank, must be responsible.

Then in the spring when the days were longer Jan and another young worker were returning from the fields in the valley when for the third time the voice rang out, "Jan Coo! Jan Coo!"

" 'Tis me they're callin' ", said Jan, "I'll go and see what 'tis." He ran back to the river bank, and a moment later his companion saw Jan picking his way across the water from boulder to boulder. Jan was adept at doing this, so his friend continued up the hill. The calling only stopped as he reached the house door. It was not until darkness had fallen that the other men became worried. But no amount of searching ever revealed what had happened to Jan Coo.

The voice of the Dart is still to be heard. Listen to it as the waters rush turbulently along.

What do they say?

Longhouses feature in several pages of this book, but this one is different: you can visit it. Some years ago the National Park Authority was able to buy it, and now, several times a year, a visit to it is the highlight of one of their guided walks starting from Bel Tor Corner. Dates and other details are posted at the starting place, and also printed in the free magazine "Dartmoor Visitor" available at all the information centres and many shops as well.

This particular longhouse was acquired because it retains unaltered so many original and typical features.

The moorland face of the house is dug deep into the hillside, and the thatch reaches right down over the upper storey.

The living quarters are on one side of the central cross passage, and the shippon is on the other. This still has its central drain, tiny windows, post holes for the animal stalls, and giant crucks supporting the roof.

In the living room the huge fireplace is still in use, and upstairs glass panels have been inserted into the ceiling in order to make the underside of the roof visible.

As Higher Uppacott is the home of a member of the Park staff it is not possible to walk in at any time. If you cannot manage one of the guided tours then enquire at the National Park Headquarters at Bovey Tracey.

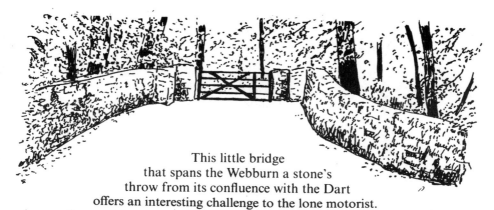

This little bridge
that spans the Webburn a stone's
throw from its confluence with the Dart
offers an interesting challenge to the lone motorist.
Across the road is a gate which has to be opened to allow a car to pass through. There is no latch, rope, or boulder to hold the gate either open or closed. The post on which it is hinged is set at a slight angle to ensure that once opened the gate will automatically swing itself shut—in less time than it takes a driver to get back into a car and engage gear.

The Webburn flows into the Dart where the greater river sweeps round a bend. Wide, sunny rock terraces here afford a perfect place to dally awhile, offering delightful and very different views up and down stream. The Dart has no more picturesque spot anywhere in its moorland journey.

Among the flowers to be found growing in cracks of the rock are the deep yellow Monkey Flower, which likes the damper crevices, and the lemon yellow Mouse-ear Hawkweed, which prefers drier ones. The long white hairs on the leaves make this plant easy to distinguish from similar species.

A five minute walk upstream along the lane will take you to another bridge. A much more unusual one. This is a suspension footbridge slung across the river under the trees.

Monkey Flower

WELSTOR CROSS

The lanes in this square tend to confine the explorer rather than allow opportunity to digress, so here are two easily recognizable plants that grow along these roadsides, and that are not mentioned elsewhere.

The pure white flowers of Jack-by-the-hedge, or Garlic Mustard, show up against the dark hedges in early spring. The leaves, if crushed, have a strong garlicky smell, and have in the past been widely used to "add flavour to the frugal diet of countrymen who could not afford more costly condiments".

In late summer two taller flowers dominate the lane sides: Rosebay Willowherb (See Square C 16) and Hemp Agrimony. The flowers of the latter form large heads of pinkish or purplish creamy blossoms that are later followed by fluffy masses of tufted seeds.

Garlic Mustard or Jack-by-the-hedge

A tea made with the dried leaves of Hemp Agrimony is said to give prompt relief if taken at the onset of a bout of 'flu.

Another common use for the leaves was to put some in the bread bin to stop the bread from going mouldy.

Hemp Agrimony

274

BELFORD MILL

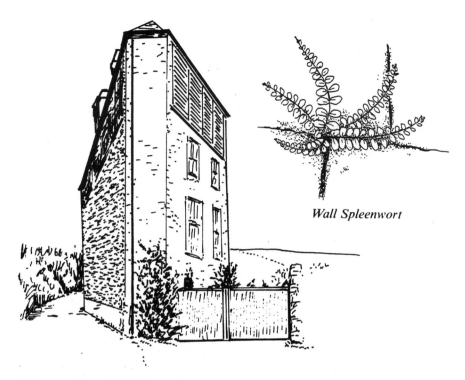

Wall Spleenwort

When approached from the south this appears to be an incongruous building to find in a rural situation. Originally, probably back in the eighteenth century, it would have been a woollen mill. The weather boarded top storey allowed the air to circulate across the wool drying floor. There is more about the local wool industry on the page about Ashburton (Square P 18). There are no obvious signs of the leat to bring in water, but the River Asburn is not very far away. During the next century the building was used as a corn mill for a while.

Growing in the crevices of the mill wall is the little fern often called Maidenhair Spleenwort in modern books. But this name only serves to confuse the plant with a rarer one called Maidenhair Fern. Its older name of Wall Spleenwort is much more suitable. If you look at the underside of the leaflets you can often see the brownish patches under which the spores develop.

Country folk used to make a tea with the dried leaves for use as a remedy against lung infections. But it is a larger fern, the Hart's-tongue, that was used to "remove obstructions from the spleen".

The spelling on the signpost offers an ornithological interpretation of the name of this crossroads.

The four hedge corners here each have different characters and different plants, but you only have to visit two of them to find Blackthorn, Blackberry, Black Bryony, and Black Knapweed.

Blackthorn fruits are always known as Sloes. These are hardly edible, but picked when really ripe and soaked for a long time in a bottle of gin, they make an excellent liqueur. Blackthorn leaves make a good tea, and at one time were used to adulterate China Tea. The wood is strong and hard and has often been used for such articles as the teeth of rakes.

On the corner with the widest verge Black Bryony spirals its way up and over the hedge. The flowers are small, but the succulent berries put on an eye catching display in early autumn, green, orange, and red ones all hanging in the same cluster. They should not be eaten, but a handful may be taken home and—as with sloes—soaked in gin. Don't drink this: use it as a lotion to rub on a bruise or a chilblain or a rheumaticky joint. If you think that is a waste of good gin then you can use shredded strips of the root for the same purpose. But remember that digging up wild plants is illegal: so it might be wiser to visit a chemist. It is the thick black roots that give the plant its name.

If you don't really fancy any of the above wild fruits then at least you can eat with pleasure a few Blackberries, or collect a handful to add to a bottle of Forest Wine.

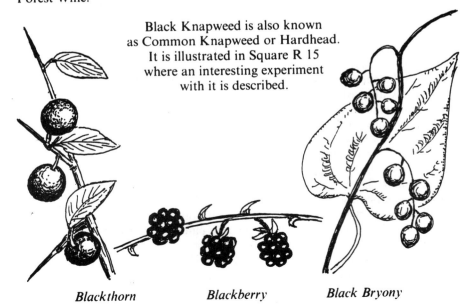

Black Knapweed is also known
as Common Knapweed or Hardhead.
It is illustrated in Square R 15
where an interesting experiment
with it is described.

Blackthorn   *Blackberry*   *Black Bryony*

HOOKS CROSS

This road junction, HOOK or HOOKS, depending on whether you read the signpost or the map, is at the apex of a small wood. In early spring the Hazel catkins hang heavily beside the path. Everyone knows the "lambs-tails", but not so obvious are the small female flowers, just tiny clusters of dark red stigmas waiting to receive pollen blown from the male catkins, in order that they may grow into nuts. Occasionally you come across a double nut. In Devon these are called "loady nuts", and are said to be a certain cure for toothache.

Here is a selection of other uses of Hazel, culled from other counties and other centuries.

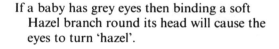

If a baby has grey eyes then binding a soft Hazel branch round its head will cause the eyes to turn 'hazel'.

To stop a nosebleed burn some Hazel bark, powder it, and blow this into the nose of the patient.

To cure deafness mix the sap of some green Hazel with honey and the juice from a House-leek, and put it into the ear.

Hazel branches, picked on Palm Sunday and fastened to the roof, will protect a house from lightening.

A forked twig of Hazel can be used to divine the presence of hidden water, metals, treasure, and criminals.

In Ireland a Hazel nut carried in the pocket will ward off rheumatism.

Finally, a leafy Hazel twig worn in the cap will bring the wearer good luck and prevent him from being kidnapped by Piskies.

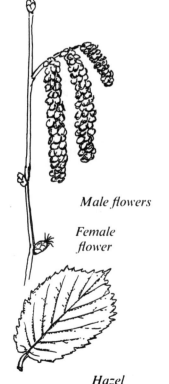

Male flowers

Female flower

Hazel

This magnificent brick viaduct used to carry the Great Western Railway from Plymouth to Tavistock and beyond, until the line was closed in 1962.

The viaduct was built in 1902 to replace an older one, of granite and wood, constructed when the line was first opened in 1859 by the South Devon and Tavistock Railway Company.

From the car park at Bedford Bridge you can walk up under the arches, examine the Staffordshire bricks from which it is made, continue past an adit to a copper mine (on the right), and up through the woods to the railway track. Access to the 200 yard long viaduct itself is fenced off for safety reasons.

An unused brick

The village bridge must be one of the oldest in Devon still open to modern traffic. It possibly dates back to the 14th century.

Immediately upstream of the bridge are a weir, a salmon leap, and below the weir a pool where children can swim and play. In the pleasant and spacious park alongside stands the fine village sign.

The village sign depicts both bridge and salmon; a nearby house is called "Salmon Leap"; and the inn on the other side of the river is the "Leaping Salmon".

Here is just a tiny hamlet, an old bridge, a grassy bank, a ford, and a seat whereon to sit and watch the river.

On a sunny day the Walkham ripples merrily on its way to Horrabridge. In autumn, if the river is running high, salmon may pass on their way upstream to spawn.

There was once a mill and an inn, but the miller, the inkeeper, and the miners who doubtless drank with him have departed, leaving only the river to chatter as it sparkles on its way.

WALKHAMPTON CHURCH HOUSE

This lovely old house is probably, apart from the church, the oldest building in the parish. A plaque on the wall gives a date of 1698 and some initials, but these may refer to some alterations, for the original parts of the house are possibly 200 years older than that.

During the sixteenth century this would have been the equivalent of a village inn. It belonged to the parishioners and was under the control of the church wardens. Its original purpose would have been to brew and sell ale, and it would have been open for custom after church services. It thus became a meeting place and a centre for celebrations of all kinds. Later it was also used for the collection of tithes, as a council chamber for the village elders, and as a centre to administer the Poor Law.

It was not until about 1895 that the Church House ceased to function as an inn.

It has now been converted into a pair of cottages. The roof has been repaired, and the stone mullioned windows, which had been walled up, restored. The mounting steps against the front wall are still in place. Inside are stone arches and a stone staircase.

The pillar in front of the house is all that remains of an ancient cross.

A preliminary ascent of Sharpitor will provide a glorious introduction to this pair of tors that dominate the local scene. Both of them resemble a gigantic pile of boulders rather than a solid mass of rock. An immense amount of clitter has rolled down from each of them. It is not easy to conjure up the original form of the tors when all the fallen boulders were on top. From the summit of Sharpitor the course of the Princetown railway can be followed for several miles as it winds its way around the hills. To the far northwest the church on Brentor stands on the horizon.

The view of Burrator Reservoir is a fine one, but even more of it can be seen from the bird's-eye viewpoint of Leather Tor.

About thirty acres of the downland round here are owned by the Dartmoor Preservation Association. There are several boundary stones inscribed DPA marking their land. One that is easy to find stands between Sharpitor and the main road.

View of Burrator Reservoir from Leather Tor

CRAZYWELL POOL

Crazywell Cross

Another of Dartmoor's surprises. Although this deep excavation on a treeless slope holds an acre of water, so well hidden is it that approached across the open heath it remains unseen until the last moment. There is surprisingly little waste material from the digging, which possibly dates back to Tudor times. But there are plenty of stories connected with the pool. Here are a few:

The water level rises and falls with the tide.

It was a favourite haunt of the Witch of Sheepstor.

The parishioners of Walkhampton once wanted to know how deep it was, so they brought up the bell ropes from the church, tied them together, and weighted the end. But they were not able to reach the bottom.

At dusk a voice from the pool calls out the name of the next person to die in Walkhampton parish.

At midnight on Midsummer Eve you can see in the still waters the face of the next person in the parish to die. This piece of romance was once put to the test by a disbelieving motor cyclist and his pillion passenger. They spent the required night by the pool and at daybreak drove back home. At a sharp bend they came off the road and were both killed.

The cross, on the old monastic route, stands about a hundred yards to the east of the pool.

A long, narrow gert runs up the slope of Cramber Hill and ends more or less at this pool. Presumably the tinners were following a vein of ore which suddenly plunged vertically into the earth. It is much smaller than Crazywell Pool in Square P 7. It is also more colourful, more secluded, and unless you strike the right gert and follow it uphill, more elusive.

The pool is clearly filled from rain seeping down its banks, but where the water goes after that is a bit of a mystery. Do not be tempted to wade in to see if there is a hole in the middle: there might be.

In the muddy water round the margins grows Bogbean, the three large leaflets on each stalk rising above the surface. If you can manage a close look at a cluster of flowers without getting wet socks you will see that the pinkish petals are enhanced by an extraordinary fringe of long white hairs. Here is an unusual and beautiful wild flower.

Another spectacle that catches the eye is the nonstop activity of Whirligig beetles gyrating endlessly on the still, dark surface of the water. A new generation of adults emerges in late summer. They can both fly and dive, so they must have an exciting life. Winter is spent buried in the mud.

Bogbean

Tracks from Whiteworks and Princetown, the Monks's Path from Buckfast, the Abbot's Way also from Buckfast, Sandy Way from Holne, a track from Eylesbarrow mine, and two branches of the old routes from Tavistock and Walkhampton all meet here, on this low col between the Newleycombe Lake to the west and Fox Tor Mire to the east.

But this mighty cross was here long before any of these tracks came into being. Its first documentary mention was in 1240 when it was called Siward's Cross, and recorded as a boundary mark of the king's forest. It is thought that the almost indecipherable inscription on its east face reads SIWARD, and possibly refers to a Saxon Earl Siward who owned land round Tavistock before the Norman Conquest.

When the light is at an acute angle the inscription on the west face is more easily made out. This reads BOC LOND, and almost certainly refers to Buckland: for the lands of Buckland Abbey near Tavistock used to extend up to this point.

Within a stone's throw stands the abandoned Nun's Cross farmhouse, with a couple of forlorn conifers to keep it company. The house was built in 1901 to replace a smaller one that had been established about thirty years earlier. It was inhabited until the mid 1960's; since when it has had occasional use by groups of young people on moorland adventure courses.

Just beyond the house the Devonport Leat flows into a tunnel for a quarter mile journey underground, on its way to Burrator reservoir. A topical warning on the "portcullis" explains why you should not attempt to wade through.

CHILDE'S TOMB

This version of the story of the death of Childe Harold in the 11th century should be sung mournfully to the tune of "My Bonnie lies over the Ocean".

Childe Harold was riding 'cross Dartmoor,
  The snow came right up to his knees,
Childe Harold was lost upon Dartmoor,
  One night when it started to freeze.

CHORUS:
What did, what did, what did poor Harold do then?
What did, what did, O what did poor Harold do then?

Poor Harold got down from his horse then,
  He'd made up his mind what to do.
He unsheathed his sword in a twinkling
  And severed its jugular through.

CHORUS

He next disembowelled the creature
  To fashion a shelter forlorn;
He snuggled right in to the carcase
  And lay down to wait for the dawn.

CHORUS

The liver he used for a pillow,
  The rib-cage provided his bed:
But the blizzard blew on to his torso
  And froze him until he was dead.

CHORUS

A party of monks found the carcase
  With Harold's stiff body inside,
One thumb was stuck out at an angle
  As if he were hitching a ride.

CHORUS

They lifted him on to a stretcher
  And carted him over the mire.
They carried his corpse to the abbey
  And thawed it in front of the fire.

What will, what will, what will poor
  poor Harold do now?
What will, what will, O what will
  poor Harold do now?

TER HILL

G.R.642706

Over the brow of this hill, where in a summer breeze the long grass rolls across the landscape like waves on a green ocean, used to run the Monks' Path. This was the track between Buckfast and the two abbeys to the west, Tavistock and Buckland. The three mediaeval crosses marking the route over the hill have all had an "up and down" existence.

During the 19th century the farmer at Sherberton removed this cross to his farmyard, thinking it would add character to his home. When he was forced to return it he dumped it near its original site, leaving others to re-erect it.

The fallen shaft and head of this cross were recorded about 1880 as being even nearer to the cross above than they are now. A few years later the pieces were moved about a hundred yards to the west, clamped together, and set up at the present site. Before long cattle using it as a rubbing post knocked it over again, this time breaking off one of its arms. It lay in the grass for many years until another splint was fixed, and the cross was reset, this time into a socket stone. During the summer of 1990 the whole cross was temporarily removed for more repair work.

The sketch was done from a photo taken a year or so earlier.

Only a quarter of a mile to the west, but out of sight, stands Mount Misery Cross. This one too has twice fallen, but fortunately remains undamaged. It was re-erected in 1885, the same year as the other two crosses. By that time the nearby early 19th century walls and gateway were already falling into disrepair.

HOOTEN WHEALS

For six hundred years and more tin has been sporadically taken from the valley of the O Brook. Near the river are the comparatively small heaps turned over in mediaeval times; in Dry Lake and up at the Hensroost are deep gerts gouged out perhaps in the 16th or 17th centuries. Here at Hooten Wheals and 500 yards northeast at Hensroost Tin Mine are the substantial ruins of the last phases of production, from about 1890 to 1920. The final *coup de grace* came during the Second World War when U.S. forces used the remaining buildings for target practice.

The terraces illustrated were the dressing floors where the crushed ore was separated from the waste material. On the lowest level are two buddles (see Square J 13) and the remains of an armature; for after about 1905 electricity for the works was generated at Saddle Bridge, downstream.

By the track below is a wheelpit, and about 50 yards up is an adit to the underground workings. This has been blocked up but a stream runs from its base.

The other interesting site nearby is labelled on the map 'Mine (disused)'. Here a wooden launder once carried water from the end of the aqueduct to a great wheel mounted above the pit.

The ghost of a wheel

This is the first cross on open moorland along the east-west Monks' Path that linked Buckfast Abbey with the abbeys at Tavistock and Buckland. Since another old track that ran southward from Dartmeet to South Brent also passed by here this spot represents a former crossroads. But which came first, the cross or the crossroads? Who knows? The north-south track can perhaps be made out coming from the direction of Combestone Tor, but of the Monks' Path only the cross remains as evidence. However the line of a prehistoric reave just a few yards away is still quite clear.

Although the battered head and the basal socket stone are original (about 14th century) the shaft is much newer. It had disappeared at some time before the end of the nineteenth century, and the present one is a replacement.

This spot was at one time known at Stacombe's Telling Place, in memory of a local shepherd who used to gather his sheep here in order to tell (count) them.

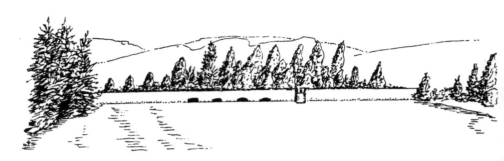

This reservoir has the advantage that from the car park at the western end, where there are toilets and a useful information board, you can circumnavigate the reservoir on foot and be back at your car in about an hour. The path is easily followed, and the way is full of interest.

The dam was completed in 1907, and its 33 acres of water supply about three million gallons a day, mostly to the Torbay area. The reservoir is fed by the Venford Brook and also by an intake from the River Swincombe about five miles to the west.

Beneath the water near the upper end of the drowned valley there was once a blowing house. A fine triple mortar stone rescued from it now stands just inside the gate through the railings at the western end of the dam. A glance over the parapet will show how steeply the brook continues its journey down to the Dart. Under the road the Holne Moor leat is piped. Its course, which used to sweep round the valley in a wide arc, was redirected when the dam was built. The tunnel down which it disappears can be found up the hill about 200 yards to the west. It reappears on the hillside to the east of the other car park.

The name of these meadows beside the Dart is misleading. The "marsh" now comprises several acres of dry, level turf where the young can play and the old can contemplate the river flowing quietly along. A thoughtful notice says that "IN THE INTERESTS OF CONSERVING THE TRANQUILLITY AND THE WILD LIFE OF THE RIVER DART FOR THE MAJORITY NO BOATING IS ALLOWED".

Among the trees and shrubs here the most notable is the colony of Alder Buckthorn, which must be one of the largest in the National Park. This is not related to the much commoner and larger Alder, though its wood has one similar property: it was once reckoned to be one of the best for making charcoal that was to be used in the manufacture of gunpowder. The inconspicuous greenish white flowers, much favoured by bees, appear in May and June. They are soon followed by small berries that will turn from red to purple in late summer.

Alder Buckthorn is the only Devon plant on which the caterpillars of Brimstone butterflies feed. The adults often overwinter among thick Ivy on walls and trees, the bright yellow males heralding Spring when they emerge in March. The females are a much paler colour. The shape and colouring of the underside of the folded wings provides such excellent camouflage that the butterflies seem to become invisible when at rest among the leaves.

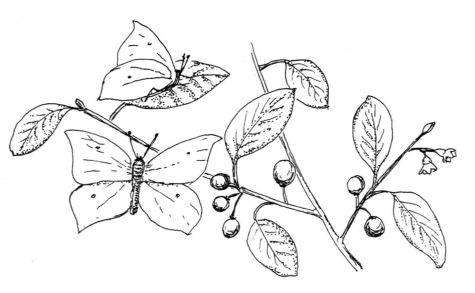

Brimstone butterfly and Alder Buckthorn

A "County" stone

About the time that young King Henry V came to the throne the bridge here was washed away. By the time he had won renown at the Battle of Agincourt the present one had been built.

If you go through the gate a little way downstream on the left bank and walk back under the bridge you can see that at some later date the main arch was widened on its upstream face.

Down here on the damp, shady slope grows Yellow Pimpernel, a relative of the smaller Scarlet Pimpernel that prefers sunnier places.

On the south side of the river there appears to be a road running downstream. This was the old route to Holne. A hundred yard walk along it will take you to what was once said to be the sharpest, steepest, hairpin bend on any proper road on the Moor. You can follow the route through the woods and emerge on to the present road near Holne Chase Hotel. On walking back to the bridge you will pass, just opposite the "Single Track Road" sign a stone set well into the high bank with a letter C cut into its face. This is a "County" stone showing the distance from the bridge (a hundred yards) for which the County was once responsible for maintaining the bridge and its approaches. The stone was originally at the hairpin bend mentioned above. There is a similar stone along the other approach road.

The attractions here are perhaps at their best on a hot summer day. The park is so large that if you don't want to swing on Tarzan ropes, or attempt the catwalk, or haul yourself across a swaying bridge, or try out the death slide or the anaconda run, or climb into a tree house, or paddle, or swim, or sit under a waterfall, or ride a pony, or take a voyage on the Kon Tiki raft, or dangle on ropes suspended over a shallow lake; even if you don't want to play a game in the meadow, or explore the riverside and woodland walks, or follow one of the nature trails; even if a leisurely stroll across the lawns to admire the fine specimen trees is too much of an effort, then you can sit and watch other people doing all those things, or learning the skills of canoeing or practising archery; or you can just have a picnic. . . . There's no difficulty in finding a quiet place to rest in either sunshine or shade.

There is a tremendous amount for children to do here, particularly if they are active and adventurous. Water plays a large part in the activities so bring them in warm weather.

All the usual facilities for visitors are available, as well as leaflets dealing with the local trees, flowers, and birds.

In no other town in the Park do the citizens meet once a year to appoint Bread Weighers, Ale Tasters, Market Viewers, Watercourse Viewers, Pig Drovers, and Leather Sealers. Ensuring that these officials perform their tasks conscientiously is one of the duties of the Portreeve, another elected citizen. For a thousand years at least there has been a Portreeve in Ashburton. The townsfolk are proud of a colourful history that stretches back to the days of Alfred the Great.

In the 13th century this became a Stannary town, and by the 16th up to 40% of all Dartmoor tin was weighed, assayed, stamped, taxed, and sold here.

The other important industry to develop was the woollen one. It grew alongside the tinning, but outlasted it well into the 19th century, bringing employment and prosperity to the town.

Washing, carding, spinning, and weaving were all done here. The little Ashburn stream running through the town centre supplied both soft water and power. Several houses with a long upper floor walled by weather boarding—used for storing, drying, and carding the wool—are still to be seen. An excellent one stands at the top end of North Street.

At the bottom of this street, above an unusual granite arch by the ironmongers, is fixed a plaque declaring that a Roundhead general stayed there in 1646 after driving the Royalists out of town. Yet only a few paces away, just round the corner, stands the "Royal Oak" where the chief Royalist of them all is plainly to be seen hiding among the branches!

River Ashburn
at King's Bridge

LINHAY HILL QUARRY

This quarry is the largest one in the Park still working to extract limestone from beneath the soil. At one time the diggings went down 300 feet below the surface. Roadstone, building stone, concrete blocks, and even animal feedstuffs are produced. Although the quarry lies rights beside the A38 it goes unnoticed by the passing traffic, because screening trees and hedges have been planted along the embankment. As the quarry is extended—and it still has another fifty years of working life—so more trees are planted.

Along the roadside bank in June every year there is a fine show of Ox-eye Daisies. These thrive in comparatively poor soils and the rootstocks are perennial, so the display should continue for many years. Among other names for these, the largest of our wild daisies, are:

Dog Daisy, Horse Daisy, Bull Daisy, Sun Daisy, Moon Daisy, Thunder Daisy, Cow's-eye, Ox-eye, Fried Egg.

The old herbalists did not discover many ills that these plants might cure, but here are two of interest:

A few stems and flowers placed in the bed of a domestic pet would banish any fleas it might harbour.

"A decoction of this herb cures all diseases that are occasioned by drinking cold beer when the body is hot."

That one is dated 1694.

Ox-eye Daisy

HARROWBEER DOWN

Q 3   G.R.508686

An abandoned aerodrome is not by nature a scenic spot, but Time and Nature are working slowly and methodically to redesign the landscape: where in 1945 there were stores, workshops, and tarmac there is now a scattering of Rowan, Hawthorn, Elder, and Gorse; and sheep and ponies graze among the Daisies.

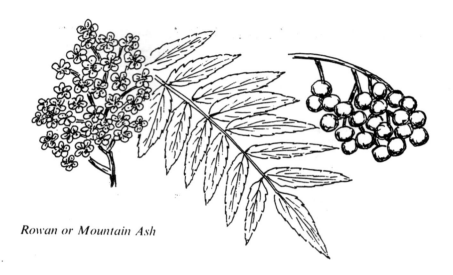

Rowan or Mountain Ash

In many moorland valleys you may notice in walking upstream that the last tree of all is a ROWAN.

Over much of Europe Rowan has for untold ages been a tree of magic. It was one of a select few whose branches, picked preferably during the first few days of May, were festooned over the door of farmhouse, shippon, or milking parlour to protect all who lived or worked therein against entry by witches. For the same reason Rowan wood was used for at least one small part of carriages, babies' cradles, and even small boats. For those on foot or horse-back then a twig carried in the pocket afforded protection against "the evil eye".

In mediaeval times Rowan wood was considered to be the best, after Yew, for making bows. Until recently the berries were dried and made into flour, or crushed to make a kind of cider, and then sometimes fermented to produce a spirit. Well ripened berries can be made into a jelly which is specially recommended to be eaten with pheasant or venison.

In different parts of Devon Rowan has other local names, several of which have a suggestion of magic or witchery about them:

WITCHBEAM, QUICKBEAM, TWICKBINE, and WIGGEN.

Q 4

Few village schools can boast such a magnificent entrance as this.

The history of the school begins in 1719 when Lady Modyford founded and endowed the school, in a cottage, probably on the same site. Originally, twenty boys were to be educated from the age of 9 to 13.

By 1785 there were thirty boys and ten girls; and during the next hundred years the number on roll rose to over a hundred, in three classes.

The older buildings had to be demolished, and in 1895 most of the present ones, including the tower and the school house, were built.

Local children of secondary age now go to Tavistock for their education, so this school caters for all the infant and junior children in the area. There is no other school in the parish.

The village has been here since Saxon times, so visitors exploring it may wonder what has happened to the church. It has not disappeared: it stands high on a hill nearly half a mile away, where it has always been. Lanes and footpaths leading to it make a very pleasant circular tour.

The church is featured in square P 5.

```
LADY MODYFORD'S
     SCHOOL
FOUNDED------1719
COMMEMORATED-1969
```

Plaque over the door

297

Besides being scenically attractive Burrator Reservoir has the added appeal of a road all round, car parking space at both ends, and an ice cream van and toilets at the S.W. corner. The reservoir is fed by the River Meavy, Newleycombe Lake, Narrator Brook, and the Devonport Leat. At the southern end are two dams, Burrator dam across the steep narrow valley of the Meavy, and Sheepstor dam across a wider, shallower valley 500 yards to the east.

The two dams are of quite different construction. Burrator dam has a massive granite facing on each side, and a core of rough granite blocks embedded in concrete. Its strength lies in its weight.

Sheepstor dam is mainly of earth with a core of puddled clay and concrete, which in places reaches down over ninety feet before settling on solid rock. This is shown in the diagrammatic cross-section. The underwater slope is faced with stone.

The reservoir was opened in 1898, and during the 1920's its height was raised by ten feet. It now holds about 1,000 million gallons. The inlet on the further bank just beyond the dam is the quarry from which much of the granite for its construction was obtained.

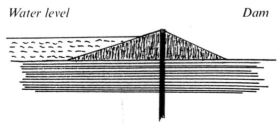

Water level   *Dam*

Core of clay and concrete

This blowing house lies beside the path that runs up from Norsorthy Bridge along the left bank of the Meavy. Some red tipped posts mark its site.

The house is in fairly ruinous condition, but the incoming leat and the wheel pit can be made out; and on the floor is an interesting collection of mortar stones. The stamps for crushing the ore were activated by the wheel, and must have been arranged something like the imaginary illustration. The heavy wooden trip hammers were shod with iron. The ore, already broken into small pieces was placed on a granite block and crushed into a coarse powder. Gradually a depression would be ground out beneath each hammer. When this became too deep for efficient operation the mortar stone would be shifted or turned. Examples of this can be found here.

The stone with a slot cut into one face is not thought to be part of the crushing apparatus. It may be of much later date, but its purpose is not known. The blowing house itself was possibly in use during the seventeenth century.

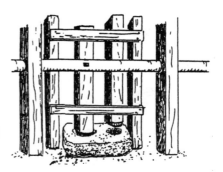

Stamps

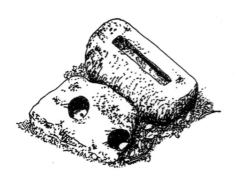

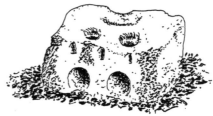

Mortar stones

A cuckoo flies past Cuckoo Rock

From whichever angle you look at this rock it has a remarkable outline, though none of them has much resemblance to a Cuckoo. Perhaps it earned its name for quite a different reason. There are certainly Cuckoos around here, and Pipits too, in whose nests they often lay their eggs.

The rock is really a miniature tor, although it is not set on a hilltop. It lies on a boulder strewn slope below Combshead Tor.

One of Dartmoor's early letterboxes used to be situated on top of the rock, but it has gone now.

Underneath is a small cave once used, so the story goes, as a cache for smuggled brandy. There are more hiding places among the other huge boulders on this hillside.

DOWN TOR ROW

Western end and cairn circle

The stone row and its associated monuments on this downland ridge are definitely one of the "not to be missed" ones on the Moor. Of the single rows perhaps only that on Stalldon (Square U 10) is more impressive, but this one has other remains to add to its interest.

The best place to begin a walk is certainly from the cairn about 150 yards beyond the row's eastern end. From that viewpoint it can be seen that the row (often called Down Tor Row) runs off in an almost dead straight line. A dip in the terrain part way along exaggerates a very slight bowing out of the row at that point. It is interesting to speculate whether this curvature could have been intended by the builders, was the result of carelessness on the part of the Bronze Age surveyor, or is due to earth slip during the last four thousand years.

The first stone in the row is as usual an extra large one, but by the time you have followed the line for about 300 yards and counted about 150 stones, the last few at the higher end increase vastly in size. The final massive menhir rises to about nine and a half feet, and it is known to extend some three feet into the ground.

Immediately beyond the terminal menhir is a stone circle. This once formed a sort of retaining wall for another cairn. The position of the burial chamber within it is obvious enough.

One last question to ponder: Why is the cairn at the higher end built right against the end of the row, while the one at the other end is a hundred and fifty yards away? The answer, of course, is not known; but a handful of entertaining answers can easily be propounded.

The track leading down to this ford is remarkably broad and well worn seeing that this lonely spot sees few travellers: the river crossing is little more than half a mile from the source of the Plym.

But this ford, and the next one downstream known as Plym Steps, once had a good deal of use. That was in the days when the Dartmoor wool industry was important. For four hundred years up to the middle of the eighteenth century fleeces were collected and delivered all over the southern Moor by "Yarn jobbers". The towns of Tavistock and Ashburton, the abbeys at Buckfast and Buckland, and numerous villages, all had a hand in the manufacture of woollen goods. Thus the Jobbers' Path came into existence, crossing some of the bleakest areas of the Moor.

The O.S. maps mark the Abbot's Way as crossing the Plym here, but there is a good deal of doubt about that, as another and better route (marked with numerous crosses) existed further north.

Perhaps the best way to come here is from Fox Tor and thence up the gully that turns into Black Lane. For then the open, gently rolling miles of blanket bog that lie beyond the hillcrest in all other directions spring freshly into view, and you can reach this entertaining guide post on Cater's Beam without having trudged weary distances across a featureless expanse of sedge, rush, and Purple Moorgrass.

Whoever carried this railway sleeper up here and stuck it firmly in a hole did a good job. If you are navigating by compass—and this is almost essential across these wastes—the post forms an excellent guide. Its position, labelled "Post", is precisely plotted on the map. The initials inscribed on the sleeper's eastern face testify to its "guiding starriness" for many a moorland tramper.

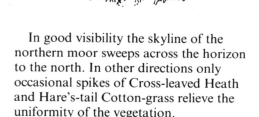

In good visibility the skyline of the northern moor sweeps across the horizon to the north. In other directions only occasional spikes of Cross-leaved Heath and Hare's-tail Cotton-grass relieve the uniformity of the vegetation.

This is a spot to be savoured by those whose spirits are refreshed by long views across untenanted expanses. Yet near at hand is Fox Tor, from where your car may well be in sight.

NAKERS HILL

Here you are right in the middle of one of the Moor's most desolate areas.
On a sunny day it has its own attraction, but if the sky is low and mists are
about, and your spirits are as grey as the clouds, you need a song to keep you
going. This one, sung to the tune of "All through the night" might help.

'Cross the more I tramp unseeing
  Shrouded in mist.
Step by step I'm slowly being
  Soaked by the mist.
Neither tor nor river showing,
Ne'er a rock to help me knowing
Whereabouts on earth I'm going
  On through the mist.

Once I hear some cattle lowing
  Lost in the mist.
Twice I cross a streamlet flowing
  Down through the mist.
Where they're off to, laughing, playing,
Though I ask them they're not saying.
So alone I go on straying
  On through the mist.

Not a breath of wind is blowing
  Here in the mist;
Naught to do but keep on going
  On through the mist.
O'er the sodden heather treading,
Through my boots the damp is spreading:
Lord alone knows where I'm heading
  On through the mist.

It is thought that between about 1,000 B.C. and 500 B.C. the climate over the high moorland changed quite rapidly and that the pleasant conditions that had lasted throughout the Neolithic and Bronze Ages deteriorated to become much colder and wetter. No longer could the high moor support permanent communities or primitive agriculture. Vast tracts of moorland were abandoned, the hut circles sheltered only wild animals, the blanket bog spread and deepened, and the valley mires became impassable.

A few of Dartmoor's deeper mires have earned a sinister reputation, for example Fox Tor Mire and Raybarrow Pool, while many others provide "walking" only for the agile or the foolish.

Aune Head mire is a desolate expanse of rush, sedge, sphagnum, and water; though in a dry summer it is quite possible to work one's way upstream to the approximate source of the river. Surprisingly, along such moorland streams the firmest ground can sometimes be found right beside the streamlet itself. For in time of flood the current has thrown up stones which have then settled in a narrow ridge along the water's edge.

An often told story, sometimes located here, sometimes at Raybarrow Pool, relates how a walker, picking his way from tuft to tuft, came upon a top hat reposing on a watery patch of Bogmoss. In fun he gave it a hefty kick, whereupon a voice from below demanded, "Hey, what yu'm adoin' to me 'at?"
"Be there someone there?" asked the walker.
"Ess, I reckon so." came the reply.
"What be you doing then?"
"Settin' on me 'oss."

SNOWDON

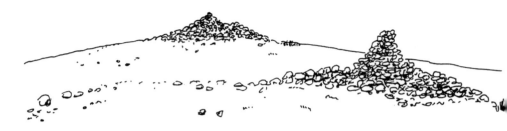

The two southern cairns on Snowdon

Here is another hill once favoured by our forefathers as a burial ground. There are four cairns running in a north to south line spaced about a hundred yards from each other. The two northernmost are not very conspicuous, being low and well grassed over. The next one is the largest. Here the loose boulders have been amateurishly rearranged to form a shelter. But it is definitely not recommended as a place of refuge in a storm, or indeed at any other time. The southernmost cairn is also mainly of loose boulders.

Assuming that each cairn was the last resting place of a local chieftain one can invent all sorts of reasons for the choice of these sites. The spirits of the inmates will certainly not be lonely. When they grow tired of each other's company then within sight there are other cairns on Pupers Hill, Eastern Whitebarrow, Huntingdon Hill, and Ryder's Hill.

Just beyond the southern cairn a mining gert comes up from the west. This is Gibby Beam that once supplied tin ore to Huntingdon Mine by the Western Wellabrook. This is mentioned in Square R 13.

Eyebright is widespread on Dartmoor. Its small white flowers are marked with purple lines and yellow spots. An eye lotion used to be made from the leaves. They were dried, powdered, and stirred into wine or beer.

Eyebright

This hamlet is well
tucked away from the *Tutsan*
"madding crowd's ignoble strife". The half dozen houses and couple of farms
find peaceful shelter here in the valley. There are some attractive cottages, a
large barn converted into a home, a small stream, and even an Elm by the
bridge. At the foot of the lane that climbs Great Combe the Foxgloves grow
six and a half feet tall.

There is a letter box in a hedge above the bridge, but it looks as if any letter
posted in it would not see the light of day for a very long time. It might be
better to walk up to Holne where there is a post office and shop.

But at least those who live here don't have to go to Holne to buy
Elastoplast. For along a shady bank grows Tutsan, whose broad leaves have
long been recommended for pressing on to small wounds to stop the flow of
blood. The large yellow flowers are succeeded in autumn by berries that turn
from red to black. The plant's name is derived from the French "toute saine"
which means something like "all wholesome" . . . for the leaves, dried and
powdered used to be made into potions and ointments for curing anything in
the nature of a cut, sore, or ulcer.

In ancient Greece and Rome it was believed that the leaves might also find
a use between the bedsheets, because "the vertue of this herbe is that he wylle
gladly kepe men and women chast".

One of the delights of this well kept village is that it lies just off a useful but minor road across the Moor.

Thus it escapes the problems of through traffic, and manages to retain a good deal of quiet charm. Since the village is "quite a long way from anywhere" it supports a well stocked shop and a post office. Roads come in from east and west and south, each one being a scenic pleasure to travel. Visitors are well "catered" for at both the Church House Inn and the Old Forge tea rooms.

In the church is a screen with forty painted panels and much intricate carving. The ceilings too are interesting, the bosses in the barrel roof of the chancel being clearly picked out in colour. Even the porch has a barrel roof and painted bosses. In the churchyard stands a remarkable Yew whose trunk has become completely hollowed out. It must have been planted soon after the church was built round about 1300 A.D.

For some people Holne would be too remote from the world that rushes by. However it is superbly sited in a south facing hollow under the heights of the open moor, and it is quite certain that villagers have been living here for at least a thousand years. In the Domesday Book of 1086 twenty families are recorded in the extensive manor of Holle, as it was then called.

Hembury is one of several Iron Age hill forts that overlook the valleys of the Teign and Dart. See also, for example, Cranbrook Castle in Square E 17.

A thousand years of natural regeneration had obscured the ramparts and the ditch until some of the trees were cleared in order to reveal the extent and layout of the fortress. On the highest point is a mound which was raised to support an early mediaeval castle, probably built of wood.

The view below was sketched from the road junction at Hockmoorhead, about three quarters of a mile to the southeast.

William Crossing recounts a story about the capture of the castle from the Danes who occupied it at one time.

Some local women allowed themselves to be seized and taken to the fortress. During the night, while their captors were sleeping soundly after an evening of "wine, women, and song" the women arose, seized weapons, slew the unsuspecting guards, and admitted their compatriots.

At any time of the year this is a delightful lane to stroll along. It is wide, has two hedgebanks full of wild flowers, and doesn't seem to go anywhere. That is to say, it makes for the River Dart and just stops when it gets there. Downstream is a private drive to an unseen house, while upstream a scramble along the riverbank takes you first past a very shallow reach of the river, and then to a bend where the water runs deep and dark beneath the steep wooded slope on the other side.

Spindle berries

In late April the lane verges, spangled with the yellows of Celandines and Primroses, are about to be overtaken by the May colour scheme of red, white, and blue. The red is supplied first by Red Campion and later by Herb Robert. For white there are banks of Greater Stitchwort and Ramsons, and here and there Wild Strawberries. The Bluebells cannot be missed, but for a purer blue look for the smaller sprays of Bird's-eye Speedwell.

Then, also in Spring, there are clumps of Wood Spurge, which bears clusters of petal-less flowers surrounded by large greenish yellow bracts.

The Early Purple Orchid grows here too, and by mid-summer . . . well, the list would be a long one.

An autumn delight that provides a startling splash of colour is the Spindle. Its berries are quite unmistakable: bright pink four-lobed capsules that open to reveal orange berries inside.

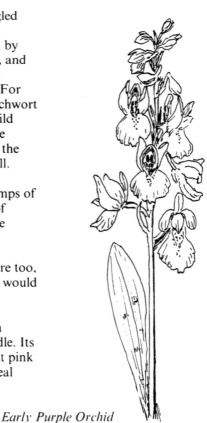

Early Purple Orchid

ROBOROUGH DOWN

A ROCK AND A LEAT

"The Rock" is a popular playground. It stands well back from the main road and is largely screened from traffic. There is level turf here, a good approach road for drivers, ponies, and an ice cream van.

The artificial banks here are all that remains of a wartime airfield that operated from 1941 until 1945. Before that time the row of shops in Yelverton had a second storey. But the runway was so near that in order to allow a margin of safety for aircraft landing and taking off, the houses had to be cut down into bungalows . . . and they have never grown up again. A story of another kind says that the top of Roborough Rock was also removed for the same reason. Well, it does have an odd outline.

Just across the main road a footpath takes you in about two minutes, first across the dry Devonport Leat, and then across the track of the Plymouth and Dartmoor Railway. This, the first iron way in Devon, was opened in 1823. A short length of rail is still *in situ*. Horse drawn trucks carrying granite from Foggintor for Nelson's Column came this way *en route* to Plymouth and London.

Another few yards will bring you to the much older Drake's Leat, which was dug in 1591 to take water to Plymouth. The granite lining slabs were put in position in 1871. Occasionally flood water can still be seen running along its course.

THE MEAVY OAK

G.R.540672

Tradition has it that this remarkable Oak on the village green at Meavy was planted when the first church was consecrated: and that was back in 1122. Although it has lost part of its upper trunk, and needs a few artificial supports, the tree is still in good health: in summer it bears a fine canopy of leaves.

The appropriately named inn nearby is also an "old timer": parts of the building date back to the fifteenth century. It has the unusual—possibly unique—distinction of being owned by the parish. This means that part of the profits are used for the benefit of parishioners.

SHEEPSTOR VILLAGE

Here is a delightful little village, too small to support shop, post office, or inn. It is named after the massive tor not far to the north, but how that got its name nobody knows. Apparently it has nothing to do with sheep.

The cross by the lych gate was found in a nearby field, rescued, repaired and remounted here in 1910. Inside the churchyard, by a wall stile, is another old cross which has also been "rescued"—but where that one came from is unsolved mystery.

The great tomb inside iron railings is that of the White Rajahs of Sarawak, whose English home was at Burrator House on the outskirts of the village.

ANIMA RESURGAT

ET   SIC
HORA   VITAE

MORS JANUA VITAE

In a niche over the church porch has been placed this curious carving which was once part of a sundial. It depicts ears of corn growing out of a skull mounted on an hourglass. The Latin tags compare the hours to a span of life, and state that death is but a doorway to a new life. It also bears the date 1640.

313

YELLOWMEAD CIRCLES

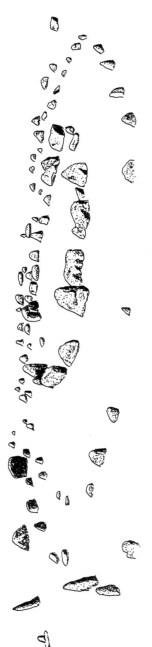

There is no other Bronze Age relic on the Moor to compare with these four concentric circles. The site is assumed to be connected with a burial although there is no sign of a grave.

A good deal of restoration, supervised by respected local archaeologists, was done in 1921, when all the fallen stones were reset in their original positions. The holes, even though filled in by accumulated soil, are usually easy to find by examining the compactness of the soil.

Counting the stones in any Dartmoor circle is always an entertaining and often a puzzling task. Walk round each of these circles and try it. There are obviously some missing stones, and the circles are not all quite circular. There were perhaps once about forty stones in each.

On the surrounding downland are quite a few other stones that possibly indicate former rows and avenues, but these are far from complete. It is likely that the local walls are the present home of many of the missing stones.

This site must once have had considerable importance: all it now needs is a little informed guesswork and a lively imagination to fill the place with our Bronze Age ancestors coming and going on the ceremonial occasions that surely took place here.

DRIZZLECOMBE

This magnificent menhir—at fourteen feet the tallest on the Moor—is just one of a fascinating assembly of prehistoric remains on the downland between Drizzlecombe and the River Plym.

The area is rated by some authorities as the most important of all such Dartmoor sites. Closely associated are three stone rows, three menhirs, three kistvaens, and seven cairns. A short walk round will soon show a geometrical pattern. The three rows each have a menhir at one end and a cairn at the other, and are aligned pointing to a fourth cairn. Another more distant menhir could also form part of the design, but this one has no row associated with it.

The three menhirs at the ends of the rows had all fallen before the end of the nineteenth century. When they were re-erected in 1893 the holes into which they fitted were deepened as a safety measure: so once they stood even taller.

The very large cairn to one side of the rows is known as The Giant's Basin.

This reach of the Plym valley and the slopes on either side contain many kistvaens (burial chambers). One of the best and easiest to examine lies about half way between the Drizzlecombe Brook and the northwest cairn.

Buzzard

Wheatear

Small Heath

Heron

Skylark

Red Admiral

The dead man who was found here was removed some two hundred years ago, and now there is nothing sinister about this tiny valley. Much of it has been deepened by tin streamers so that part of it resembles a miniature gorge. In it sheep find shelter, butterflies breed, birds seek food, and fish dart through the shallows.

On a calm summer day the scene is alive with wings. Once during a ten minute rest on the bank I watched a Buzzard soar low overhead, a Heron take off from the rushy river foot, two young Skylarks, a Wheatear, a Red Admiral, several Small Heaths, two pairs of Small Whites, a single Large White, and a Hawker dragonfly.

Once there was a pool here about an acre in extent, but at some time it was drained by the tinners, and now there are only a few small shallow pools where Sphagnum, Bogbean, and Marsh Violet find a home. But the area is a marshy one, and the slight depression in which the "pool" is situated is surrounded by blanket bog. There are no tors within a mile—which makes finding the place none too easy.

The second oldest of all the Dartmoor letterboxes is located here. It is one of the only two (the other is at Cranmere Pool) to have a permanent site. The canister, stamp and book were placed here in 1938 to commemorate the life and work of William Crossing. His famous "Guide to Dartmoor" was for sixty years the only near-comprehensive guide to exploring the Moor. It is still regarded as essential reading by enthusiasts.

IN MEMORY OF
WILLIAM CROSSING
AUTHOR OF MANY INSPIRING
BOOKS ON DARTMOOR. WHOSE
GUIDE IS A SOURCE OF
INVALUABLE INFORMATION
TO ALL LOVERS OF THE MOOR.
DIED 3RD SEP 1928 AGED 80

The "stamp" and the plaque on the large boulder

REDLAKE PIT

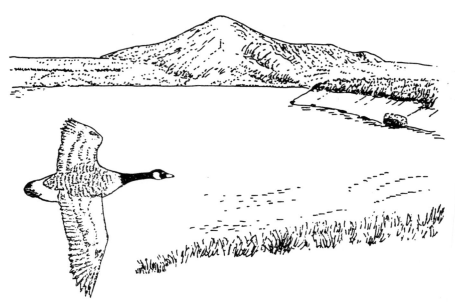

This huge white pyramid in the very centre of the southern wastes is a beckoning curiosity as well as a useful landmark. Known as 'the sky tip' it is simply the pile of waste material derived from the china clay diggings at its foot. The pit was worked from the early years of this century until 1932, over a hundred men being employed here at one time. Some would come up daily along the 8-mile railway from near Ivybridge, others would spend several weeks at a time at the hostel on the site.

After the topsoil had been removed the clay was washed out with high pressure hoses, pumped into mica pits for a first cleansing, and then run in suspension down twin pipes to the drying sheds near Bittaford.

The abandoned pit holds well over a million gallons of water. During the droughts of 1976 and 1989 some of this was pumped out to help feed the Avon reservoir.

The smaller storage ponds to the east of the main pit have been the home of a pair of Canada Geese during several recent summers.

Canada Goose

HUNTINGDON WARREN FARM

Only a ghost of a house is to be seen here now. The warrener's home that once stood beside the Sycamore was lived in until 1956. Soon after its last occupant moved out the house was severely damaged by fire (by visiting cadets) and a few years later the tottering ruins were well and truly demolished.

Rabbit warrening was carried on here throughout the whole of the nineteenth century and well into this one, but the difficulties of getting rabbits to market from this remote spot finally put an end to the business. The buries in which the rabbits lived are easily found on the slopes of the hill to the south, as also is the kennel field—the smaller of the two enclosures to the right of the track that comes up from the clapper bridge.

The numerous walls in the vicinity of the house still support a quite extraordinary number of gateposts.

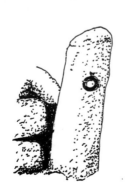
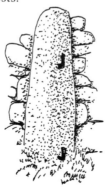

KEBLE MARTIN'S CHAPEL
R 13   and HUNTINGDON MINE   **G.R.667667**

Tinners were once active along the banks of the Western Wella Brook. Mounds, pits, and short gullies are everywhere, and stretches of a leat are evident here and there. All is now covered in a blanket of grass, rush, and heather, offering interesting exploration and a wealth of wild life. Pipits, Skylarks, and Wheatears abound, and on one memorable occasion a family of six Ravens was playing in the sky overhead. One obvious mining relic stands firmly near the stream, the 19th century Huntingdon Mine wheelpit, the gable end of which gives it from afar the appearance of anything but a pit. There is no sign of the water channel, for this came in on a long wooden launder which might have been twelve feet or more above ground by the time it reached the pit.

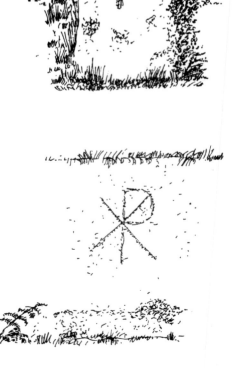

During the summers prior to the Great War a group of young men used to camp a short way upstream from here. One of them was to earn wide recognition many years later as artist and botanist for his *Concise British Flora in Colour*—the Reverend Keble Martin. In a little dell they piled up boulders to form the walls of a tiny chapel. They cut a simple cross into an upright stone and the CHI RHO symbol into a horizontal one. These are both still to be seen.

In 1904 or 1905 a child of the warrener at nearby Huntingdon Warren Farm was baptized here, and in May 1990 a wedding was celebrated. This time the chief participants were keen "letterboxers". A small board recently set into the chapel wall records also that an act of divine worship was held here in July 1982.

This is not a chapel that has frequent use, but a few minutes sojourn here can be a refreshing experience, especially if your rucksack contains a thermos flask.

DEAN BURN CLAPPER

At any season this is a picturesque spot. A ford, a clapper, and an over-hanging Oak make an appealing scene, one into which more light falls in winter than in summer.

The clapper bridge is worth examining carefully. The northern impost (slab) has several dates cut into its surface. Halfway across near the down-stream edge 1737 can be made out fairly easily, though the initials above it are not clear. At the midstream end is another date more difficult to decipher. It might be 1705. Only guesses can be made as to what these may signify. There are also some smaller, more recent letters and figures elsewhere on the slab.

The notice on the gate through which the track leads declares, like the map and the fingerposts, that this is the Abbots' Way: but it is thought likely nowadays that this route is merely part of the Jobbers' Path, which is also mentioned in Square S 12. The route used by monks in journeying from Buckfast to Buckland and Tavistock finds a place in Squares P 9, P 11, and R 16.

Just beyond the gate stands an impressive row of ancient Beeches. They are growing so close to each other that even the number of individual trees may be open to doubt.

CROSS FURZES

The first map reference refers
to the road junction labelled
Cross Furzes on the map.
Here a carefully cut granite
waymark has been pointing
the way to Buckfastleigh,
Ashburton and Tavistock for
at least a couple of hundred
years, and should continue to
do so for another thousand.
The lane heading moorwards is the
shortest route to Huntingdon Warren.

Two hundred yards to the southeast at
another junction stands a "signpost"
which, at any rate in 1990, did not point
the way to anywhere. One day it may be
replaced, and then a much weathered old
friend will have disappeared. For there is
room to park half a dozen cars here,
making it a popular taking off point for
the open moor. A rough track opposite
the post is the start of the moorland
section of the Abbots Way.

Hardheads grow on the verge here.
Their hard heads and purple flowers
decorate many a laneside in high summer.

Girls wanting to know if their love will
blossom should pluck a single head, pull
off the expanded flowers, and place the
bare head inside their blouse. If within an
hour or so any new petals have
blossomed, then so will their love.
To ensure satisfaction it may be worth
carrying out experiments at different times
of the day.

Hardhead or Knapweed

This tree well deserves its name. From a distance it certainly has an unusual appearance. A walk round it close to the trunk will bring more than one surprise. The work of a tree surgeon with both iron and concrete shows the affection with which the tree must once have been held; for it would have been easier to fell what remained of its storm battered trunk than to take so much trouble to repair it.

This lane junction is on the Monk's Path that used to run from Buckfast Abbey across the moor to the abbeys at Tavistock and Buckland. That gives rise to a thought: which came first, the oak or the cross?

It needs careful examination to see that the cross too has been repaired. For some years the upper part of it stood on a bank a short way along the lane at Hawson Farm, having been moved there from the road junction. In 1952 a new shaft was grafted on, and the whole cross restored to its ancient position.

Booklets and pictures telling the story of the origin of the abbey and its rebuilding 900 years later are obtainable in the abbey grounds. So here is a different view: the one seen if you can stand with your back to the abbey church. In it are three items older than any building around you: two ancient crosses unearthed in the National Park and one Giant Sequoia.

SKYLARKS at CLEARBROOK

If there is one bird to bring joy into a moorland walk it must surely be the Skylark. Anywhere on Dartmoor where the walking is grassy or heathery, at any time of the year, its vibrant singing may be heard from the sky. The song is particularly vigorous in spring and autumn, when it may last for five unbroken minutes: yet, to stand and listen on a winter day to a burst of song from a pale blue sky, or in summer when a mist totally conceals the sky to hear its melody drifting down from above adds a bonus to an outing.

Skylarks build their nest on the ground, often in a slight hollow beside a grassy tuft. Only chance will reveal one, for the birds always land and take off some yards away, giving little help to a human who wants to find one.

You can stand outside "The Skylark" inn and hear its aerial namesake singing in the sky above the downland on the other side of the road.

Most of the china clay workings on the southwest fringe of Dartmoor lie outside the National Park. But there are many remains of past activity to be seen within its boundary. Old diggings, spoil heaps, pipelines, drying sheds, and tracks leading to them are to be found without difficulty on the southern Moor.

These pits are small compared to the colossal ones to be seen in the distance on Shaugh Moor, but they are much more friendly. The slopes are gentle, and the grassy banks invite you to sit and contemplate the scene.

Some of the pools have been stocked with fish for the pleasure of anglers.

The aquatic plant with broad floating leaves is Broad-leaved Pondweed. In summer it may produce spikes of greenish flowers that rise above the surface.

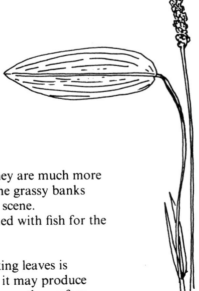

Broad-leaved Pondweed

In 1909 some of the fallen stones of this circle were put back into their holes. There are now twenty four standing stones together with a few half buried ones and a number of fragments. So in its present state the circle must provide a fairly complete picture of its original appearance, except perhaps that the turf is more thoroughly grazed than it was during the Bronze Age. What it was used for of course still remains a mystery.

If you approach the circle along the wall uphill from the east and find your access barred by a high fence, then continue for another hundred yards to a gate that will allow you through on to Ringmoor Down and beyond. If you come from the west through the tiny settlement of Brisworthy you will pass what is probably the largest collection of old tractors and other farm machinery to be found on Dartmoor – an open air museum that just needs a little tidying up.

The suffix "worthy" often means an enclosed homestead. Two other examples in this area are Trowlesworthy, which can be seen across the Plym, and Ditsworthy, which is not far up the valley.

LEGIS TOR

A VERMIN TRAP

One or two of the rabbit warrens along the Plym valley were in business for over 600 years (see also square S 8), and predators must always have been a problem. Stoats and Weasels are probably the most rapacious of these. Keeping the land free of such animals would have been a continuous exercise. One kind of trap that evidently worked reasonably well (for about fifty have been found in the warrens of Trowlesworthy, Ditsworthy, and Legis Tor) was built of granite and slate. These are now known as vermin traps.

In principle, walls, tinners' mounds, or purpose built rows of boulders were used as funnels along which the predators became accustomed to travel. At the narrowest part was the trap. This would have a flat granite base and roof. One side would be formed by a single slab and the other by two shorter ones. Slate shutters would slide up and down in grooves near the ends of the projecting side walls. The trip plate operated by the vermin when well inside must have been connected through the side opening by wire or cord to some pegs and levers fitted into holes on the cover stone. Stepping on the plate would cause the shutters to descend.

It is unfortunate that these traps went out of use so long ago that no exact explanation of the method of operation has been recorded.

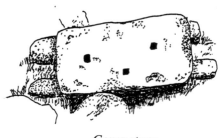

Cover stone

DITSWORTHY WARREN HOUSE

It is unusual to find a farm house still in habitable condition so far out on the Moor. But this one is maintained and used by several adventure training groups.

Rabbit warrening has a history spanning nearly 700 years on Dartmoor, and certainly the warrens in this area (Ditsworthy, Trowlesworthy and Legis Tor) were among the earliest to be established.

The warreners piled up mounds of earth and small stones in which the rabbits could burrow. These oblong buries were usually about twenty yards long. The map sometimes labels them as 'pillow mounds'. Several hundred pairs of rabbits would be in residence on a warren.

Nets and dogs were used to catch the animals, and there would be a special building for cleaning the carcases before transporting them to Plymouth or, in later days, the railway station at Yelverton or Dousland.

The small field beside the house still contains several kennels built into the thickness of the wall.

After the last war the farming of rabbits was made illegal in Devon, and another moorland industry came to an end.

Kennel in a wall

329

The open slopes above Langcombe Brook, which runs down to the Plym, were once a favoured burial area for our Bronze Age ancestors: the hills hereabouts are dotted with kistvaens – considerably more than are shown on the map. This is one of the finest, with its own name, "Grim" being another name for Satan. It is the only one in the vicinity that has a retaining circle – nine hefty stones that look as if they had been blow outward by a volcano erupting through the grave in the centre. What appears to be the cover stone is in two pieces. In the nearby stream are quite a number of similar-sized boulders, a clue as to where the gravestones came from.

This is a lonely place to be buried, on the edge of the vast, soggy mass of Langcombe Hill. Only one tor is in sight – Sheeps Tor to the west-north-west.

Did the original occupant of the grave choose the site himself?

Deergrass

Purple Moor-grass

For those who enjoy being alone an hour or two spent on the empty fastness of Langcombe Hill is a rewarding experience. Here you can sit and muse surrounded by nothing but a nearly featureless mile of waving sedge and grass in every direction. If visibility is less than a mile then not even a distant tor is to be seen.

On the northern spur of the hill stands this boundary stone, dividing the parishes of Shaugh and Cornwood. The inscribed "BB" stands for Blachford Boundary, one of the manors in Cornwood.

Common Cottongrass

Hare's-tail Cottongrass

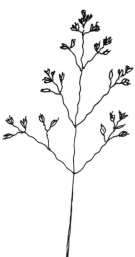

Wavy Hair-grass

The best introduction to the four pounds on the eastern slopes above the Erme is a walk along the west side of the valley, high enough above the river to get a bird's-eye view of the shapes and positions of the enclosures. From this side each one can be clearly seen, though towards the northern end the walls become a jigsaw of lines and shapes. A search among the pounds will reveal a stone row, a small retaining circle, and many hut circles, some within the walls, others on the downland above.

The walls of the northernmost enclosure – the one now called Erme Pound – were at some time rebuilt, and used at least until the end of the eighteenth century for folding animals. Many of the boulders on the slope inside have fallen from the hut circles that were once there.

The care of cattle and horses in such a remote spot would have meant that the herders needed proper shelter, so two huts were built just outside the wall. The upper one is unusual in that substantial seating has been included in it, almost the whole way round.

There is a **Bronze Age** hut just a little way above it.

BOUNDARY CROSSES

G.R.653654 and 664662

A sad history attaches to PETRE's CROSS on Western White Barrow. During the last century peat cutters at Red Lake thought this a convenient spot to build a house. Loose stones from the Bronze Age cairn were at hand for wall building, and the 400-year old cross, once its arms had been knocked off, made an excellent chimney support.

Later when the house had become a ruin the cross was retrieved and re-erected. However its head was so mutilated that it was decided to set it up upside down . . . and that's why the tenon, cut to fit into a socket stone, now points to the sky.

PETRE'S CROSS

HUNTINGDON CROSS, like Petre's Cross above, was also set up to mark the boundary of the Manor of Brent by Sir William Petre in the 1550's.

It stands on the approximate route of the Jobbers' Path, an important track used by the wool jobbers whose trains of packhorses once carried bales of wool across the Moor. Because the mediaeval abbeys owned great flocks of sheep on the hills, monks too would have used the track – which possibly accounts for its later renaming as the Abbots' Way.

HUNTINGDON CROSS

This is the newest of the large reservoirs, being completed in 1957. The dam is not much short of 300 yards in length. Access is so easy from Shipley Bridge, a mile and a half away, that the road to the dam (closed to vehicles) makes a popular stroll.

In a year of drought when the water level is really low the ruins of a mediaeval settlement are uncovered along the shore to the west of where the Brockhill Stream flows in. There are prehistoric hut circles here too, but the rectangular water washed walls of the farmstead make a much more unusual discovery. This was possibly also the home of the shepherd from Buckfast who guarded the abbey flock here during the first half of the fourteenth century.

This mediaeval farmstead is now usually under water.

WATER OAK CORNER

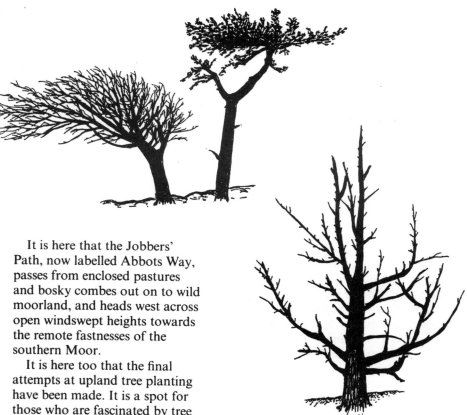

It is here that the Jobbers' Path, now labelled Abbots Way, passes from enclosed pastures and bosky combes out on to wild moorland, and heads west across open windswept heights towards the remote fastnesses of the southern Moor.

It is here too that the final attempts at upland tree planting have been made. It is a spot for those who are fascinated by tree shapes. The Oaks that presumably gave the place its name have long since disappeared, but other trees have been introduced. The cluster of Sycamores looks as if it will survive for many years yet, but for the more mature Pine and Beech along the highest edge of the plantation life is a tough experience. Several alien conifers have also been planted, and have grown into trees of fantastic form.

One, perhaps a Silver Fir, died some years ago, but it still stands like a giant skeleton in silhouette against the sky. Two others cling desperately to life, bearing tight clusters of green needles at the ends of gaunt branches. One of them indeed pulsed into life again in 1990 and put on a show of new foliage.

A small area has very recently been replanted with treelets, Scots Pine, Beech, and Oak among them. It will be interesting to watch their growth in the years to come.

Along one side of the only lane that crosses this square mile a number of Holly trees have been planted. Red berried holly finds a frequent place on Christmas cards, but it was used for winter festival decoration long before the first Christmas. So firmly implanted was the custom that the church decided it was best to adopt Holly as a Christian symbol. Later it played a leading part in several popular Christmas carols. Although tradition demands that Christmas decorations should be removed by Twelfth Night, this does not apply to Holly. This may be left in place until Candlemas Eve (February 1st).

Female flower  *Male flower*

Those who collect sprays of Holly for winter decoration are often disappointed to find that many trees bear no berries at all. This is almost certainly because they are male trees. The flowers of these trees have stamens but no ovaries. The difference is shown in the drawings above. Any one Holly tree will normally bear flowers of only one sex, and of course it is only the female trees that have berries! Holly seeds only germinate readily if they have passed through the digestive track of a bird. If you want to grow your own holly hedge from berries collected at Christmas you will have to keep them for about fifteen months in damp sand before sowing. Alternatively you could feed them to a pet bird and sow the droppings!

Holly wood is hard, fine grained, and almost white. It stains well, and is often dyed black in imitation of ebony. It is used for such articles as chess men, teapot handles, and mathematical instruments.

Finally, here is an experiment you might like to try if you wish to dream of your future spouse. In silence, at midnight on any Friday, pick nine she-holly leaves (ones without prickles), tie them with nine knots into a three-cornered handkerchief, and put them under your pillow.
Pleasant dreams!

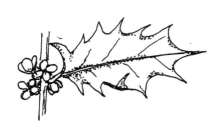

WALLAFORD CROSS

What a pity it is that whoever planted this Beech over a hundred years ago cannot be here to see the results of his hour's handiwork. He would surely be pleased.

Beech trees do not live as long as Oaks but their wood is as strong, and has the advantage of being more durable in wet conditions. It was used in mediaeval times for the foundation piles of buildings – Winchester Cathedral is such a one. Its best known modern use is for furniture: traditional beechen chairs are still being manufactured.

In a "good mast year", that is when there are plenty of nuts, many animals make the most of the abundant food, from woodmice to pigs, which used to be driven into the beechwoods to forage. The nuts may be ground to provide a substitute for coffee, and the oil pressed from them can be used in cooking or for lamps.

The soft furry catkins which fall so abundantly in late spring make an excellent filling for pillows; and a mattress filled with leaves newly fallen in autumn will outlast one stuffed with straw, and will be more comfortable into the bargain.

In the "good old days" travellers between Plymouth and Exeter passed at a leisurely trot through the streets of Buckfastleigh. Then came the A38 so that cars could whizz by without slowing down. Now that road also has been superseded, and lorries thunder past all the way to London without once leaving a dual carriageway.

This leaves the village in comparative peace, and you can wander unhurriedly along its narrow streets, peeping down the numerous colourful alleys that run off under wide arches. For visitors there are three free car parks.

In days gone by the village was a thriving and prosperous centre of the wool industry, the moorland behind providing both sheep and water. Some of the mills are still to be seen, as also are the long wooden shuttered lofts of the houses where the wool was dried.

The way to church

The church is unusual – at least in the National Park – in having a steeple. It is set on a high bluff above the village centre. The shortest way to it is up the 196 steps which start near the brook. After that there is just a long incline to the top!

SHAUGH BRIDGE

Choose this spot for a day's idleness during a summer heatwave. You can park your car under the shade of an Oak, Ash, Beech, Birch, Hazel, Holly, Hawthorn, Alder, Willow, or Sycamore. There is a bridge for cars and another for pedestrians, both across the Plym, while between them the Meavy runs in to join its bigger sister.

Footpaths go off in all directions. You can walk along the Plym to stare up at the mighty Dewerstone, or up the steps by the car park and through the woods for half a mile to look down on it from the opposite bank. One path will take you up to the summit rocks and prehistoric earthworks, and another up a disused tramway to an old cable station that once allowed a line of granite laden trucks going downhill to haul up a line of empty ones coming up.

The ruins by the car park are those of kilns for drying clay; those near the confluence of the two rivers were once part of an iron mine; and the shell of a small building not far up the right bank of the Plym belonged to an early paper mill . . . But nowadays all is quiet except for the singing of the river or the wind through the leaves.

Hawthorn

Oak

Ash

Hazel

Beech

Birch

Willow

Alder

Sycamore

339

THE DEWERSTONE

A good many youngsters have experienced some of their earliest thrills of supervised rock climbing here. The Dewerstone offers the highest near-vertical granite face in Devon, with climbs of up to 150 feet on the main stack. There is room for half a dozen small groups at a time.

The area is also popular with non-climbers, for its setting is as picturesque as could be wished. A path from Shaugh Bridge will lead you to the foot of the rock, and there you can sit on a boulder in the river or under the shade of the oaks, and watch dragonflies or wagtails or young climbers.

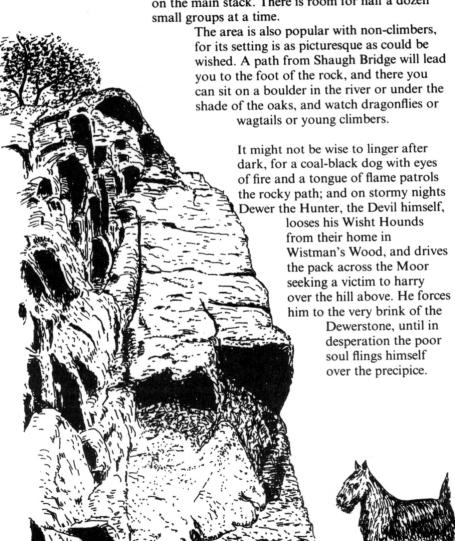

It might not be wise to linger after dark, for a coal-black dog with eyes of fire and a tongue of flame patrols the rocky path; and on stormy nights Dewer the Hunter, the Devil himself, looses his Wisht Hounds from their home in Wistman's Wood, and drives the pack across the Moor seeking a victim to harry over the hill above. He forces him to the very brink of the Dewerstone, until in desperation the poor soul flings himself over the precipice.

Once upon a time – back in the 1820's – there was a grandiose scheme to erect a large flagpole in Devonport. For its base a magnificent cylinder of granite was designed. Here among the plentiful moorstone round the Trowlesworthy Tors a suitable boulder was found and the stonecutters set to work. However by the time it was finished (all except the central hole) the project had collapsed. So here it rests, a block of such size that 170 years have passed without anyone finding a use for it.

Exploration of the two Trowlesworthy Tors will show that a good deal of quarrying and stonecutting has been done here. This was during the last century when the local pink granite was in demand. When polished it has a most attractive appearance. There is still plenty to be seen.

Some of the lichens that grow flat on rock surfaces are difficult to identify. But here are two, to be found in this area, that are comparatively easy to name – a reason why they are among the few to have vernacular names.

CROTTLE (*Parmelia saxatilis*) usually grows in a rosette-like patch in several shades of grey.

ROCK TRIPE (*Umbilicaria pustulata*) is of a more olive colour and has an unmistakable pustular surface, to which it owes its name.

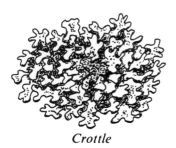

Crottle

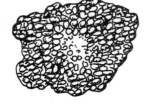

Rock Tripe

PENN BEACON
and SHELL TOP

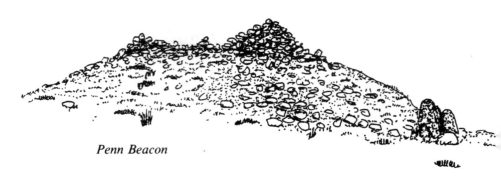

Penn Beacon

A climb up here is rewarded with a fine view, including one of the best of Plymouth to be seen from the Moor; though nearer than that the great spoil heaps of the china clay industry hardly lend enhancement to the view. The cairn on the summit is well grassed over, but a sizable pile of loose boulders has been neatly rearranged.

The upper slopes on the southern side are well clothed in Whortleberry, but this changes quite suddenly to Ling and Purple Moorgrass as you continue on up SHELL TOP.

There is a tiny tor on this height, and the views extend even further than from Penn Beacon. They include more of a bird's-eye view of the china clay works below, and show them stretching further into the distance. Round to the west and northwest the hills of Cornwall can be seen. It is said that in good visibility it is possible to make out the china clay country there too. A lonely triangulation pillar stands aloof on the crest of the down about half a mile away to the northwest.

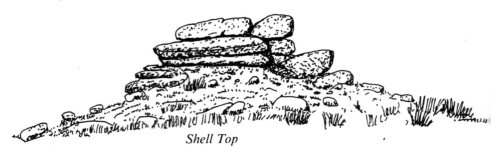

Shell Top

The remains of part of a circle of stones round the summit outcrop suggests that once there may have been a cairn here. If so were the missing boulders used to build the reave that runs along the watershed to Penn Beacon and beyond?

If you have walked up valley to get here, perhaps from YEALM STEPS (Square T 10), you will have clambered across numerous heaps of small boulders thrown up by the tinners who used the blowing house above the falls. After four or five hundred years many of these are still bare except for a few lichens discolouring their surface. When you reach a wide depression where two other streamlets run in from the west there may well be no surface water to be seen at all. Even up here hefty boulders are strewn around as if the tinners in their frenzied search tossed them carelessly aside.

About two hundred yards up the central of the three little valleys this boundary stone stands against the bank on your right hand side. BB stands for Blachford Boundary. This was a manor whose coat of arms is still to be found on the drinking fountain in Cornwood village. See square W 9.

Yealm Head is still several hundred yards further on. Like Langcombe Hill to the north (Square S 10) it is a venue for those who enjoy the solitude of remote and lonely places under wide skies. There are no great tors at hand, only a few pimples on distant horizons; and for a mile or more in every direction except southward down the valley the fen stretches into hazy distances.

Yet, perhaps only a little more than two miles downstream, your car awaits you, . . .

. . . and you can hardly lose the way.

Red Grouse

The 'steps' are the boulders that the infant Yealm dances down during its sudden descent from the high moor.

There is not often a great deal of water coming down here for the river's head is less than a mile away, but this steep section of the stream's course must be nearly a hundred feet in height, so there are many cascades and pools to discover in a five minute clamber. The drawing above was done while sitting on a level patch of short turf by one of the little pools.

This is altogether a delightful place to spend a sunny hour.

If you want to be energetic there are two blowing houses to be explored, one on the right bank above the steps, the other on the left bank below them. At each blowing house there are two mould stones. For an illustration of a mould stone see Square N 11.

THE DANCERS

*Milkwort,
blue or white or purple,
is frequent in this area*

The story is told that the twenty six stones in this circle were once happy girls who liked dancing. One Sunday they came up here, where they thought they would be unobserved, for a party and a dance. Unluckily they were spotted by the local guardian of morals, and turned into stone as a lasting example to others who might be similarly tempted. Moorland walkers should therefore carefully check the calendar before skipping round the circle.

The line of stones that heads north from the circle raises some interesting questions. If you go to the other end you will have walked, according to one antiquary, 2 miles, 3 furlongs, 19 yards, and 8 inches. On the way you will have climbed up and down hills, forded the River Erme, jumped over Red Lake, and come to a final halt on the summit of Green Hill.

Now what could have been the purpose of such a row? Why did the bones buried in the grave at each end need to be linked together in this way? The stones in the row are not large, and some are now covered with vegetation. Some are almost certainly missing. The line is not dead straight, but the general direction is north.

This is the longest such primitive row known anywhere in the world.

PETRE'S PITS

The 'pits' are the widened and deepened upper reaches of the Bala Brook. Twice during the last century and once in this one undertakings have been started to extract china clay from this small area. Nearby ran the abandoned Zeal Tor tramway (Square T 13): so during the second period of operations at Petre's Pits a short branch line was constructed to link it with the new diggings. The clay ran down in suspension along leats or pipes to the works at Shipley Bridge which had been adapted for drying the clay.

However the quality of the clay was not high, and not one of the ventures (in the 1850's, 1870's, and 1920's) prospered.

Today this is a rather forlorn site.

Whatever remains of the works of man is hidden under rushes and water, lying forgotten between steep banks on a windswept moor.

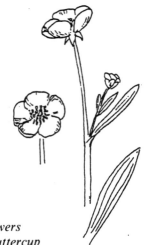

Lesser Spearwort has flowers (but not leaves) like a Buttercup

ZEAL TOR TRAMWAY

**G.R.665646
to 672633**

This stretch of the old line makes an easy mile of walking. The railway was built in 1847 to transport men and materials between the peat cuttings near Red Lake and the works at Shipley Bridge. There naphtha, used in making candles, was extracted from the raw peat.

The rails were of wood, fastened to granite sleepers with iron spikes. Quite a number of these broken off spikes are still to be seen protruding from sunken setts. The trucks were drawn by horses, which must have had a difficult task on the much steeper slopes near the two termini.

The enterprise failed after only three years.

Three times during the next seventy five years the line was again put to use, when the works at Shipley Bridge were converted for drying china clay which was taken from Petre's Pits. (See Square T 12). But these ventures too were short lived.

A 'milestone' by the track

Spikes for securing rails

*A GHOST
AND A MEMORIAL*

A fine mansion stood here for over a century until, being abandoned, it had to be demolished in 1968. Here is the entrance to the garden area, but of the house, stables, barns, dairy, servants' quarters, cottage, kennels, and gardens, nothing but heaps of rubble remain. All this was the hub of a 3,000 acre estate, mostly on the west side of the Avon.

The ghost was that of a nursemaid who suffocated one of her small charges. She too disappeared with the house.

The memorial stands on a ledge under dark evergreens to the left of the road as you come upstream. It commemorates Margaret, the young daughter of Francis Meynell, who died after a riding accident. The spot was not then so gloomy as it is now: the Cherry Laurels had not grown, and there was a lily pond at the foot of the rock.

> M.M.
> MARCH 27TH 1865
> MY LOVELY LITTLE LILY
> THOU WERT GATHERED VERY SOON
> IN THE FRESH AND DEWY MORNING
> NOT IN THE GLARE OF NOON.
> THE SAVIOUR SENT HIS ANGELS
> TO BEAR THEE HENCE MY OWN,
> AND THEY'LL PLANT THEE IN THAT GARDEN
> WHERE DECAY IS NEVER KNOWN.

MOOR CROSS

The fine A on this old waymark points towards Ashburton, and the P on the opposite face the Plympton. The two T's stand for Totnes and Tavistock. It stands on a former track that ran from Buckfast Abbey to cross the Avon near Shipley Bridge, then on past Corringdon Ball Gate and Spurrell's Cross, and down to the priory at Plympton.

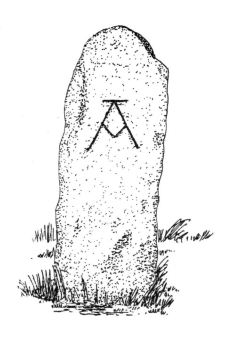

Across the track by the waymark grows a plant which is thought to have been introduced into this country by mediaeval monks as a valuable healing herb. Its leaves boiled, or even taken fresh when young, make spicy eating, but it is the roots which are of particular value. Bruised, boiled, and then used as a poultice they were widely recommended for curing gout and sciatica. Thus it earned one of its common names, Goutweed. It is also known as Bishopweed and Herb Gerard, because it was dedicated to St Gerard, a saint who was said to have a special interest in such afflictions.
    However by the early sixteenth century herbalists were writing such warnings as:

"It groweth by itself without sowing, and is so fruitful that where it hath once taken root it will hardly be gotten out again."

Modern gardeners, who usually call this plant Ground Elder, know this only too well!

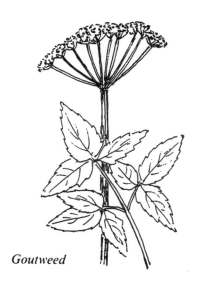

Goutweed

In this house there once lived a weaver named Knowles. He had built his loom in an upstairs room where he worked long hours weaving cloth of such excellent quality that he became a prosperous man. However it appears that his dedication to work was due more to greed than to a desire to provide for his family.

On his death he was given a magnificent funeral, and buried at Dean Prior church, less than a mile away. The service was followed by a restrained celebration, for money was not lacking, and many of those attending were not sorry to be paying their last respects.

But the very next morning his son was horrified to hear once more the familiar clack-clack of the loom working in the room overhead. A hurried and fearful peep showed him that his father was there, working away as usual. The young man hurried off to the vicarage, explained to the parson what he had seen, and entreated him to return to the house. The strong minded parson took up a handful of soil from the newly filled grave, and made haste to the weaver's home. Arrived there he stood at the bottom of the stairs and peremptorily ordered weaver Knowles to come down. The weaver at first demurred, but after a second and sterner command came downstairs. The parson thereupon threw his handful of soil into the phantom's face, causing the apparition to turn into a black dog. "Follow me!" he ordered the dog, and led it out through the woods down to the Dean Burn.

On the way he picked up an empty hazel nut. Presently the pair, priest and dog, arrived at a deep pool in the brook. The parson gave the nutshell to the dog with the instruction, "Not 'til you have emptied this pool with this nut will your spirit be at rest."

You can still visit the pool, which is called, appropriately, Hound Pool. It still contains water, for the nut had been scooped out by a woodmouse, leaving a large hole at one end. They say the best time to see the dog at work is during the few moments when the church clock is striking twelve.

The gate of Weaver's Cottage, Deancombe

SHAUGH PRIOR

 This cross, standing at the road junction just above the church, is probably the oldest hand fashioned object in the village. Although it cannot be certain that it has never been moved it is likely that it has stood here, or nearby, for best part of a thousand years. At one time it may have served as a meeting point for the villagers with monks who came here from Plympton Priory on their circuit of preaching and evangelizing. That would have been before the first church was built, which was round about the time of King Stephen.

 St Edward, to whom the church is dedicated, was crowned King of England in the year 975, at the age of fourteen. Four years later he was murdered by his stepmother.

 Inside the church the most notable object is the towering eight foot high cover of the font.

 During the course of five hundred years it has been carved, used, misused, discarded, forgotten, found, and finally replaced.

 The figure on the pinnacle represents a bishop giving his blessing.

351

The tip seen from the southern flank of Penn Beacon

A view such as this may strike horror into the heart of a lover of the upland wilderness, or of one who thinks that National Parks should be places where such devastation of the landscape should not be allowed. Be that as it may, we should sadly miss the products of these china clay pits in a dozen ways if all activity here were suddenly to cease. The very paper on which these words are printed is made smooth and shiny by the addition of clay from this – or another – pit.

China clay pits that are still operating are not open to the general public, but if ever you get the chance of a conducted tour then watching a worker gouge out a cliffside with nothing more than a jet of water is a sight to be stored in the memory. The force of the water coming out of the monitor (a sort of water gun) is such that a step in front of it would be the last step you ever took. It's quite impressive.

The illustration below was traced from a photograph taken in another china clay pit.

Washing out china clay with a monitor

HIGH HOUSE WASTE

This little pool in Broadall Lake lies only a yard or two outside the wall enclosing High House Waste. Higher up the slope the wall is built on top of part of an older wall surrounding a prehistoric settlement. This probably accounts for the curious kinks in it.

It can be a fascinating pastime to stand on the spot at which the sketch was made and see, in the imagination, the men, women, and children of the Bronze Age village coming down to draw water, wash clothes, or just splash about. Of course some of the boulders will have been moved by floods during the last three thousand years, but there is no reason why the scene should have greatly changed.

If you go up to inspect the village it will be difficult to sort out the fallen walls. A better plan is first to view the site from further off, ideally from the slope to the northeast. The layout of the huts and enclosures can then be more easily understood.

In the western wall of the Waste, that runs parallel with Ford Brook, are two sheep creeps, still in regular use. The upper one is a particularly good example.

STALLDON ROW

Stone circle half way along row

This is the grandest of all Dartmoor's stone rows. At the southern end the stones are about four feet high and four or five yards apart, but 500 yards further on at the northern end they have increased in height to between six and eight feet and stand roughly at ten yard intervals. Beyond the last huge stone lies a recumbent one of about the same size. Very few stones are fallen or missing, and since this open windswept ridge cannot have changed much in the last three thousand years, the impression the row now gives – from a distance it looks like a line of giants marching along the horizon – must be very similar to the one intended by its builders.

About half way along the row is a small ruined circle which might have been a burial site.

On the hilltop not far to the east are several cairns, one of which features in Square U 11.

HILLSON'S HOUSE

Stalldown Barrow forms the southern prominence of a wide ridge that strides for two and a half open, windswept miles northwest to Langcombe Hill (in Square S 10). On the summit, a few hundred yards east of the magnificent stone row featured in Square U 10, stands a large Bronze Age cairn. This has been somewhat disarrayed by the building of a small house – now also rather ruinous – among its stones.

The story is told that a moorman once found an abandoned child on Stall Moor. He took it home and he and his wife brought the boy up as their own son, giving him the appropriate name of Hillson.

When he became a man Hillson built himself this tiny house among the boulders of the cairn, and became something of a hermit. However he had in the meantime learned a trade, and was able to make a living by building eight-day clocks. This seems an unlikely craft to pursue in such a remote spot, but William Crossing once wrote that a Mr Hillson who lived in Cornwood, the nearest village, possessed one of these clocks.

The little house was obviously built by someone who needed a weather-proof shelter, for the lower stones of its walls were carefully, chosen and well laid. But the supposition that this was a permanent home and workshop is not easily to swallow.

. . . But if you are seeking a room with a view, you would be hard put to it to find a better . . .

What a magnificent place to spend the rest of eternity.

When the cloud base is lower than the hilltop – which is over 1,500 feet high – and from the central cairn you can't see either of the others, then a splendid sense of isolation enwraps this burial place in the sky.

In clear weather the views are superb. Visit all three cairns, for the two end ones offer different landscapes to the beholder.

If, as historians say, these great piles of boulders are the last resting places of some of our prehistoric ancestors all sorts of fascinating speculations arise.

Why three cairns? Was the site chosen by those who were buried beneath them or by those who carried the boulders? Was the quantity of stone available nearby the determining factor? The workers who cleared the stones from the hilltop certainly did a good job, for all is now grass and heather, making for easy walking.

It is an interesting exercise to stand up here and watch, in the imagination, hundreds of men (and women and children?) toiling up the slopes, each with a boulder on his back. If there were a hundred builders how long did it take them? For one cairn? For all three cairns?

Then there is the great reave to be considered, the one that sweeps up from the south to the very hillcrest and disappears away to the north. It is marked on the map as "Boundary work". Was this well defined bank of earth and stones already here when the cairns were built? Or did it come later? There was obviously a good reason for this summit to be used for two quite different purposes.

Here the Red Brook
tumbles down through
a trough or traw that
has delighted many a
Dartmoor walker. The
dancing stream leaps down
over tiny cascades and
through swirling pools,
whisking its happy way round
mossy boulders.

A little way back from the left bank is the ruin of a mediaeval or Tudor hut
known as Garth the Tinner's House. This is the scene of one of Crossing's
"Gems in a Granite Setting" wherein he tells the following story.

One morning Garth was making his way upstream by the traw when the cry
of a child arrested his attention. A short search revealed a toddler lying on a
blood stained cloak among the rocks. She was a girl perhaps three years old
who knew only her name, Melys. Nothing else was to be found. Garth took
the infant home, where he also had a small son, and the two of them were
brought up together.

Fourteen years passed. The youngsters had fallen in love with each other
and planned to wed. But one wintry day Garth was accosted by a rider, clearly
a person of rank. The horseman explained that fourteen years previously he
had been riding this way with his infant daughter when he had been thrown
from his horse, injured, and lost consciousness. It had been many hours before
his companions, whom he had lost in a mist, found him. After a fruitless search
for the child they had to continue their journey to take a ship to Spain. He had
been captured by the Moors and imprisoned for many years. Now he had
returned to try to learn if anyone might have news of the child.

Garth told his story, and with the utmost anguish he and his son brought
Melys to her father, and watched them ride away. The young man's despair
was so great that at dark he walked out into the snow, and lay down to die
beside the brook where he and his love had spent so many happy hours. But
Melys too was so heart broken that her father, anxious to see her happy,
promised that she could wed the tinner's son. So next day they returned to the
Red Brook . . .

. . . but, alas, it was too late.

This curious building with narrow vertical openings was once part of the drying shed of a clay works. The clay came in suspension through a pipe into settling pits which may be explored by taking the path up the slope to the left of the building. When dry the clay was heaped up where the car park has been levelled. The diggings were at Petre's Pits. (See Square T 12.)

This building replaced an earlier one in which machinery had been installed to extract naphtha from peat. The peat, which was dug from the vicinity of Red Lake, was transported along the Zeal Tor Tramway. (See Square T 13.)

All these enterprises were short lived. They are further described in the squares noted above.

By the streamlet that runs along the edge of the car park are some patches of Chamomile. This plant was once used to make lawns. Bruise one of the finely dissected leaves between your fingers and smell it to "see" why. The flowers are very similar to the much commoner Mayweed. Another delightful little plant on the drier slopes round here is the yellow flowered Trailing St John's Wort. Bend down to admire it but do not pick any.

Trailing St John's Wort   *Chamomile*

BLOODY POOL

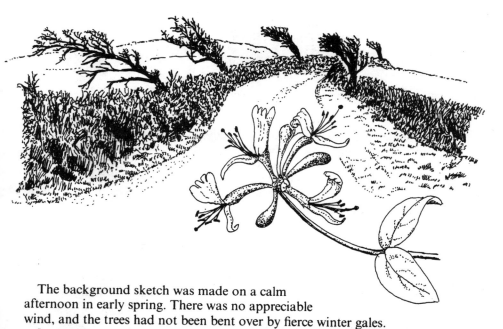

The background sketch was made on a calm afternoon in early spring. There was no appreciable wind, and the trees had not been bent over by fierce winter gales.

In some areas where the wind direction is fairly constant one of its effects is to prohibit bud growth on the windward side of trees. Buds on the leeward side develop more or less normally: so as the years pass the trees become more and more lop-sided. Some species are affected more than others, and it doesn't seem to happen everywhere. The five trees here comprise three Hawthorns, and Oak and an Ash. In the leafless season it needs a close inspection to decide which is which.

At this season Honeysuckle in the hedges was already sporting its first leaves, but it would be several months before its golden trumpets would decorate the wayside.

The flowers often open in the evening, and the scent given off after dark attracts long-tongued hawkmoths to feed on the nectar and pollinate the flowers. If you find small holes near the base of the flower tubes you can be sure that other tinier insects have been sipping the nectar, but have bored their way either in or out to avoid the long crawl through the throat of the flower.

Honeysuckle used to be one of the plants that were fixed above the doors of farm buildings to keep out witches. For the same purpose it was often trained to grow over the porch of a cottage.

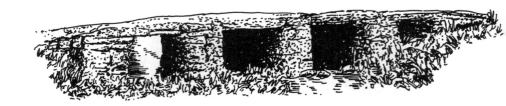

The hamlet of Harbourneford lies quietly on a minor road that was once the most direct route between South Brent and Buckfastleigh. It was there when the Domesday Book was compiled, affording a livelihood for six families, and it doesn't seem to have grown much since. In the days of Queen Victoria a letterbox was installed in the wall of Rose Cottage, but there is no post office, shop, or church.

The old clapper bridge is well looked after. It even has a handrail for frail pedestrians, though this has not been included in the sketch.

On the other side of the road are some fine, mature Alders. This tree is often known as Aller in Devon, and a number of Dartmoor place names are derived from this form of the word.

Alder leaf

Alders only grow beside water, and the wood has been renowned for centuries for its durability in wet conditions. The Romans used it for making water pipes. The Venetians for the foundations of their bridges, the Dutch for building dykes and making clogs. A quite different use for the wood was to produce a high grade charcoal which was particularly suitable for manufacturing gunpowder.

Male catkins and female cones are borne on the same tree. The little cones remain on the branches throughout the winter after they first open.

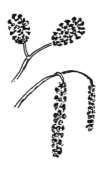

Female cones and male catkins

360

WISDOME

The often hidden stream that gurgles down this valley is the Redaven. It is one of two of the same name, though the other one (under Yes Tor) is spelt with two hyphens.

This, according to the map, is Wisdome Bridge. About a quarter of a mile upstream, at Wisdome Mill, is another bridge, which has only one arch, and is much more humpy than this one. One can't help wondering why that bridge is not Wisdome Bridge, especially as the cottages beside this one are clearly named "Vicarage Bridge Cotts". But then . . . Where would the vicarage be? The nearest church is a mile away. On the other hand, of the two bridges this is the one nearer to Wisdome Farm.

At Wisdome Mill House it is worth clambering down to the water's edge to discover the remains of the wheel in the huge pit behind the mill itself.

Wisdome Mill Bridge

Along the western border of the National Park there are a number of lanes running between enclosed fields and heading straight for the open moor. At the end of these lanes is a gate and parking space for a few cars. These form excellent means of access to the high moor. New Waste, in spite of its uninviting name is such a place. All the Yealm and much of the Erme are within easy reach.

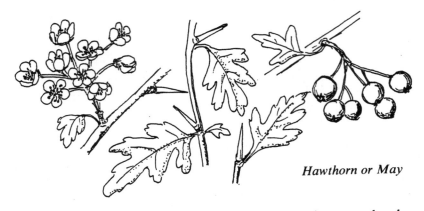

Hawthorn or May

On the lower slopes beyond the gate Hawthorns grow into more handsome trees than those that cling desperately to a windy life on the higher hills.

Hawthorn, like Rowan (See Square Q 3) used to be an important tree of magic and protection. Flowering branches of May blossom would be cut on May Day to be fixed on house and cattle shed as a protection against lightning, witches, and "evylle ghosts". They would also be woven into crowns and wreaths for binding to the maypole. A small spray carried in the pocket provided personal insurance against ill luck. Until 1752 it was much more likely than it is now that May would be in blossom by May 1st: for in the autumn of that year eleven days were deleted from the calendar . . . and they have never been replaced!

Hawthorns standing alone on a hillside or in a field have always been reckoned as special trees. They belonged to the fairies and were never damaged or cut down. They can be used as wishing trees by hanging a small token on a branch. But woe betide any who misuse it to make an improper wish. A wheel of fire will spring out from the base and scorch the wrongdoer.

The superstition that it is unlucky to bring May blossom indoors is a comparatively modern one. It seems that one of the ingredients of its scent is trimethylamine. This substance is also a constituent of the smell associated with putrefaction, a smell which became all too common at the time of the Great Plague.

TRISTIS ROCK

The best thing about this small tor is the delightful view from the top. Come here in Bluebell time, and if you have walked from Harford Gate and crossed the Erme you will have seen acres of hillside painted blue. From the top of the rock further acres can be seen extending up the valley. By nature Bluebells are woodland plants, so this probably indicates that the valley was once well wooded. Indeed, the view up river extends as far as Higher Piles Copse, which is the third highest, in altitude, of Dartmoor's three upland oakwoods. The other two are Wistman's Wood (See Square L 9) and Black-a-tor Beare.

There is an unusual thicket of young Rowans between the rock and the river.

Bluebell bulbs contain a sticky mucilage which can be scraped off and used as glue. It was much employed at one time by bookbinders; and also by fletchers for fixing feathers to arrow shafts. Women of Tudor times used it as a starch for stiffening muslin.

Herbalists of old found little use for the Bluebell, although there was once a belief that the roots boiled in wine and drunk would make "hair grow upon the beardless".

Among other local names for the Bluebell are CUCKOO'S BOOTS and GRANFER GRIGGLESTICKS.

Bluebell

Near the summit cairn the map
marks a menhir with the words
"Longstone" and "recumbent". But
as can be seen from far off this hefty
boulder now stands upright again,
surveying the grassy hills and tors
that stretch all round into hazy
distances. The menhir was
presumably re-erected in its original
hole, but it is a pity that the 19th
century bondstone stands quite so
close.

If you walk southwards along the
boundary line that climbs up here
from Western Beacon the second
stone you come to will be seen to
have a small cross engraved on one
face. This is Hobajohn's Cross,
known locally as "Hoppyjon".

It is suspected by several earlier
writers that this stone is a
replacement for a larger and proper
cross that was removed from here
about 1557 and set up on Three
Barrows as a boundary marker for
Brent Manor. Unfortunately that
cross was later broken up, and has
now disappeared.

Two more boundary markers of
the same manor are featured in
Square S 12. There is a suspicion
that those crosses also were "found
nearby" and put to a new use. It is
suggested that it would have been
less trouble to shift a ready made
cross a mile or so on a sled than to
carve a new one from a lump of
moorstone.

The crosses so used would
probably originally have been set up
as waymarks.

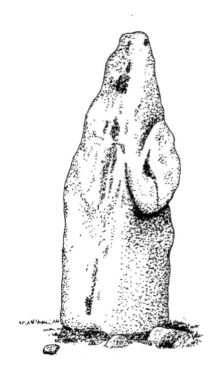

Hobajohn's Cross

CORRINGDON BALL GATE AND BARROW
G.R.670613

This is quite a remarkable pair of gateposts to find, especially if you come across them suddenly during a misty walk over the open moor. The small court beyond was built for sorting livestock. The track that comes through the gate and out over the moor was once used by wool jobbers and clay diggers.

On the moorland side of the gate is Corringdon Ball Barrow. The few large slabs of granite and the low mound are all that is left of a Neolithic burial chamber. It is firmly stated by Pettit in "Prehistoric Dartmoor" that this barrow and another one about two miles away are "the oldest constructions of man to remain on Dartmoor".

The stone slabs would have formed a chamber at one end of a gallery which might have been up to forty yards long. The whole would have been covered by a mound of earth, but this has largely disappeared.

A date somewhere between 3,000 and 2,000 B.C. has been suggested, but where the tomb builders lived is not known.

The Neolithic tomb

LYDIA BRIDGE

G.R.696606

By far the best way to approach Lydia Bridge is to walk upstream along the river bank. Take the path that runs off the road just past the church and goes down under the former railway bridge. Coming up to the old packhorse bridge from below provides a real appreciation of its site, raised high above the narrow gorge, just below a waterfall.

There used to be a plaque on the parapet stating that the bridge would not supports weights beyond "THE ORDINARY TRAFFIC OF THE DISTRICT" and that "DRIVERS OF LOCOMOTIVES WERE WARNED AGAINST ATTEMPTING THE PASSAGE OF THE BRIDGE WITH-OUT THE CONSENT OF THE COUNTY SURVEYOR".

By the bridge is Lydia Mill, which was rebuilt in 1669 after the previous mill was destroyed by a flood. It started as a flour mill, and later became a wheelwright's shop and forge. The wheel is still in place, but is no longer in working order.

The Avon runs under Lydia Bridge

SOUTH BRENT

If *"The Guinness Book of Records"* had been in existence several hundred years ago it seems that South Brent would have appeared in it more than once, sometimes as the Smallest Town in England, sometimes as the Largest Village. It all depends . . . who . . . and how . . .

The town is a lot quieter now that the dual carriageway rushes past without stopping, though the narrow streets in the town centre still offer problems to motorists who don't know about the large free carpark in the former station yard. On the toll house near the Anchor Inn the list of charges to be made on Market days includes one penny for any cart drawn by a donkey, two pennies for one drawn by a horse, and 2s 6d for a caravan. So be warned!

The church claims a record not held by any other in England save Canterbury Cathedral. On 7th June 1436 at the end of Evensong, intruders entered, dragged the parson out, and beat him to death. The door through which they hauled him is the small one (now walled up) in an angle at the northeast corner.

High up on the southern transept is a sundial. A colony of bees have built a nest behind it. When the summer shadow thrown by the dial's gnomon tells the proper time the bees fly busily in and out. An interesting contrast to this old dial is the new one near the town centre commemorating two jubilees.

Three-cornered Leek

One of the surprises in Cornwood is the magnificent village school that displays its motto across three gable end windows, and dwarfs all other buildings in sight. In the square next to the village shop is the former smithy. A mounting block still stands outside. The jubilee fountain opposite bears the arms of the Manor of Blachford.

To find the church cross the main road past the inn and bear left up the slope. Although unseen from the square it occupies a glorious position on the crest of a ridge with wide views across valleys to both east and west. It is probable that the oldest parts of the village would once have been up here.

In the churchyard grows a profusion of Three-cornered Leek, a plant that at first sight looks like a white Bluebell. But take note of the cross section of the stems, and then crush a leaf and smell it. What better name could it have?

HALL FARM

In the house across the yard from this barn there was born in 1720 a girl whose beauty and talents would one day bring both the king and queen to her wedding reception, and bestow upon her two titles, Countess of Bristol and Duchess of Kingston, at the same time. For she managed to marry a second husband without divorcing her first.

The girl was Elizabeth Chudleigh. Her father died when she was six years old, and she spent much of her childhood with her mother here at Hall Farm. Her first serious love affair happened when she was about fifteen, and by the time she was twenty the Earl of Bath, having met her by chance, arranged for the two women to move to London. Three years later she became maid of honour to the Princess of Wales.

Her next love affair was with the young Duke of Hamilton, but unfortunately his letters to her were intercepted, and she supposed he had deserted her. It was possibly in a fit of pique that she then married the grandson of the Earl of Bristol, but not wanting to lose her job at court she kept the marriage a secret. It was a stormy partnership, and the pair soon parted.

During the 1750's it is said that the king, George II, exhibited a pretended attachment to her, and that she helped the Prince of Wales in one of his love affairs.

Elizabeth's own next 'attachment' was to the Duke of Kingston, whom she married bigamously in 1769. However he died four years later, leaving her his whole estate on condition that she remained a widow.

A year and a half later her first husband succeeded to the title of Earl of Bristol. He now wanted a divorce, in order to remarry, and the case came to court. Elizabeth was tried and found guilty of bigamy, but was allowed to keep her fortune. The Earl of Bristol only lived another three years.

During the next ten years Elizabeth travelled through France, Germany, Italy and Russia, still apparently living luxuriously and scandalously. She died in Paris in 1788.

As a postscript to throw a different light on Elizabeth's life, here are some of the adjectives used by other writers about her conduct: whimsical, self-indulgent, indelicate, coarse, generous.

All in all she was quite a character!

It is surprising that this remote hamlet, which seems to consist only of a handful of houses and an E VII R letterbox, should support such a fine mediaeval church. Rooks nest in the great Beeches round the churchyard and jackdaws in the tower: otherwise all is peaceful. There is no more picturesque and tranquil churchyard along the southern borders of the Moor, especially as its very existence is so unexpected.

In the belfry, cemented against the wall, are four slate memorials that commemorate the lives of villagers who were living here when the Spanish Armada sailed up the English Channel.

Long before that, in 1086, the Domesday Book records twelve families living in Harford. The Lord of the Manor owned 20 sheep, 11 goats, 5 oxen, 5 pigs, and 2 slaves. This does not seem much livestock seeing that the manor lands encompassed perhaps 500 acres of pasture and enough arable land to require three ploughs. But the recorded figures almost certainly do not include any animals belonging to the villagers. Although it was not part of the brief of the King's Commissioners to record the belongings of the Saxon farmers, it can be imagined that these took care that on the day the officers arrived there was not much of their own livestock in evidence.

SPURRELL'S CROSS
and REDLAKE TRAMWAY

G.R.659599

If you have walked up here from Harford Gate you have been following an old route that ran from Plympton Priory to Buckfast Abbey. The cross marks the spot where that track crossed another one running north-south. Perhaps that is why this unusual cross does not stand on the skyline where it would have been more easily seen. As the shaft is a twentieth century replacement the head may of course have been moved, though it has certainly been just here for several generations.

Another nearby track which you can't possibly miss is the Redlake Tramway. The line was completed in 1912 and used to transport men and materials to and from the clayworks at Red Lake (See Square R 11). The rails were laid on oaken sleepers set into the track bed. The single line track had a gauge of 3'0". Steam engines hauled the trucks and carriages, as many as a hundred men travelling each way at one period. The clay came down in suspension in pipes.

The total length of the tramway from Red Lake to the drying sheds at Cantrell was just over eight miles. Except for a two year break from 1919 the line operated until 1932.

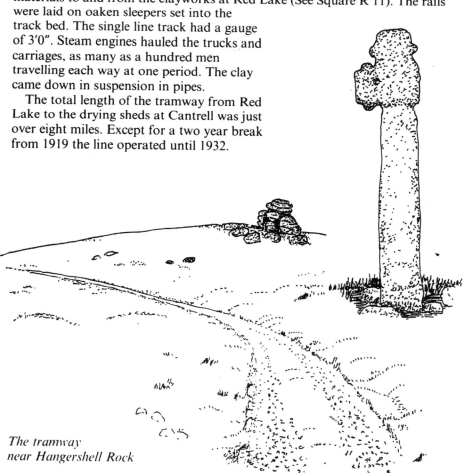

The tramway
near Hangershell Rock

UGBOROUGH BEACON

G.R.669591

Here stands the southernmost tor of Dartmoor. Ugborough's partner, Western Beacon, lies very slightly further south, but there is not really a tor on that hill.

It is pleasant to sit here in a detached sort of way, looking far out across the South Hams, or watching the speeding traffic on the A 38 sliding along in unending file like warrior ants on the move.

On the largest outcrop are four small rock basins. For more about these phenomena see Square L 6. Down below South Brent snuggles close under the edge of the moor, and a little to the north the East and West Glazebrooks tumble down from the heights.

The smaller outcrop on the summit of this hill must at one time have been almost hidden by the cairn built around it, but the stones have been considerably re-arranged by modern cairn builders, doubtless energetic young men with strong arms and backs.

There is good evidence that there was a signal beacon here in the days of Charles I and II.

The small yellow flowers of Tormentil spangle the turf on these hills for a long season every year. They normally have four petals, but now and again you may find a lucky one that has five.

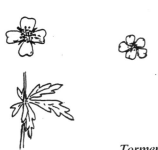

Tormentil

LADY'S WOOD

This small nature reserve is open to the public. A path leads to it from the lane to the south, under the magnificent Glaze Viaduct, past the wood, and on up to Owley. Inside the reserve a footpath runs all round the perimeter. Several low banks run through the wood showing that for some reason it was once divided into small plots.

The wood is only eight acres in extent but it has a rich variety of trees and shrubs, typical of oakwoods in south Devon. It was regularly coppiced until the 1930's, and this has now been started again in order to ensure the continuation of the ground flora.

The presence of Oak, Hazel, and Honeysuckle provides a habitat that finds particular favour with Dormice, entrancing creatures that are all too rare in the countryside nowadays. In this wood their small summer nests for daytime sleeping are usually a little above ground level in thick vegetation. A larger nest for rearing the young is also built. Winter nests, in which they hibernate from October to April, are more usually underground among roots and leaves. The nests are constructed of leaves, grass, moss, and shredded Honeysuckle bark.

At night Dormice are active in the trees and shrubs, scrambling about with great agility. They feed on nuts, berries, seeds, and insects.

Dormice

If you have walked the short but steep half mile up to here from the centre of Ivybridge to follow the "Two Moors Way" to Lynmouth then you have only another hundred and one and a half miles to go. This long distance footpath passes over high moorland, through deep woodlands, and along farm tracks. The suggested time needed to follow the path—according to the official guidebook—is anything up to a fortnight, depending upon the number of side excursions you might wish to make.

This stone, commemorating the opening of the way in 1976, stands by the side of Stowford railway bridge. From here about twelve miles of open moorland lie ahead, by far the longest such stretch on the route. Much of the rest of the way follows old tracks and waymarked paths. Inevitably some short stretches of road walking are necessary. The official "TWO MOORS WAY" guide includes large scale maps of the entire route, and information about things to see on the way.

This point is also the southernmost tip of the National Park—well almost; for to be exact, less than a mile to the east the park boundary bulges about 300 yards further south.

But here, opposite the TWO MOORS stone, stands the southernmost DARTMOOR NATIONAL PARK emblem, another appropriate memorial to the hills, valleys, farms, villages, rivers, and woodlands ahead. As the crow flies it is 24 miles from here to the northernmost roadside emblem, and in between, spreading out east and west are 365 square miles of Dartmoor National Park.

WESTERN BEACON

This is the southernmost hill of Dartmoor. It has an altitude of about 1080 feet. On the summit are at least four prehistoric cairns, and along the easy undulating walk northwards to Piles Hill there are many more. Perhaps our Bronze Age ancestors also appreciated the glorious view southward to the English Channel. But the South Hams would then have been much more thickly forested, and not covered with a jigsaw of fields and hedges as they are now. A short study of the shapes below will soon show you a point where six fields meet at a single focus.

The railway line between the foot of the hill and the dual carriageway here forms the boundary of the National Park. The viaduct at Bittaford nearby was built of granite from the quarry just below these cairns.

If you walk north along the line of boundary stones that separates the parishes of Harford to the west and Ugborough to the east you will soon come to Black Pool. This has no resemblance whatever to either the glittering resort in Lancashire or the sandy cove in south Devon, but at least you can still see how it got its name.

Round-leaved Crowfoot

Blinks

These two flowers are to be found in wet, muddy places in the entrances to the quarries. They both have white petals.

This 366th location is included just in case it is leap year!

The headquarters of the Dartmoor National Park does not lie within the park boundary—though it is less than half a mile outside—but it cannot sensibly be omitted from a survey like this. Even the map has a marginal extension in order to include it.

As well as the headquarters in Parke House there is an information and interpretation centre here, a pleasant picnic lawn, a peacock or two, paths, lawns, some fine specimen trees, a tea room, and a separate reserve specializing in rare breeds of farm animals.

No exploration of Dartmoor could be complete without a visit to Parke.

INDEX

to squares

VERSES

To remind you of:	at:	in Square:
Good King Wenceslas . . .	Branscombe's Loaf	D 6
To be or not to be . . .	Walla Brook	E 11
It's a long way to Tipperary . . .	Amicombe Brook	H 7
D'ye ken John Peel . . .	Fur Tor	H 8
She'll be coming round . . .	Cut Hill	H 9
Away in a manger . . .	Warren House Inn	I 13
The Ancient Mariner	The Four Ace Fields	I 14
While shepherds watched . . .	Brent Tor	J 1
The Quartermaster's Store	Upper Walkham valley	J 7
The Raven (Once upon a midnight . . .)	Chaw Gully	J 14
Billy Boy (Where have you been . . .)	Jay's Grave	J 16
The Mermaid (One Friday morn . . .)	Bowerman's Nose	J 17
Smugglers' Song (If you wake . . .)	The Hairy Hands	K 11
Tom Pearse, Tom Pearse . . .	Haytor Down	K 19
Hiawatha (Should you ask me . . .)	Vixen Tor	N 5
At the Zoo (Christopher Robin)	The Crock of Gold	N 9
Lines and Squares (Christopher Robin)	Devonport Leat	O 9
My bonnie lies over the ocean . . .	Childe's Tomb	P 10
All through the night . . .	Nakers Hill	Q 11